China's Global Image Making

The Belt and Road Initiative
Interdisciplinary Perspectives

Series Editor

Jia Wenshan

Vol. 3

Muhammad Khalil Khan

China's Global Image Making

The Belt and Road Initiative in the Islamic World

PETERLANG

New York - Berlin - Bruxelles - Chennai - Lausanne - Oxford

Library of Congress Cataloging-in-Publication Data

Names: Khan, Muhammad Khalil, author.
Title: China's global image making : the Belt and Road Initiative in the Islamic world / Muhammad Khalil Khan.
Description: New York : Peter Lang Publishing, Inc., 2024. |
Series: The Belt and Road Initiative : interdisciplinary perspectives, 2689-7970 ; Vol. 3 | Includes bibliographical references and index.
Identifiers: LCCN 2024001607 (print) | LCCN 2024001608 (ebook) |
ISBN 9781433195570 (hardback) | ISBN 9781433195808 (ebook) |
ISBN 9781433195815 (epub)
Subjects: LCSH: Yi dai yi lu (Initiative : China) | China—Foreign public opinion, Islamic countries. | China—Foreign relations--Islamic countries. | Islamic countries—Foreign relations—China. | China—Foreign economic relations—Islamic countries. | Islamic countries—Foreign economic relations—China.
Classification: LCC HF1604 .K4726 2024 (print) | LCC HF1604 (ebook) |
DDC 327.51017/67—dc23/eng/20240203
LC record available at https://lccn.loc.gov/2024001607
LC ebook record available at https://lccn.loc.gov/2024001608
DOI 10.3726/b19534

Bibliographic information published by the Deutsche Nationalbibliothek.
The German National Library lists this publication in the German National Bibliography; detailed bibliographic data is available on the Internet at http://dnb.d-nb.de.

Cover design by Peter Lang Group AG

ISSN 2689-7970 (print)
ISSN 2689-7989 (online)
ISBN 9781433195570 (hardback)
ISBN 9781433195808 (ebook)
ISBN 9781433195815 (epub)
DOI 10.3726/b19534

Published by Peter Lang Publishing Inc., New York, USA
info@peterlang.com - www.peterlang.com

This publication has been peer reviewed.

To my beloved parents,
whose innumerable prayers and endless cooperation encouraged me in all aspects of life.
To my wife, who always stood firmly beside me on all occasions of happiness and sadness, and
To my beloved sons, and
To my beautiful daughter who has always wished me with their innocent prayers.

Contents

List of Tables

List of Figures

1 Introduction

The growing international discourses on China's status as an "emerging global power" has reinvigorated the Chinese government's commitment to focus more on China's positive image promotion in the foreign public to convalesce its long-lost right of say in global affairs (Zheng, 2005; Cull, 2009; Gong, 2021; Jacob, 2020; Wang, 2011). It employs the new public diplomacy initiatives—the Belt and Road Initiative (BRI) strategically to magnify its soft image and neutralize the stigmatization of China's reputation in the globalized mediated societies.

The rapid information flow and digital transformation have revitalized the importance of a country's reputation and favorable image in globalized and mediated societies. A country's reputation and favorable image abroad have become more exigent than "territory, access, and raw materials" (Gilboa, 2008, p. 56) as they define the country's political standing and space for political action through mutual understanding in the international system (Gilboa, 2008; Leonard et al., 2002; Schatz & Levine, 2010; Vickers, 2004; J. Wang, 2006). Therefore, nation-states dedicate all-out efforts to raise the country's soft power, soft image, and soft esteem by establishing a strong, stable, and reputable country image in an antagonistic global environment (Kunczik, 2003; Melissen, 2005; Nye, 2005; Price, 2003; Werron, 2013).

A country's image critically impacts its geopolitical influence and its action in the global governance system (Gilboa, 2008; Kunczik, 2016; Leonard et al., 2002; Sun, 2008; Van Ham, 2008; Vickers, 2004); international consensus-building (Wang, 2006); foreign direct investment (Kotler & Gertner, 2002; Kunczik, 2002); promotion of exports (Barr, 2012; Papadopoulos, 1993); attractiveness for foreign skilled labors (Papadopoulos, 2004), the opulence of national tourism industry (Gertner, 2010; Tapachai & Waryszak, 2000); educational systems (Gertner, 2010; Srikatanyoo & Gnoth, 2002); economic growth, national security, and advancing national interests (d'Hooghe, 2014; Han et al., 2012; Hartig, 2019). It has become even more critical in the newly mediated environment and is consistently rated and compared by foreign media, international organizations, and the foreign public based on its effectiveness and morality in political values, economic stability, domestic development, international policy, cultural prestige, etc. Therefore, the political leadership is always worried about a country's overseas image (Kunczik, 2003; Price, 2003; Werron, 2013) and employed best communication practices to manage and promote the country's positive image within the national state system and abroad (Dinnie, 2015; Dyke & Verčič, 2009; Kunczik, 2016; Snow & Taylor, 2008).

A nation's image contributes to its international relations. Scholars (Leonard et al., 2002; Schatz & Levine, 2010; Vickers, 2004; Wang, 2006) argue that a favorable perception of a country by the foreign public can enhance its political standing and space for political action through mutual understanding in the international system. A positive national image is an important component of the nation-state's strategic communication that enhances its soft power to attract, influence, and even shape the preferences of other nations without any punitive or coercive measures (Nye, 2005; Nye & Jisi, 2009). A country's positive image builds public trust and strengthens public confidence in the country's future. This public trust and confidence in the state later works as a currency for its future international credit ratings, foreign investments, and foreign exchange rates (Kunczik, 2003).

China's multi-billion US dollar BRI enchants unique opportunities that can boost China's global image. Scholars (Khan & Pratt, 2019) argue that BRI facilitates regional connectivity, improves financial integration, promotes free trade, strengthens systematic policy coordination, and people-to-people bonds in the developing world and, therefore, "it attracts global attention and is intent on improving China's political stature, sociocultural reach, and economic standing on the global stage, not least in [Islamic] countries" (Khan et al., 2022, p. 2).

Enabled by BRI, China's economic engagements in the Islamic world can propel China's positive image in the Islamic World and attract foreign public attention to promote trade, business, investment, exports, tourism, public diplomacy, and foreign policies abroad (Voon & Xu, 2020).

The Islamic world is beset with lingering regional disputes and faces subtle economic challenges. It needs substantial financial capital to rejuvenate its economic growth and renovate the much-needed infrastructure to deal with the evolving challenges of the 21st Century. China's BRI aims to facilitate infrastructural development and cultural and policy dialogues among divergent national states. It promises regional connectivity, infrastructural development, financial and economic support, and unimpeded trade among Islamic countries that will eventually improve China's global image and stature as a trustworthy global partner in the Islamic world (Jin et al., 2016; Khan & Pratt, 2019). China is hoping that the large investment in the shape of BRI will facilitate the "Chinese dream" of global leadership. It will stimulate a new wave of share globalization through the share development model which could improve the existing global governance and China's image as a new global leader (Khan et al., 2018).

In recent years, China's national image studies have received significant attention from communication researchers around the globe, particularly in Chinese academia (An & Feng, 2022; Buhmann & Ingenhoff, 2015; Meng, 2020; Xie & Page, 2013). Researchers are focusing more on China's image-building (Allison, 2013; Barr, 2012; Guo et al., 2015; Zhang & Cameron, 2003), public diplomacy (d'Hooghe, 2014; Jia & Li, 2020; Schliebs et al., 2021; D. Scott, 2015), charm offensive (Eliküçük Yıldırım & Aslan, 2020; Kurlantzick, 2007; Lee & Hao, 2018), and related concepts "with an enthusiasm rarely seen in other parts of the world" (Rawnsley, 2012, p. 126, 2014). China National Knowledge Infrastructure (CNKI) database indicates that Chinese academicians used the word "national image" over 2700 times in their research titles between 1998 and 2017. Scholars argue that the global discursive debate about China's status as an "emerging global power" has encouraged the Chinese government to focus more on China's positive image perception in the foreign public to recuperate its long-lost right of say in global affairs (Cull, 2009; Zheng, 2005). Recently, the Chinese government has shown great concern, sensitivity, and enthusiasm to project China's soft image around the world (d'Hooghe, 2014; Rabinovitch, 2008). Wang Chen, a prominent member of the Political Bureau of the Communist Party of China (CPC) Central Committee, Vice Chairman, and Secretary-General of the Standing Committee of the 12th National People's Congress (NPC) consistently voiced for grasping the precious historical opportunity to create and built a favorable image of China on the global stage (Xie & Page, 2013).

But scholars like Ramo (2007, p. 12) still believe that "China's greatest strategic threat today is its national image . . . For one of the few times in its history, this famously inward-looking nation is vulnerable to how it is seen abroad. How China is perceived by other nations—and the underlying reality that perception reflects—will determine the future of Chinese development and reform". As a result, Chinese scholars are avidly probing the question of China's image abroad but the focus remained broadly in the Western media and the Western world, particularly in the United States (Barr, 2012; de Moura et al., 2011; Ding, 2011; Dinnie & Lio, 2010; Han & Wang, 2014; Liu & Yang, 2015; Wekesa, 2013; Zeng et al., 2014). China's image construction in the Islamic world is ignored. Even though few scholars tried to inquire about the relationship between China and the Arabic Islamic world, most studies merely focus on the economic and strategic relationship (Dorraj, 2013; Elmagherbi, 2010; Elmagherbi & Wang, 2011; Hayoun, 2013; Makar, 1985; Olimat, 2010; Sekkal, 2013; Xiaodong, 2013; Zhu, 2010). This has left a huge scope for communication scholars to probe the Islamic English news media's role in building and shaping China's image in the Islamic world. Particularly, the impact of China's huge investment in the shape of BRI on its image construction in Islamic English news media.

Purpose of the study

China's problematic image abroad poses a "strategic threat" to its dream of rejuvenation into a new global power (Ramo, 2004, 2007). It is often considered a "major issue" and challenge to China's peaceful rise, and its role in global governance and leadership (Hayden, 2012; Khan et al., 2022; Kurlantzick, 2022a; Ramo, 2007). In recent years, China has devoted sufficient resources to boost its positive image abroad. But Western media steadily disparage China's role in international politics and the new world order due to its alleged exponential expansionism abroad, an abridgment of the freedom of speech, and alleged human rights violations (Armony, 2012; Hayden, 2012; Kurlantzick, 2007, 2022a). China's flimsy political image abroad made it vulnerable, particularly in the West, therefore, China needs to strengthen its positive image to counter evolving propaganda of the "China threat" in international media (Corkin, 2014; Li, 2008). Chinese scholars argue that international media possess ideological biases and often distorted facts to "demonize" China's image (Xiang, 2013). There is international misunderstanding and unwarranted criticism of China's development owing mainly to the negative reporting of Western media. China needs to talk back and communicate the "real" and "true image" of China to the world to converse the frivolous negativity and demonizing of China's image by Western media (Gao et al., 2016; Hartig, 2016, 2019; Zhao, 2017). Therefore, China should manage and utilize all available means to communicate and establish China's positive image abroad i.e., the effective use of Chinese media and communication tools and public diplomacy to strengthen its soft power and improve China's national image abroad (Kurlantzick, 2007).

The Western allies, particularly the United States, United Kingdom, Canada, and Australia have started to galvanize collective actions against China's alleged human rights abuses in Xinjiang by announcing the diplomatic boycott of the Beijing Winter Olympics Games on the allegations of "genocide and crimes against humanity" against ethnic Uyghur Muslim minority (Mather, 2022, p. 1). France which had decided against the diplomatic boycott earlier adopted a resolution just a week before Beijing Winter Olympics that "officially recognizes the violence perpetrated by the People's Republic of China against the Uyghurs as constituting crimes against humanity and genocide" and directed the French government to initiate "the necessary measures within the international community and in its foreign policy towards the People's Republic of China" to halt Beijing's actions in Xinjiang (Al-Arabia News, 2022). Such Western countries (e.g., the U.S., UK, and Canada) have also imposed human rights sanctions on China due to the alleged forced labor and human rights violations in Xinjiang. However, Beijing historically denies those accusations and terms them "slanderous attacks" and "serious interference in China's internal affairs"(CNBC, 2021). Chinese Foreign Minister Wang Yi told the U.N. Human Rights Council in February 2021 that the "basic facts [e.g., social stability and economic development] show that there has never been so-called genocide, forced labor, or religious oppression in Xinjiang," and "[s]uch inflammatory accusations are fabricated out of ignorance and prejudice, they are simply malicious and politically driven hype and couldn't be further from the truth."(Nebehay, 2021, p. 1 emphasis added).

However, the powerful Western narrative about human rights issues in Hong Kong, Tibet and particularly labeling China's actions in Xinjiang as "suppression" and alleged "genocide" of Uyghur Muslims, have reverberated the Islamic English news media (Al-Arabia News, 2022; Al-Jazeera, 2020; Roache, 2021). For example, Al-Jazeera on December 9, 2021, published an unofficial and independent UK-based tribunal report under the title "China guilty of Uyghur genocide in Xinjiang, tribunal rules" aligning its editorial judgment with the popular Western media narrative (Roache, 2021). Similarly, Al-Watan (a Saudi Arabic newspaper) published an eyewitness account of a teacher on February 19, 2021, under the headline "They flaunt rape stories"... A shocking testimony "from inside the Uyghur camps". The article explicitly highlighted the alleged sexual abuse of women by Chinese administrations and described the events at Uyghur campus as "so disturbing that it made her ill" (Alhura, 2021; Ezell, 2021, p. 17). Protest in support of Uyghur Muslim rights in Xinjiang has also been witnessed in a few Islamic countries (e.g., Turkey, Malaysia, Kazakhstan, and Indonesia) in recent years (Al-Jazeera, 2022; Ezell, 2021). For example, in June 2015, the Turkish Ministry of Foreign Affairs alleged China imposed a so-called "Ramadan ban" and did not allow the Uyghur Muslims in Xinjiang to fast during Ramadan resulting in an anti-China media campaign and an outbreak of large-scale anti-China public demonstration in Turkey on July 5, 2015 (Chen, 2020).

The Islamic world and its leadership refrain from openly criticizing the Chinese policies in Xinjiang to avoid China's provocation in fear of losing the lucrative investment from China and a big Chinese market (Kelemen & Turcsányi, 2020). However, the Islamic English news media has shown a steady trend of picking up stories from the Western media to sensitize the Uygur Muslim issues in the Islamic world, making China's fragile political image vulnerable in the Islamic world (Al-Jazeera, 2022; Ezell, 2021; Kelemen & Turcsányi, 2020; Yusuf, 2020). The Islamic world is an ardent participant and backbone of the BRI. Almost the entire Islamic world (48 Islamic countries) has officially joined the BRI (Table 1.1). Five out of six economic and energy corridors pass through the Islamic countries, making them indispensable partners of the BRI (Khan & Pratt, 2019). Therefore, China needs to strengthen its communication strategies and public diplomacy to boost its favorable image in the Islamic world and counter the Western media's evolving propaganda about mistreating its Muslim minority in the Islamic world (Corkin, 2014; Khan et al., 2022; Li, 2008).

Table 1.1: Geographical Distribution of Muslim and Non-Muslim Countries Associated with the Belt and Road Initiative.

Geographical Regions	Muslim Countries (N = 48)	Non-Muslim Countries (N = 105)
East Asia & Pacific (N = 25)	Brunei, Indonesia, Malaysia.	Cambodia, China, Cook Islands, Fiji, Kiribati, South Korea, Lao PDR, Micronesia, Mongolia, Myanmar, New Zealand, Niue, Papua New Guinea, Philippines, Samoa, Singapore, Solomon Islands, Thailand, Timor-Leste, Tonga, Vanuatu, Vietnam.
Central Asia & Europe (N = 35)	Albania, Azerbaijan, Bosnia and Herzegovina, Kazakhstan, Tajikistan, Turkey, Uzbekistan, Kyrgyz Republic, Turkmenistan.	Armenia, Austria, Belarus, Bulgaria, Croatia, Cyprus, Czech Republic, Estonia, Georgia, Greece, Hungary, Italy, Latvia, Lithuania, Luxembourg, Moldova, Montenegro, North Macedonia, Poland, Portugal, Romania, Russian Federation, Serbia, Slovak Republic, Slovenia, Ukraine.
Middle East and North Africa (N = 20)	Algeria, Bahrain, Egypt, Iran, Iraq, Kuwait, Syria, Jordan, Lebanon, Libya, Morocco, Oman, Qatar, Saudi Arabia, Tunisia, United Arab Emirates, Yemen, Palestine.	Israel, Malta.
South Asia (N = 7)	Afghanistan, Bangladesh, Pakistan, Maldives.	Bhutan, Nepal, Sri Lanka.
Sub-Saharan Africa (N = 47)	Djibouti, Mauritania, Somalia, Sudan, Niger, Nigeria, Mali, Senegal, Sierra Leone, Chad, Burkina Faso, Guinea, Gambia, Comoros.	Central Africa, South Sudan, Tanzania, Angola, Benin, Botswana, Burundi, Cabo Verde, Cameroon, Democratic Republic of the Congo, Republic of the Congo, Côte d'Ivoire, Equatorial Guinea, Eritrea, Ethiopia, Gabon, Ghana, Guinea-Bissau, Kenya, Lesotho, Liberia, Madagascar, Mozambique, Namibia, Rwanda, Seychelles, South Africa, Togo, Uganda, Zambia, Zimbabwe, Sao Tome & Principe, Malawi.

Continued

Table 1.1: *Continued*

Geographical Regions	Muslim Countries ($N = 48$)	Non-Muslim Countries ($N = 105$)
Latin America & Caribbean ($N = 19$)	None	Antigua and Barbuda, Barbados, Bolivia, Chile, Costa Rica, Cuba, Dominica, Dominican Republic, Ecuador, El Salvador, Grenada, Guyana, Jamaica, Panama, Peru, Suriname, Trinidad and Tobago, Uruguay, Venezuela.

Source: <https://www.yidaiyilu.gov.cn>, April 1, 2022

China's image has also become a core concern in China's foreign policy. It is also evident from President Xi Jinping's keynote at the 19th National Congress of the Communist Party of China (CPC) held on October 18, 2017, where he categorically signifies the importance of improving the Chinese "capacity for engaging in the international communication. . . to tell China's stories well, present a true, multi-dimensional, and panoramic view of China, and enhance [the] country's cultural soft power" (Xi, 2017c, p. 39 emphasis added). Scholars and policymakers consistently make efforts to analyze China's image abroad to develop a strategic framework that justifies China's rise as a global power, boosts its global standing, and fosters its influence on the global stage (Hayden, 2012). Within the scope of this significance, this study is designed to analyze China's image in the Islamic world. The findings of this study will hopefully help improve a better global understanding of China and help improve China's international communication system which eventually helps it to build a strong positive image in the Islamic world.

Significance of the study

China and the Islamic world are becoming influential players in the newly evolving international order as powerful allies under the auspice of BRI that started to bind the Chinese and Muslim communities. They found mutual respect and trust in each other. China has extended the BRI to every corner of the Islamic world and connected Afro-Eurasian communities across Africa, Asia, and Europe through the Indian Ocean, the Atlantic, and Western Pacific shores. The BRI bids China for global leadership and strengthens China's connectivity with the

Islamic world, "with the global economy, and with rapidly changing transnational political order" (Bianchi, 2019; Khan et al., 2018; Khan & Pratt, 2019).

The Islamic world has emerged as an indispensable partner in China's BRI due to its geostrategic, geo-economic, and geopolitical importance in global governance (Khan & Pratt, 2019). It includes 50 Muslim-majority countries that account for more than 24% of the world's landmass (Majoka et al., 2012; World Population Review, 2022). In addition, a total of 1.9 billion people (24.1%) around the world adhere to the Islamic faith (World Population Review, 2022). According to the Pew Research Center, Islam is the world's second-largest and fasting growing religion that will surpass Christianity at the end of this century (Pew Research Center, 2015). Finally, more than 62% of the Muslim population live in close vicinity to China's geographical location in Asia (Khan & Pratt, 2019; Li, 2018; Sherani, 2013).

The Islamic world upholds an influential and powerful "Islamic political bloc of 57 nation-states under the banner of the Organization of Islamic Cooperation (OIC)"—the second-largest intergovernmental body in the world after the United Nations (UN) that animated the geostrategic and geopolitical standing of the Islamic world in global politics (Khan & Pratt, 2019). It also controls abundant natural resources, mainly oil and gas. The Islamic world holds 75% of the world's proven oil reserves and 42–55% of the world's natural gas reservoirs (Cooper & Yue, 2015; Majoka et al., 2012). It is the backbone of the world's natural energy supply; "the Middle East contributes 42% of oil and 26% of natural gas to the world's energy supply chain and it possesses 65.36% of the world's proven oil reserves and 51% of the world's total natural gas resources" (Khan & Pratt, 2019, p. 124). Muslim countries like Saudi Arabia, Iraq, Iran, Kuwait, and Qatar are among the world's largest oil and gas exporters and are vital for the entire world's economic growth, social development, energy security, and human prosperity. China heavily relies on Islamic countries (e.g., Saudi Arabia, Iran, and Iraq) for its petroleum products to sustain its economic growth and social development (Chen, 2011; Cooper & Yue, 2015; Khan & Pratt, 2019; Majoka et al., 2012).

China's unprecedented economic growth and alleviation of more than 800 million people out of poverty entice the international community and strengthen China's image as an emerging global power. Subsequently, the United States' (US) competitive favorability advantage over China declined to 12 from 25 countries, where the US enjoys a more favorable image than China (Vice, 2017). However, Kurlantzick (2022a) argues that China's global image has been weakened in the last few years, not only in rival countries such as Japan, Australia, and the U.S. with whom it has grumpy relations, but also among the developing countries in Asia, Africa, and Europe where it had enjoyed positive or at least neutral relations during the past two decades before COVID-19. He noted various reasons for the decline of China's soft power and the deteriorating China's global public image: (a) rising authoritarianism at home, (b) initial cover-up of the COVID-19 outbreak, (c) repressive actions in Xinjiang and Hong Kong, (d) aggressive "wolf warrior" diplomacy, (e) use of economic coercion against other states and multinationals (companies); and (f) zero-COVID strategy that miff foreign public perception against China and undermine people-to-people contacts that cast doubt on Chinese development model—even within China (Kurlantzick, 2022a, 2022b; Yuan, 2022).

A new Pew Research Center survey (2022) also indicates that in the past four years, China's global image has been damaged intensively in Asia Pacific, Europe, and North Africa and negative public perception about China is at "historic highs" in many of the 19 countries in the Asia Pacific, Europe, and North America. A majority of the people in those regions showed strong resentment and negative opinions toward China's human rights policies (79%), China's growing military power (72%), economic contest with China (66%), and China's involvement in domestic politics of other countries (59%). The U.S. favorability over China has also increased in those regions except Singapore and Malaysia (a Muslim country) where the public still views China more favorably than the U.S. (The Pew Research Center, 2022). In the last four years, the negative public perception of China's image increased in Japan from 78% in 2018 to 87% in 2022, negative public perception in Australia increased up to 87% in 2022, and the U.S. witnessed an increase from 79% in 2019 to 82% in 2022, in South Korea negative public perception about China raised from 60% in 2018 to 80% in 2022. Public perception in European countries that once held a positive view of China in 2018 also changed into negative perceptions in 2022. For example, China's negative perception in Poland increased from 37% in 2018 to 55% in 2022, in Hungary from 47% to 52%, in Greece from 48% to 50%, in Spain from 48% to 63%, in the UK from 35% to 69%, and negative public perception about China in Italy raised from 60% in 2018 to 64% in 2022. China's negative public perception in Israel also rose from 25% in 2018 to 46% in 2022. However, Singapore (34%) and Malaysia (39%) observed relatively low negative public perception of China in 2022 (Silver et al., 2022; The Pew Research Center, 2022). China's public perception in some Islamic countries is also negative and hostile. For example, the majority of the population in four major Islamic nations—Turkey, Jordan, Egypt, and Lebanon hold a negative view of China (Pew Research Center, 2017; Xie & Page, 2013).

The Pew Research Center, Global Indicators Database on global image survey from 2005 through 2019 reported variation in China's unfavorable image perception in some main Islamic countries from an average of 4% to 56% between 2005 through 2019 (Figure 1.1).

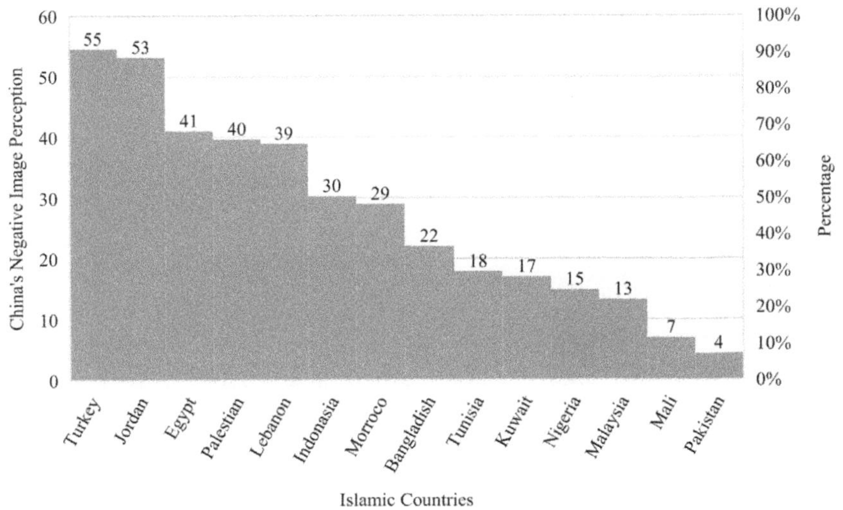

Figure 1.1: An Average of China's Unfavorable Image Perception in the Islamic World between 2005 and 2019.
Source: Pew Research Center, Global Indicators Database 2005–2019

Similarly, an average of more than 50% of the people from the four major Islamic countries, namely Turkey, Jordan, Egypt, and Palestine, self-reported distrust in the Chinese Government's claim to do the right things regarding world affairs between 2014 and 2019 (Pew Research Center, 2014–2019) (Figure 1.2). Public perception of China in some other Islamic countries in the Middle East (e.g., Saudi Arabia) and Africa is also negative, even hostile in some cases (Al-Sudairi, 2013; Khan, Pratt, & Akhtar, 2023; Wekesa, 2013). The favorable perception of China as an emerging global power is still under the shadow of the strong Western narrative in the Islamic world. Therefore, BRI projects can facilitate China's public diplomacy endeavors to enhance its favorable image in the Islamic world.

People's perception of foreign countries mainly depends on how a foreign country is projected in local and international media (Mcnelly & Izcaray, 1986; Semetko et al., 1992; Wanta et al., 2004). Therefore, it is imperative to analyze how Islamic English news media portrayed China's image in the Islamic world during the last decade and how a different dimension of China's image has been interpreted, constructed, and disseminated in Islamic English news media. Particularly, how the influential Islamic English news media outlets (i.e., *Arab News, The Nation, Daily Sabah, Tehran Times, Daily News Egypt,* and *Al-Jazeera English*) of the most influential and powerful Islamic countries i.e., Saudi Arabia,

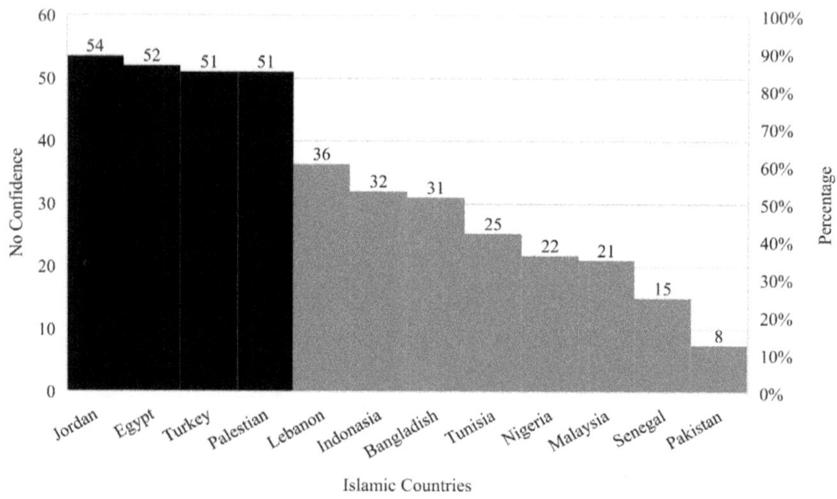

Figure 1.2: How Much Confidence Do You Have in Chinese Leadership to Do the Right Thing Regarding World Affairs?
Source: Pew Research Center, Global Indicators Database 2014–2019

Pakistan, Turkey, Iran, Egypt, and Qatar have presented China as an emerging global power in the Islamic world.

Objectives of the study

The primary objectives of this study are as follows:

1. To analyze and measure China's overall image in the Islamic world. Particularly in the most influential and powerful Islamic countries such as Saudi Arabia, Pakistan, Turkey, Iran, Egypt, and Qatar due to their strong political, economic, and cultural influence in the world and particularly in Muslim countries/Ummah.
2. To examine how Islamic English news media such as *Arab News, The Nation, Daily Sabah, Tehran Times, Daily News Egypt,* and *Al-Jazeera English* have constructed, interpreted, and disseminated China's image in the Islamic world over the last decade.
3. To explore how much attention is paid by Islamic English news media to China's overall image and its particular image dimensions such as political, economic, cultural, social, technological, and so on in the Islamic world.

4. To examine whether the different dimensions of China's image in the Islamic world interrelate and affect each other.
5. To highlight the opportunities and obstacles to China's favorable image in the Islamic world.
   (a) Opportunities and obstacles to China's favorable image in a particular country.
   (b) Opportunities and obstacles to China's favorable image in a particular dimension.
6. To examine the impact of China's economic relationship (imports and exports) with particular Islamic countries such as Saudi Arabia, Pakistan, Turkey, Iran, Egypt, and Qatar on its image in that particular county's media.
7. To measure the impact of the political system (government system) of particular Islamic countries such as Saudi Arabia, Pakistan, Turkey, Iran, Egypt, and Qatar on China's image in that particular county's media.
8. To examine the effects of BRI on China's image construction in the Islamic world
9. To provide policy guidelines to improve China's international communication system that eventually helps her to build a strong positive image in the Islamic world.

Research questions

This study is designed to investigate China's image in the Islamic world. Therefore, the following research questions are proposed: -

RQ1: What is the intensity of the overall attention paid to China-related news by the Islamic English news media and how does the media attention change over time?

RQ 2: How does the Islamic English news media construct China's image in the Islamic world and how did it change over time?

RQ 3: How does Islamic English news media construct different dimensions of China's image in the Islamic world and how do these dimensions change over time?

RQ 4: How do different dimensions of China's image in the Islamic world interrelate and affect each other?

RQ 5: What impact, if any, does China's economic relationship (imports and exports) with particular Islamic countries (i.e., Saudi Arabia,

Pakistan, Turkey, Iran, Egypt, and Qatar) exert on China's image in that particular country's news media?

RQ 6: What impact, if any, does the degree of compatibility in the political system (government system) between China and particular Islamic countries (i.e., Saudi Arabia, Pakistan, Turkey, Iran, Egypt, and Qatar) have on China's image in that particular country's media?

RQ 7: What impact, if any, does the Belt and Road Initiative affect China's image construction in the Islamic world (i.e., Saudi Arabia, Pakistan, Turkey, Iran, Egypt, and Qatar) and how does BRI relate to the different dimensions of China's image in the Islamic world?

An overview of the book

This book comprises eight chapters. Each of those highlights the different aspects of this study. The first chapter encompasses a short introduction to the study and highlights its primary purpose, significance, and objectives. It introduces the research question and provides the scheme of this study.

Chapter II discusses historical connections and highlights immanent challenges and futuristic prospects of Sino-Islamic relations. Chapter III focuses on the trajectory, landscape, challenges, and prospects of the BRI, and its impact on China's global image and political and economic standing in the Islamic world.

Chapter IV provides a well-articulated review of literature related to national/country image construction, interpretation, and dissemination. It focuses on China's image framing in international media, providing a broader view of China's image construction in international and Islamic media. Chapter V reviews China's image perception around the world. It provides a broader picture of China's global image standing in the Islamic and Western world and explores China's image perception on the African continent.

Chapter VI explains the research methodology adopted in this research study. The methodological section defines the procedures, methods, and research protocols adopted in a systematic way to answer the proposed research questions. Quantitative longitudinal content analysis is used as a method of analysis. The researcher strictly followed the recommended guidelines of Wimmer & Dominick (2013) for content analysis to get better results. The study design encompasses the following steps: (a) formulation of research questions, (b) definition of population, (c) selection of an appropriate sample from the population, (d) selection of the unit of analysis, (e) construction of distinct categories of content, and

(g) establishing the quantifications system. The method of intercoder reliability and intercoder agreement is also discussed in this chapter.

Chapter VII highlights the data analysis and results of the study. The researcher used descriptive statistics i.e., frequency tables, and graphs (bar charts, pie charts, and line charts) to examine the frames embedded in the texts and to show the changes and variations in China's image construction, interpretation, and dissemination in different Islamic English news media. The researcher used the Chi-square test to find the significant difference in China's image construction in different Islamic countries. Whereas correlation analysis is used to explore the relationship between China's image construction and particular Islamic English news media. Regression analyses were used to measure the effects of independent variables (e.g., political system, economic relations, and BRI) on China's image construction, interpretation, and dissemination in the Islamic world.

Chapter VIII presents the discussion and conclusion of the study of China's image construction, interpretation, and dissemination in Islamic English news media. It highlights the research findings, discusses its theoretical and practical implication for China's image construction in the Islamic world. It also acknowledges the limitations of the research study and outlines future research directions.

References

Al-Arabia News. (2022, January 20). French parliament officially denounces China's "genocide" against Uyghur Muslims. *Al-Arabia News*. <https://english.alarabiya.net/News/world/2022/01/20/French-parliament-officially-denounces-China-s-genocide-against-Uyghur-Muslims>

Al-Jazeera. (2020, December 18). US Muslim groups accuse OIC of abetting China's Uighur "genocide." *Al-Jazeera English*. <https://www.aljazeera.com/news/2020/12/18/us-muslims-press-organization-of-islamic-cooperation-on-china>

Al-Jazeera. (2022, January 23). Uighurs in Turkey call for boycott of Beijing Winter Olympics. *Al-Jazeera English*. <https://www.aljazeera.com/news/2022/1/23/uighurs-in-turkey-call-for-boycott-of-beijing-winter-olympics>

Al-Sudairi, M. T. (2013). China in the eyes of the Saudi Media. *Gulf Research Center, February*(February), 1–38. <https://www.ictsd.org/sites/default/files/downloads/2013/04/china-in-the-eyes-of-the-saudi-media.pdf>

Alhura. (2021, February 19). "They Flaunt Stories of Rape". A Shocking Testimony from inside the Uyghur Camps [“يتباهون بقصص الاغتصاب”.. شهادة مفزعة من داخل معسكرات الأويغور]. *Al-Watan*. <https://alwatannews.net/article/926244/World/يتباهون-بقصص-الاغتصاب-شهادة-مفزعة-من-داخل-معسكرات-الأويغور>

Allison, S. (2013, July 5). Fixing China's image in Africa, one student at a time. *The Guardian*, 1–7. <https://www.theguardian.com/world/2013/jul/31/china-africa-students-scholarship-programme>

An, J., & Feng, Y. (2022). Do the "Dragon's Gifts" improve China's national image? An empirical analysis of the economic relations and public perceptions of China in Africa. *Journal of Chinese Political Science*, 1–24. <https://doi.org/10.1007/s11366-022-09793-4>

Armony, A. C. (2012). A view from Afar: How Colombia sees China. *The China Quarterly*, *209*, 178–197. <https://doi.org/10.1017/S0305741011001536>

Barr, M. (2012). Nation branding as nation building: China's image campaign. *East Asia*, *29*(1), 81–94. <https://doi.org/10.1007/s12140-011-9159-7>

Bianchi, R. R. (2019). *China and the Islamic World: How the New Silk Road is transforming global politics* (1st ed.). Oxford University Press. <https://doi.org/10.1093/oso/9780190915285.001.0001>

Buhmann, A., & Ingenhoff, D. (2015). The 4D model of the country image: An integrative approach from the perspective of communication management. *International Communication Gazette*, *77*(1), 102–124. <https://doi.org/10.1177/1748048514556986>

Chen, J. (2011). *The emergence of China in Middle East* (Issue 271, pp. 1–8). National Defense University, Washington, DC. <https://doi.org/10.1111/j.1539-6975.2009.01318.x>

Chen, Y. (2020). Developments in China–Turkey relations: A view from China. *Critical Sociology*, *46*(4–5), 777–787. <https://doi.org/10.1177/0896920519885001>

CNBC. (2021, December 12). U.S. imposes sweeping human rights sanctions on China, Myanmar and North Korea. *CNBC*. <https://www.cnbc.com/2021/12/13/us-imposes-human-rights-sanctions-on-china-myanmar-and-north-korea.html>

Cooper, W. W., & Yue, P. (2015). Global oil flow and strategic geography of the Muslim World Article information. In W. W. Cooper & P. Yue (Eds.), *Challenges of the Muslim World* (1st ed., pp. 60–101). Emerald Group Publishing Limited.

Corkin, L. J. (2014). China's rising soft power: The role of rhetoric in constructing China-Africa relations. *Revista Brasileira de Politica Internacional*, *57*, 49–72. <https://doi.org/10.1590/0034-7329201400204>

Cull, N. J. (2009). How we got here. In P. Seib (Ed.), *Toward a new public diplomacy* (pp. 23–47). Springer. <https://doi.org/10.1057/9780230100855_2>

d'Hooghe, I. (2014). *China's public diplomacy*. Martinus Nijhoff Publishers.

de Moura Engracia Giraldi, J., Ikeda, A. A., & Campomar, M. C. (2011). Reasons for country image evaluation: A study on China's image from a Brazilian perspective. *Journal of Database Marketing & Customer Strategy Management*, *18*(2), 97–107. <https://doi.org/10.1057/dbm.2011.10>

Ding, S. (2011). Branding a rising China: An analysis of Beijing's national image management in the age of China's rise. *Journal of Asian and African Studies*, *46*(3), 293–306. <https://doi.org/10.1177/0021909611405830>

Dinnie, K. (2015). *Nation branding: Concepts, issues, practice*. Routledge.

Dinnie, K., & Lio, A. (2010). Enhancing China's image in Japan: Developing the nation brand through public diplomacy. *Place Branding and Public Diplomacy*, *6*(3), 198–206. <https://doi.org/10.1057/pb.2010.20>

Dorraj, M. (2013). *Iran's expanding relations with China and their strategic dimensions* (12th ed.). Emirates Center for Strategic Studies and Research.

Dyke, M. A. Van, & Verčič, D. (2009). Public relations, public diplomacy, and strategic communication: An international model of conceptual convergence. In K. Sriramesh & D. Vercic (Eds.), *The global public relations handbook, revised and expanded edition: Theory, research, and practice* (2nd ed., pp. 822–842). Routledge. <https://doi.org/https://doi.org/10.4324/9780203889374>

Eliküçük Yıldırım, N., & Aslan, M. (2020). China's charm defensive: Image protection by acquiring mass entertainment. *Pacific Focus, 35*(1), 141–171. <https://doi.org/10.1111/pafo.12153>

Elmagherbi, F. I. (2010). A case study of China's relations with the Arab world. *2010 2nd IEEE International Conference on Information and Financial Engineering*, 646–650. <https://doi.org/10.1109/ICIFE.2010.5609442>

Elmagherbi, F. I., & Wang, R. (2011). Optimum plan to improve the economic relation between China and Arab world. *Modern Applied Science, 5*(6), 181–187. <https://doi.org/10.5539/mas.v5n6p181>

Ezell, C. (2021). Human Rights abuses in Xinjiang: Perspectives and responses from the Islamic World and the Middle East. In *Center for Open Science*. SocArXiv. <https://doi.org/10.31219/osf.io/mk7q6>

Gao, J., Ingram, C., & Kee, P. (2016). *Global media and public diplomacy in Sino-Western relations*. Routledge.

Gertner, R. K. (2010). Similarities and differences of the effect of country images on tourist and study destinations. *Journal of Travel & Tourism Marketing, 27*(4), 383–395. <https://doi.org/10.1080/10548408.2010.481572>

Gilboa, E. (2008). Searching for a theory of public diplomacy. *The Annals of the American Academy of Political and Social Science, 616*(1), 55–77. <https://doi.org/10.1177/00027162073121>

Gong, L. (2021). Humanitarian diplomacy as an instrument for China's image-building. *Asian Journal of Comparative Politics, 6*(3), 238–252. <https://doi.org/10.1177/20578911211019257>

Guo, Q., Wang, H., Yu, T., Tang, X., Chen, R., & Li, P. (2015). A study on Chinese National Image under the background of Beijing Olympic Games. *International English Education Research, 8*, 5–11. <http://en.cnki.com.cn/Article_en/CJFDTOTAL-TYKX200908002.htm>

Han, F., Zhao, K., & Ke, Y. (2012). *Gonggong waijiao gailun [Introduction to public diplomacy]*. Peking University Press.

Han, G. K., & Wang, X. C. (2014). Analysis finds U.S. newspapers use six frames for "Made in China". *Newspaper Research Journal, 35*(2), 6–24. <https://doi.org/10.1177/073953291403500202>

Hartig, F. (2016). How China understands public diplomacy: The importance of national image for national interests. *International Studies Review, 18*(4), 655–680. <https://doi.org/10.1093/isr/viw007>

Hartig, F. (2019). A review of the current state of research on China's international image management. *Communication and the Public, 4*(1), 68–81. <https://doi.org/10.1177/2057047319836495>

Hayden, C. (2012). *The rhetoric of soft power: Public diplomacy in global contexts*. Lexington Books.

Hayoun, M. (2013). Strange Bedfellows: China's Middle Eastern Inroads. *World Affairs, 175*(5), 89–96. <http://www.jstor.org/stable/43554744>

Jacob, J. T. (2020). "To Tell China's Story Well": China's international messaging during the COVID-19 pandemic. *China Report, 56*(3), 374–392. <https://doi.org/10.1177/000944552 0930395>

Jia, R., & Li, W. (2020). Public diplomacy networks: China's public diplomacy communication practices in Twitter during Two Sessions. *Public Relations Review, 46*(1), 1–12. <https://doi.org/10.1016/j.pubrev.2019.101818>

Jin, X., Li, D. D., & Wu, S. (2016). How will China shape the world economy? *China Economic Review, 40*, 272–280. <https://doi.org/10.1016/j.chieco.2016.07.006>

Kelemen, B., & Turcsányi, R. Q. (2020). It's the politics, stupid: China's relations with Muslim countries on the background of Xinjiang crackdown. *Asian Ethnicity, 21*(2), 223–243. <https://doi.org/10.1080/14631369.2019.1677145>

Khan, M. K., & Pratt, C. B. (2019). China's Belt and Road Initiative: Its landscape (and trajectory) in the Islamic World. In A. Visvizi, M. Lytras, X. Zhang, & J. Zhao (Eds.), *Foreign business in China and opportunities for technological innovation and sustainable economics* (pp. 117–142). IGI Global. <https://doi.org/10.4018/978-1-5225-8980-8.ch006>

Khan, M. K., Pratt, C. B., & Akhtar, N. (2023). China's public diplomacy for image making in Islamic North Africa: Frames of the Belt and Road Initiative in Daily News Egypt. In: A. A. Anani-Bossman, T. E. Mudzanani, C. B. Pratt, I. A. Blankson (Eds.), *Public relations management in Africa Volume 1*. Cham: Palgrave Macmillan. <https://doi.org/10.1007/978-3-031-26704-8_5>

Khan, M. K., Sallam, M. H., Pratt, C. B., & Farid, T. (2022). Stereotyping the Chinese in Arab Nations: The effects of media use, perceived realism and Chinese-Arab relations. *The Social Science Journal*. <https://doi.org/10.1080/03623319.2021.2025197>

Khan, M. K., Sandano, I. A., Pratt, C. B., & Farid, T. (2018). China's Belt and Road Initiative: A global model for an evolving approach to Sustainable Regional Development. *Sustainability, 10*(11), 4234. <https://doi.org/10.3390/su10114234>

Kotler, P., & Gertner, D. (2002). Country as brand, product, and beyond: A place marketing and brand management perspective. *Journal of Brand Management, 9*(4), 249–261. <https://doi.org/10.1057/palgrave.bm.2540076>

Kunczik, M. (2002). Globalisation: News media, images of nations and the flow of international capital with special reference to the role of rating agencies. *Journal of International Communication, 8*(1), 39–79. <https://doi.org/10.1080/13216597.2002.9751921>

Kunczik, M. (2003). Transnational public relations by foreign governments. In K. Sriramesh & D. Vercic (Eds.), *The global public relations handbook: Theory, research, and practice* (pp. 399–424). Mahwah, NJ: Lawrence Erlbaum.

Kunczik, M. (2016). *Images of nations and international public relations*. Routledge.

Kurlantzick, J. (2007). *Charm offensive: How China's soft power is transforming the world*. Yale University Press.

Kurlantzick, J. (2022a). *China's collapsing global image: How Beijing's unpopularity is undermining its strategic, economic, and diplomatic goals* (Issue July, pp. 1–38). Council on Foreign Relations. <https://www.cfr.org/report/chinas-collapsing-global-image>

Kurlantzick, J. (2022b, July 22). China's poor global image is undermining its strategic goals. *The Diplomat.* <https://thediplomat.com/2022/07/chinas-poor-global-image-is-undermining-its-strategic-goals/>

Lee, M., & Hao, Y. (2018). China's unsuccessful charm offensive: How South Koreans have viewed the rise of China over the past decade. *Journal of Contemporary China, 27*(114), 867–886. <https://doi.org/10.1080/10670564.2018.1488103>

Leonard, M., Stead, C., & Smewing, C. (2002). *Public diplomacy.* Foreign Policy Centre.

Li, F. (2018). The role of Islam in the development of the "Belt and Road" Initiative. *Asian Journal of Middle Eastern and Islamic Studies, 12*(1), 35–45. <https://doi.org/10.1080/25765949.2018.1439617>

Li, M. (2008). *Soft power in Chinese discourse : Popularity and prospect.* <http://hdl.handle.net/10220/4552>

Liu, X., & Yang, Y. E. (2015). Examining China's official media perception of the United States: A content analysis of people's daily coverage. *Journal of Chinese Political Science, 20*(4), 385–408. <https://doi.org/10.1007/s11366-015-9340-8>

Majoka, M. I., Sahibzada, H. E., & Khan, M. S. (2012). Resources of the Muslim World: A reflection on the Muslim World's Resources, their development and utilization. *Journal of Islamic Thought and Civilization, 02*(01), 73–87. <https://doi.org/10.32350/jitc.21.05>

Makar, S. H. (1985). *The People's Republic of China's policy toward the Arab world in the 1970s* [New York University]. <https://doi.org/10.3102/00346543067001043>

Mather, V. (2022, January 5). The diplomatic Boycott of the Beijing Winter Olympics, explained. *The New York Times.* <https://www.nytimes.com/article/diplomatic-boycott-olympics.html>

Mcnelly, J. T., & Izcaray, F. (1986). International news exposure and images of nations. *Journalism & Mass Communication Quarterly, 63*(3), 546–553. <https://doi.org/10.1177/107769908606300315>

Melissen, J. (2005). The new public diplomacy: Between theory and practice. In *The new public diplomacy* (pp. 3–27). Springer.

Meng, X. (2020). Perceptual barriers to China's national image and their causes. In *National Image* (pp. 19–62). Springer.

Nebehay, S. (2021, February 22). China rejects genocide charge in Xinjiang, says door open to U.N. *Reuters.* <https://www.reuters.com/article/us-china-rights-idUSKBN2AM1UX>

Nye, J. S. (2005). *Soft power: The means to success in world politics.* Public affairs. <http://www.tinyurl.com/mug36ku>

Nye, J. S., & Jisi, W. (2009). Hard decisions on soft power: Opportunities and difficulties for Chinese Soft Power. *Harvard International Review, 31*(2), 18. <https://www.hks.harvard.edu/publications/hard-decisions-soft-power-opportunities-and-difficulties-chinese-soft-power#citation>

Olimat, M. S. (2010). The political economy of the Sino-Middle Eastern relations. *Journal of Chinese Political Science, 15*(3), 307–335. <https://doi.org/10.1007/s11366-010-9114-2>

Papadopoulos, N. (1993). What product and country images are and are not? In N. Papadopoulos & L. A. Heslop (Eds.), *Product-country images: Impact and role in international marketing* (pp. 3–38). New York, NY: International Business Press.

Papadopoulos, N. (2004). Place branding: Evolution, meaning and implications. *Place Branding, 1*(1), 36–49. <https://doi.org/10.1057/palgrave.pb.5990003>

Peng, Z. (2004). Representation of China: An across time analysis of coverage in the New York Times and Los Angeles Times. *Asian Journal of Communication, 14*(1), 53–67. <https://doi.org/10.1080/0129298042000195170>

Pew Research Center. (2015). *The future of world religions: Population growth projections, 2010–2050.* <https://www.pewresearch.org/religion/2015/04/02/religious-projections-2010-2050/>

Pew Research Center. (2017). *China Image: Do you have a favorable or unfavorable view of China?* <http://www.pewglobal.org/database/indicator/24/survey/17/response/Unfavorable/>

Price, R. (2003). Transnational civil society and advocacy in world politics. *World Politics, 55*(4), 579–606. <https://www.jstor.org/stable/25054239>

Rabinovitch, S. (2008). The rise of an image-conscious China. *China Security, 4*(3), 33–47.

Ramo, J. C. (2004). *The Beijing Consensus.* Foreign Policy Centre London.

Ramo, J. C. (2007). *Brand China.* Foreign Policy Centre.

Rawnsley, G. (2012). Approaches to soft power and public diplomacy in China and Taiwan. *Journal of International Communication, 18*(2), 121–135. <https://doi.org/10.1080/13216597.2012.695744>

Rawnsley, G. (2014). "Thought-Work" and propaganda: Chinese Public Diplomacy and Public Relations after Tiananmen Square. In *Oxford handbook of propaganda studies* (pp. 147–162). Oxford University Press.

Roache, M. (2021, December 9). China guilty of Uighur genocide in Xinjiang, tribunal rules. *Al-Jazeera.* <https://www.aljazeera.com/news/2021/12/9/china-guilty-of-uighur-genocide-beyond-reasonable-doubt-report>

Schatz, E., & Levine, R. (2010). Framing, public diplomacy, and anti-Americanism in Central Asia. *International Studies Quarterly, 54*(3), 855–869. <https://www.jstor.org/stable/40931139>

Schliebs, M., Bailey, H., Bright, J., & Howard, P. N. (2021). *China's public diplomacy operations: Understanding engagement and inauthentic amplifications of PRC diplomats on Facebook and Twitter.* Programme on Democracy and Technology, Oxford University. <https://ora.ox.ac.uk/objects/uuid:427320a1-c677-40d4-b4a5-1759e563e7ed>

Scott, D. (2015). China's public diplomacy rhetoric, 1990–2012: Pragmatic image-crafting. *Diplomacy and Statecraft, 26*(2), 249–265. <https://doi.org/10.1080/09592296.2015.1034563>

Sekkal. (2013). Upheaval in the Arab World and China-Arab Cooperation. *China International Studies, 41*(July/August), 84–89. <https://heinonline.org/HOL/LandingPage?handle=hein.journals/chintersd41&div=8&id=&page=>

Semetko, H. A., Brzinski, J. B., Weaver, D., & Willnat, L. (1992). TV news and US public opinion about foreign countries: The impact of exposure and attention. *International Journal of Public Opinion Research, 4*(1), 18–36. <https://doi.org/10.1093/ijpor/4.1.18>

Sherani, S. (2013, August 12). Economies of the ummah. *Dawn.* <https://www.dawn.com/news/1035026>

Silver, L., Huang, C., & Clancy, L. (2022, June 29). Negative views of China tied to critical views of its policies on human rights. *The Pew Research Center.* <https://www.pewresearch.org/global/2022/06/29/negative-views-of-china-tied-to-critical-views-of-its-policies-on-human-rights/>

Snow, N., & Taylor, P. M. (2008). *Routledge handbook of public diplomacy.* Routledge.

Srikatanyoo, N., & Gnoth, J. (2002). Country image and international tertiary education. *The Journal of Brand Management, 10*(2), 139–146. <https://doi.org/10.1057/palgrave.bm.2540111>

Sun, H. H. (2008). International political marketing: A case study of United States soft power and public diplomacy. *Journal of Public Affairs, 8*(3), 165–183. <https://doi.org/10.1002/pa.301>

Tapachai, N., & Waryszak, R. (2000). An examination of the role of beneficial image in tourist destination selection. *Journal of Travel Research, 39*(1), 37–44. <https://doi.org/10.1177/00472875000390010>

The Pew Research Center. (2022, June 29). U.S. receives more positive ratings than China in most countries. *The Pew Research Center*, 1. <https://www.pewresearch.org/fact-tank/2022/06/29/across-19-countries-more-people-see-the-u-s-than-china-favorably-but-more-see-chinas-influence-growing/ft_2022-06-29_chinaus_01/>

Van Ham, P. (2008). Place branding: The state of the art. *The Annals of the American Academy of Political and Social Science, 616*(1), 126–149. <https://doi.org/10.1177/0002716207312274>

Vice, M. (2017). *In global popularity contest, U.S. and China—not Russia—vie for first.* <http://www.pewresearch.org/fact-tank/2017/08/23/in-global-popularity-contest-u-s-and-china-not-russia-vie-for-first/>

Vickers, R. (2004). The new public diplomacy: Britain and Canada compared. *The British Journal of Politics and International Relations, 6*(2), 182–194. <https://doi.org/10.1111/j.1467-856X.2004.00133>

Voon, J. P., & Xu, X. (2020). Impact of the Belt and Road Initiative on China's soft power: Preliminary evidence. *Asia-Pacific Journal of Accounting and Economics, 27*(1), 120–131. <https://doi.org/10.1080/16081625.2020.1686841>

Wang, H. (2011). Soft power in China: Public diplomacy through communication. In J. Wang (Ed.), *Palgrave Macmillan* (1st ed.). Palgrave Macmillan.

Wang, J. (2006). Managing national reputation and international relations in the global era: Public diplomacy revisited. *Public Relations Review, 32*(2), 91–96. <https://doi.org/10.1016/j.pubrev.2005.12.001>

Wanta, W., Golan, G., & Lee, C. (2004). Agenda setting and international news: Media influence on public perceptions of foreign nations. *Journalism & Mass Communication Quarterly, 81*(2), 364–377. <https://doi.org/10.1177/107769900408100209>

Wekesa, B. (2013). The media framing of China's image in East Africa: An exploratory study. *African East-Asian Affairs: The China Monitor, 1*, 15–42. <https://doi.org/10.7552/0-1-2>

Werron, T. (2013). On public forms of competition. *Cultural Studies? Critical Methodologies, 14*(1), 62–76. <https://doi.org/10.1177/1532708613507891>

Wimmer, R. D., & Dominick, J. R. (2013). *Mass communication research: An introduction* (10th ed.). Cengage Learning.

World Population Review. (2022). *Muslim Majority Countries 2022.* <https://worldpopulationreview.com/country-rankings/muslim-majority-countries>

Xi, J. (2017, October 18). Secure a decisive victory in building a moderately prosperous society in all respects and strive for the great success of socialism with Chinese characteristics for a new era. *Xinhua*, 1–66. <http://www.xinhuanet.com/english/download/Xi_Jinping's_report_at_19th_CPC_National_Congress.pdf>

Xiang, D. (2013). China's image on international English language social media. *Journal of International Communication, 19*(2), 252–271. <https://doi.org/10.1080/13216597.2013.833535>

Xiaodong, C. (2013). Creating a bright future for China-Arab relations. *China International Studies, July/August*, 69–78.

Xie, T., & Page, B. I. (2013). What affects China's national image? A cross-national study of public opinion. *Journal of Contemporary China, 22*(83), 850–867. <https://doi.org/10.1080/10670564.2013.782130>

Yuan, L. (2022, April 1). Covid, Russia and economy put the "China Model" to the test. *The New York Times*. <https://www.nytimes.com/2022/03/31/business/china-covid-economy-russia.html>

Yusuf, H. (2020, July 27). Silence won't pay. *Dawn*. <https://www.dawn.com/news/1571363>

Zeng, G., Go, F., & Kolmer, C. (2014). The impact of international TV media coverage of the Beijing Olympics 2008 on China's media image formation: A media content analysis perspective. *International Journal of Sports Marketing & Sponsorship, 12*(4), 319–337. <https://doi.org/10.1108/IJSMS-12-04-2011-B004>

Zhang, J., & Cameron, G. T. (2003). China's agenda building and image polishing in the US: Assessing an international public relations campaign. *Public Relations Review, 29*(1), 13–28. <https://doi.org/10.1016/S0363-8111(02)00198-4>

Zhao, K. (2017). China's public diplomacy for international public goods. *Politics and Policy, 45*(5), 706–732. <https://doi.org/10.1111/polp.12223>

Zheng, B. (2005). China's "peaceful rise" to great-power status. *Foreign Affairs*, 18–24. <https://www.foreignaffairs.com/articles/asia/2005-09-01/chinas-peaceful-rise-great-power-status>

Zhu, W. (2010). On the strategic relationship between China and Islamic countries in the Middle East. *Journal of Middle Eastern and Islamic Studies (in Asia), 4*(3), 1–27. <https://doi.org/10.1080/19370679.2010.12023159>

II

China and Islamic World: The Mutually Beneficial Relationship

The historic linkages between the world's two greatest civilizations—the Islamic and the Chinese stretched back to the early age of the Islamic caliphate (empire) when the Umayyad caliphate dispatched several Arab diplomatic missions, including a diplomatic mission headed by the historic Islamic figure, Hazrat Sad ibn Abī Waqqas (buried in Guangzhou, Guangdong Province, China), a close relative of Prophet Muhammad (The founder of religion Islam and the most sacred figure in the Islamic faith) to Guangzhou (China) to establish peaceful relation and to strengthen the economic and sociocultural exchange between the Islamic empire and Tang dynasty during 651 through 750. However, the expansionist approach in the early rise of both new empires: the Islamic Empire—Abbasid caliphate's Eastward push into Central Asia and the Tang dynasty's Westward expansion, resulted in a Battle of Talas at Taraz, Kazakhstan between the Chinese army and Islamic forces in 751. The first and only military clash between the Islamic and the Chinese societies over military and political supremacy in Central Asia resulted in a dwindling of trade along the overland routes of the Silk Road but later stimulated a new maritime Silk route to facilitate the trade and cultural contact between China and the Islamic world during the 8th Century (Jones-Leaning & Pratt, 2012; Park, 2012). The battle of Talas draws permanent frontiers between the Islamic and Chinese empires and provides opportunities for close interaction between two great civilizations that help facilitate mutual learning from each other's experiences, for example, the transmission of papermaking technology to the Islamic world by the Chinese prison of war (Frankel, 2016; Gernet, 1982; Jones-Leaning & Pratt, 2012; Li, 2018).

China and Islamic empires established a strong strategic relationship as early as five years after the battle of Talas in 756 when Abbasid's emperor al-Mansur, dispatched 22,000 Arab Muslim mercenary soldiers to China on the Chinese emperor's request to squash the growing rebellion led by a Chinese General An Lushan against the Tang dynasty and help retake the fallen capitals of Luoyang and Chang'an during 755 through 763. Those Muslim mercenaries later settled down in the rural and urban parts of Western China along the Silk Road. They intermarry Chinese women and become the Muslim pioneers of the Hui minority in China (Frankel, 2016). The embedment of Islamic culture into Chinese society not only enhances the socio-cultural exchanges between the two great civilizations, but the subsequent generations of Chinese Muslims also facilitate the economic relations (trade and business) and diplomacy (political and cultural dialogue) between China and the Islamic world during the rise and fall of the two empires—the Islamic and Chinese during 960–1279 and afterward (Frankel, 2016; Li, 2018; Park, 2012; Rossabi, 1985).

Historical Silk Road connections

Historically, the Silk Road integrated the two great civilizations and connected China to the Islamic world. It significantly contributed to mutual understanding, peaceful coexistence, and mutual cooperation between the two civilizations for mutual benefits and prosperity (Khan & Pratt, 2019; Zambelis & Gentry, 2008). The Islamic preachers and merchants from Central Asia, Western Asia, and the Arab Peninsula used the Silk Road to visit China to spread Islamic culture and trade into the Chinese societies, informing them about their native lands, religion, and neighboring countries. Reciprocally, Silk the Road facilitated the Chinese civilization in spreading its dogmas and practices, crafts, and trade to Central Asia, East Asia, South Asia, West Asia, Africa, and Europe through Muslim countries (Park, 2012; Zhu, 2011).

Park (2012) argues that the Silk Road contributed greatly to the Islamic world and China's economic and cross-cultural development from 700 through 1500. The information flow and cross-trade between China and the Islamic world promoted mutual learning, enhanced mutual understanding, and strengthened the relationship between the two civilizations. Muslim traders imported porcelains, tea, and Silk from China to the Islamic world. At the same time, Chinese traders acquired spices, precious stones, gold, and fragrances through the Silk Road from the Islamic world. The Islamic and Chinese societies' love for science and technology also brought them closer to one another (Sekkal, 2013). Prophet Muhammad instructed his followers to seek knowledge even if they had to travel as distant as China. Therefore, China as a land of wisdom and science at the time provided a prodigious environment for both Islamic and Chinese societies to interact, understand, and initiate cultural dialogues (Sekkal, 2013). The Islamic world learned various technological inventions from China, notably paper-making techniques, and the Compass while Chinese scholars learned advanced knowledge about Mathematics, Astronomy, Medicine, and Engineering from the Islamic world. The historians, writers, and mapmakers of both societies consistently recorded, updated and added new geographical, cultural, economic, and social information about China and the Islamic world. Consequently, both societies had developed a mutual understanding as Muslims of Central Asia, West Asia, the Middle East, and North Africa got a better understating of Chinese society and the Chinese learned more about the Islamic world than other societies during the 18th Century (Benabdallah, 2018; Bianchi, 2019; Park, 2012).

Modern Sino-Islamic relations

China and the Islamic world relationships are as old as Islam itself (Frankel, 2016). But the modern diplomatic relationships between China (People's Republic of China) and the Islamic world were established when Chinese Premier Zhou Enlai visited Indonesia to participate in the Bandung conference to discuss peace, economic development, and decolonization of Asia, the Middle East, and African countries in 1955. The conference was co-hosted by newly decolonized countries: Indonesia, Pakistan, India, Sri Lanka, and Myanmar (Burma) and delegates from 29 countries from Asia, Africa, and the Middle East participated in the conference (*Bandung Conference*, 1955). The Bandung conference provided an opportunity for the Chinese leadership to interconnect with Islamic leaders from Indonesia, Pakistan, Egypt, Sudan, Saudi Arabia, Libya, Afghanistan, and representatives from other Islamic countries like Palestine, etc. Chinese Premier Zhou Enlai used the platform to attenuate the mistrust between China and the Islamic world regarding China's social, ideological, and religious policies. He emphasized China's five diplomatic principles of cooperation and peaceful coexistence with the Islamic world—political choice of self-determination, non-interference in internal affairs, non-aggression, equality, and mutual respect for sovereignty and territorial integrity. He reiterated China's commitment to seek common ground while putting aside differences to foster mutual understanding and strengthen the friendly relationship with the Islamic world (Khan & Pratt, 2019; Yu, 2006; Zhan, 2006). The Islamic leadership lauded the Chinese leadership's goodwill gestures and Egyptian President Gamal A. Nasser promised Zhou Enlai to send the Egyptian diplomatic missions to Beijing to fortify bilateral relations in 1956. Egypt was the first Arab and African country that recognize the People's Republic of China in 1956. Subsequently, China provided financial aid and staunch support to Egypt during the Suez Crisis of 1956 (Abbasi, 1989).

The Bandung conference opened the diplomatic doors for China and several Muslim countries, such as Egypt, Indonesia, Syria, Yemen, and Iraq to establish diplomatic relations with the People's Republic of China in the 1950s (Bhola, 1986; Elmagherbi, 2010). Pakistan was the first Islamic country that establish diplomatic relations with China in 1950. Later, Islamic countries such as Pakistan and Egypt facilitated China's smooth relations with the Islamic world and other countries in Africa, Asia, and the Latin American region (Khan & Pratt, 2019; Zhu, 2011). Pakistan strongly supported China's claim to a permanent seat in the United Nations Security Council (UNSC) on September 25, 1950, when Pakistani Foreign Minister Zafar Ullah Khan stalwartly backed China's stance in the UN general assembly:

> "China is not applying for admission to the UN. It is a member state, a permanent member of the Security Council, one of the big five … it is entitled as of right to be represented in the United Nations like every other member state." (Abbasi, 1989, p. 44)

Since then, China has enjoyed strong and friendly relationships with the Islamic world. Despite the facts, some Arab countries stayed odd with China over some religious, cultural, economic, and diplomatic issues (e.g., only 8 Arab countries recognized the People's Republic of China till 1965). After China's Cultural Revolution (1966–1976), Arab countries significantly realigned their relationship and established diplomatic relations with China due to the growing security challenges in the Arab world, particularly in the Middle East. Subsequently, Kuwait, Iran, and Turkey established a diplomatic relationship with China in 1971; Jordan in 1977; Oman in 1978; the United Arab Emirates (UAE) in 1984, and lately Saudi Arabia in 1991 (Abbasi, 1989; Frankel, 2016).

Mutually beneficial relationship

The strong political, economic, and strategic relations between China and the Islamic world have many historic and futuristic dimensions in common. First, historically, the Silk Road opened a gateway for China to communicate with the Islamic world, particularly with the Arab world through Pakistan. Silk Road amplified the huge potential of trade, culture, and diplomatic exchanges between the two major superpowers of the time. The robust exchanges and intercultural flow between the two civilizations enhanced mutual understanding and enriched each other. Even, the congenial cultural exchanges give birth to a new Muslim ethnic community "Hui Zu" in China (the largest Muslim ethnic group in China) which strengthens the mutual understanding between the two civilized cultures (Abbasi, 1989; Rossabi, 1985). Bianchi (2013) argues that China appraises Muslim culture as an addition to its rich culture and national resources due to its indigenous creation rather than subversive dangers—foreign implants and, therefore, trying to blend Chinese tradition with Islamic principles to enlarge China's friendly relations with the Islamic world. President Xi also acknowledged the positive contribution of the Islamic civilization that "enriches Chinese civilization". He also praised the Muslim scholar and explorer Ibn Batuta in promoting China and Chinese culture in the Islamic world while addressing the "Conference on Dialogue of Asian Civilizations" held in Beijing on May 16, 2019 (Hussain, 2022).

China hosts more than 23.3 million Chinese Muslim population who make up 2% of the Chinese total population. There are 10 official Muslim ethnic minorities in China. The most prominent are Hui, Uyghur, Kazakh, Dongxiang, etc. A majority of them live in Northwestern parts of China i.e., Xinjiang, Ningxia, Gansu, and Qinghai. In addition, a substantial number of Muslim communities also exist in big Chinese cities such as Guangzhou, Beijing, Shanghai, Tianjin, etc. China is among the top three non-Islamic countries (India, China, and Ethiopia) that host more than 20 million Muslim minorities (Grim & Karim, 2011; Li, 2018). Historically, those Muslim communities played a crucial role in nurturing the cordial relationship between China and the Islamic world (Khan & Pratt, 2019).

Second, the Islamic world as a strategic geographic bloc—is a third potential force in the international power equation that will have a consequential role in the global strategic balance of power or future world wars (Abbasi, 1989; Sheikhneshin et al., 2020). The Western countries, particularly the U.S.' recent shift of policy toward Taiwan exodus the "One China" principle. U.S. President

Joe Biden categorically announced to use of U.S. forces to defend Taiwan's independence in case of war with China during his maiden visit to Japan on May 23, 2022 (*Reuters*, 2022). The U.S. is gradually retreating from the long-held "strategic ambiguity" doctrine toward Taiwan and openly expressing "America's unwavering commitment to supporting Taiwan's vibrant Democracy". Recently, Nancy Pelosi, the highest-ranking U.S. official and Speaker of the House of Representatives visited the "self-ruled Taiwan" after the lapse of 25 years despite China's strong opposition on August 2, 2022, further elucidating the U.S. future strategy policy to contain China's rise through the Taiwan card. Pelosi in her opinion piece in Washington Post shortly after she arrived in Taipei strongly criticized China's domestic and global policies and actions and extended univocal U.S. support to the democratic government in Taiwan. She wrote that "In the face of the Chinese Communist Party's (CCP) accelerating aggression, our congressional delegation's visit should be seen as an unequivocal statement that America stands with Taiwan," (Pelosi, 2022).

The West's blockade of Russia over the Ukraine war has already destabilized the strategic balance in the region as the entire Western countries stand firm against Russia and alienated it from the global economic and political landscape. The Western bloc led by the United States can potentially use the Taiwan issue to encircle China and seclude it from the international economic and political institutions. The Western bloc can even wage an all-out war on China on the pretext of the Taiwan issue as evident from President Biden's recent comments during Japan's visit. China is already facing rivalry in the region in the form of a quadrilateral security alliance "the QUAD"—comprising the U.S., India, Australia, and Japan that aims to promote democratic values and protect freedom of navigation in the South China Sea. But, the purpose seems to encircle China and confine its growing influence in the region as former U.S. Secretary of State Mike Pompeo stated that the alliance is determined to "protect our people and partners from the Chinese Communist Party's exploitation, corruption, and coercion" during the alliance meeting in October 2020 (Pompeo, 2020). In such a scenario, any potential conflict over Taiwan will jeopardize China's energy and trade routes in the Pacific and Indian Oceans which are largely controlled by American warships. The Islamic world provides alternative lifelines to China's energy and trade corridors through land and sea. For example, Central Asia and Middle East regions can become a gateway for China to connect with South Asia, Europe, and Africa through the Western Pacific as well as Latin America (Bianchi, 2013; Kaplan, 2011). Therefore, China perceives the Islamic world as a potential strategic partner that can help China to resist Western pressure and fortify its standing against the Western hegemony in the region (Khan & Pratt, 2019; Malik, 2002). The Islamic world supports the "One China" principle and does not recognize Taiwan as an independent country. Therefore, China always appraises the Islamic world for its staunch support and principled stance on the Taiwan issue (Bhola, 1986; Elmagherbi, 2010).

Third, the Western civilization enthralls historical enmity toward China and Islam (Confucian and Islamic civilizations) as they consider both as a potential threat to the Western identity and supremacy even if "Confucian and Islamic societies attempt to expand their own economic and military power to resist and to "balance" against the West" (Huntington, 1997, p. 29). China and the Islamic world are sister civilizations that suffered similar repression and humiliation from Western imperialism which ruined their glorious culture, exploited their national resources, and displaced their status as world-leading powers during the 19th and 20th Centuries (Bianchi, 2013; Legrenzi & Lawson, 2015; Ryter, 2018). Therefore, China and the Islamic world are mending their relations under a comprehensive strategic partnership framework to enhance their political, economic, and strategic leverage on the global stage (Moniruzzaman, 2013, 2020).

Fourth, over the years, the Islamic world has shown strong resentment against the growing U.S. hegemony and political meddling in the internal affairs of sovereign Islamic countries. Particularly, the U.S.'s coercive actions by means of waging full-fledged wars and ruining the sovereign Islamic countries (e.g., Iraq, Syria, Libya, and Afghanistan) under the pretense of freedom, democracy, and counterterrorism. The Islamic world is looking for an alternative global power (a substitute to the U.S.) that can help them refurbish their shrinking economies and settle their lingering political disputes. Khan and Pratt (2019) argue that China has emerged as a new substitute to the U.S. in the Islamic world that respects state sovereignty and believes in non-interference in countries' domestic affairs. It has the potential as a permanent member of the UNSC to ameliorate and solve political disputes peacefully in the Islamic world (Elmagherbi, 2010; Hayoun, 2013; Zambelis & Gentry, 2008; Zhu, 2011). The recent Saudi-Iran peace agreement further solidified China's position as a peace broker in the Islamic world. The Islamic world appraises China's consistent support for an independent Palestine and strong denouncement of U.S. interference, invasion, and occupation of Islamic countries (e.g., Iran, Libya, Iraq, Syria, and Afghanistan). Therefore, Saudi King Abdullah unequivocally described China as a reliable and trustworthy friend that "always stands on the side of truth and justice, always on the side of the just cause of the Palestinian people and the Arab people" (Khan & Pratt, 2019, p. 125; Zhu, 2011, p. 8).

Fifth, the U.S. is losing its strategic posture in the Islamic world due to its repressive foreign policies toward Islamic countries (i.e., waging wars, political meddling, economic sanctions, an arms embargo, etc.,). The former U.S. allies (e.g., Pakistan, Egypt, Iraq, Saudi Arabia, etc.,) that were once considered as U.S. virtual peripheries have significantly revised their foreign policies and strengthened their strategic relationship with China. Consequently, more and more Islamic countries are moving out of U.S. influence (e.g., Pakistan, Turkey, Egypt, Iraq, etc.,) and adhering to the independent foreign policy to court Chinese diplomatic support, military cooperation, economic capital, trade, and financial investment for infrastructural development. Recently, Indonesia vetoed a U.S. mediation offer over a territorial dispute with China (Bianchi, 2013).

Sixth, the Islamic world moved toward China due to the evolving security challenges in the Islamic world. It has boosted defense cooperation with China as a new potential arms supply dealer to the Islamic world after the U.S. embargo on sophisticated weaponry sales to South Asian and West Asian Islamic countries. Recently, the U.S. has refused to provide a Patriot surface-to-air missile system to Turkey and also frozen all major arms sales (Insinna et al., 2020). In addition, when NATO withdrew from joint military exercises with Turkey due to the exclusion of Israel, the Chinese Air Force filled the gap, making history in the strategic defense cooperation between China and Turkey (Bianchi, 2013). Similarly, Pakistan and the United Arab Emirates purchased the 4.5 generation modern J-10C fighter aircraft from China to strengthen its national defense capabilities in 2022. It is pertinent to mention that the U.S. government refused to provide modern F-16 fighter aircraft to Pakistan against its original commitments to subsidize the sale of eight F-16 fighter aircraft to Pakistan under the U.S. foreign military financing program in 2016 (Gul, 2022; Hussain, 2022; Upadhyay, 2016).

Seven, China has become the world's largest economy, and to sustain its economic and industrial growth, it needs unhindered access to natural resources (i.e., oil and gas). The Islamic world possesses the world's largest known natural resources (e.g., oil and gas), and the largest chunk of Chinese oil imports came from the Islamic world (Chen, 2011; Cooper & Yue, 2015; Khan & Pratt, 2019; Majoka et al., 2012). For example, China's oil imports from Saudi Arabia rose to 38%, making it China's largest oil supplier in 2021. In addition, Islamic countries like Iraq, Oman, the United Arab Emirates, and Iran are listed among the top 10 countries that supplied oil to China in 2021 (Aizhu, 2022). Therefore, China's strategic relationship with the Islamic world is pivotal for China's steady economic growth, socioeconomic development, and dream of becoming a great global power. It is also evident from China's Arab policy of "oil and gas plus," which synergizes the Chinese-Arab relationships to a new level of benevolence as well as a strategic partnership to ensure political stability and peace in the Middle East region. China believes that its socio-economic development is intertwined with political stability and peace in the Middle East region (Chinese Government, 2016; Wang, 2018). Chinese Government's (2016) Arab policy paper clearly illustrates that "friendship between China and the Arab States goes back to ancient times. Over two thousand years ago, the land and maritime Silk Road already linked the Chinese and Arab nations" into deep-rooted friendship and brotherhood (Zreik, 2021a, 2021b).

Eight, despite the abundance of national resources (oil, gas, minerals, etc.,) and a market of 1.9 billion people, the Islamic world plunges into an economic drought due to the lack of industrial modernization, technological advancement, and the absence of modern communication and infrastructure development. Halsall et al. (2022) argue that a country's economic prosperity largely depends on technological innovations, agriculture, and industrial development. On the other hand, the Chinese economy has shown robotic growth in recent years due to a meteoric rise in technological innovation, technical advancement, industrial development, and agricultural production. However, China faces a new challenge of overcapacity in certain sectors of the construction and manufacturing industries. Particularly, the construction industries (i.e., steel, aluminum, and cement) are the biggest industries that face overcapacity challenges in China (de L.T. Oliveira et al., 2020; Fasslabend, 2015; Huang, 2016; Swaine, 2015). China must find new foreign markets to address the issues of overcapacity in the manufacturing and industrial sectors to maintain sustainable socio-economic growth. The Islamic world possesses huge potential as a foreign market of 1.9 billion people and a lucrative place for infrastructural investment by China to accommodate its overcapacity of industrial and manufactural sectors under the auspice of BRI.

Lastly but more importantly, the BRI has kick-started a new transnational collaboration between China and the Islamic world that promises state sovereignty and political choice without trading off the national interests for economic gain in the China-led shared development model for mutual benefits and a "win-win" outcome (Huang, 2016; Khan et al., 2018; Swaine, 2015). Therefore, the Islamic world has started to realign its economic visions (e.g., Pakistan Vision 2025, Saudi Vision 2030, Egypt Vision 2030, the Abu Dhabi Economic Vision 2030, United Arab Emirates 2030 Agenda for Sustainable Development, and Kuwait Vision 2035) with China's vision of BRI to cultivate the optimal benefits from the Chinese investments in modern infrastructures and socio-economic development to uplift their stagnant economies and modernizing their infrastructure for better socio-economic development. For example, the China-Pakistan Economic Corridor (CPEC)—a leading project of China's BRI worth US$62 billion Chinese investment in Pakistan shares an analogous vision with Pakistan's long-term development plan—Pakistan Vision 2025. It includes four portfolios: Infrastructural and transportation investments; Energy infrastructure and corridor; Industrial development and cooperation; and development of Gwadar Port to improve trade flow and regional linkages between South Asian, Central Asian, and West Asian states. The government of Pakistan Vision 2025 officially cited CPEC as a core element of the country's development policy to achieve key elements of modernizing transportation and energy infrastructure, industrial development, energy mix, and regional connectivity (Ali, 2020; Government of Pakistan, 2014; Khan et al., 2020).

Saudi Arabia's ambitious Vision 2030 aims to expand its petroleum-based economy to more diversified sectors like technology, tourism, and renewable energy. It is intended to attract external investment, improve the business environment, increase non-petroleum trade, and develop modern infrastructure in Saudi Arabia to attain sustainable economic growth, create jobs, and improve the welfare of Saudi citizens. China's BRI holds vast capital for investment in infrastructure, technology, renewable energy, and other businesses. Therefore, it possesses a natural synergy for closer cooperation with Saudi Vision 2030. Saudi Crown Prince also pointed out that "The Silk Road initiative and China's strategic orientation are very much in line with the kingdom's Vision 2030" during his visit to Beijing in 2019 (Blanchard, 2019; Fulton, 2020, p. 364). Similarly, Chinese President Xi Jinping's state visit to Egypt in January 2016 and later Egyptian President Sisi's visit to China in September 2017 to meet President Xi and to attend a BRIC meeting in Xiamen strategically dock China's BRI with Egypt's Vision 2030 (Sun & Xu, 2022). During meetings, both leaders signed various agreements and MoUs to integrate the development strategies of the two countries (i.e., China's BRI and Egypt's Vision 2030), and President Xi emphasized the need to "make use of the two great opportunities for infrastructure construction and production capacity to jointly forge Egypt a pillar country along the Belt and Road" (Chinese Government, 2017).

During President Erdoğan's state visit to China in July 2019, also facilitated the integration of Turkey's ambitious regional transportation corridor—the Trans-Caspian East-West-Middle Corridor, (also known as the Middle Corridor) with China's BRI to get much-needed infrastructural investment for the realization of the fundamental project (Middle Corridor) for its opening to East as well as Caucasus region, Central Asian states, and China for enhancing trade and investment opportunities and to make Turkey a hub and transit point of trade and energy corridor between Asia and Europe. The Middle Corridor starts from Turkey and passes the Caucasus region through Georgia and Azerbaijan, passes the Caspian Sea, then traverses Central Asian states (Kazakhstan, Kyrgyzstan, Uzbekistan, and Turkmenistan) to reach China—a vital component of the ancient Silk Road that has enthralled the landlocked countries in the region. The Middle Corridor overlaps China's BRI—Central Asia-West Asia Economic Corridor by the exclusion of Iran is central to both China and Turkey's core interests and it is not only enhancing the economic, commercial, and investment relations but also strengthening cultural and political relationship between and beyond the surrounding regions (Arkman, 2019; Chen, 2020; Guo & Fidan, 2018).

The Islamic world sees the Chinese economic engagement under the BRI framework as an effect of the "Beijing Consensus"—a pragmatic and relaxed approach based on the principle of non-interference in a country's internal affairs. It finds it more attractive than the "Washington Consensus" that often entangled the U.S. economic engagement with political demands such as freedom of expression, human rights agenda, and democracy. Therefore, the Islamic world is aligning its economic agenda with China's BRI. For example, Saudi Crown Prince Mohamed bin Salman declared BRI as "one of the main pillars of the Saudi Vision 2030 which would seek to make China among the Kingdom's biggest economic partners" during his maiden visit to Beijing in August 2016 (Khan et al., 2018; Salman, 2016).

BRI injects a new strategic in-depth initiative into the relationship between China and the Islamic world. Capri (2017) argues that "If Beijing's OBOR [One Belt, One Road] strategy comes to fruition, it will be a catalyst for shifting power alliances and the changing fortunes of nation-states." China sees a new "future-oriented strategic partnership of comprehensive cooperation and common development" with the Islamic world (Xi, 2018). China has become the largest foreign investor in the Islamic world. Under the auspices of BRI, China pledges to invest a sizable amount of capital in large-scale infrastructural and development projects in the Islamic world which will change the fortunes of nation-states and reshuffle the power alliance in the Islamic world. According to Chinese Foreign Minister Wang Yi, China has already pledged to invest US$ 400 billion in 54 Islamic countries (W. Yi, 2022). For example, China is committed to investing US$62 billion in "China-Pakistan Economic Corridor"; US$16 billion in Saudi "Haramain high-speed rail project"; US$10.7 billion investment in the "Sino-Oman Industrial City"; more than "US$50 billion investment in Egypt's new capital, and the Suez Canal cooperation zone"; along with some other major investments in Algeria, United Arab Emirates, and Tunisia (Khan et al., 2022; Khan & Pratt, 2019; Kliman & Grace, 2018; Lehr, 2018). Additionally, President Xi has announced an economic package of US$20 billion in loans and US$100 million in economic support to the war-torn Arab countries (e.g., Palestine, Jordan, Syria, Lebanon, and Yemen) for the revitalization of industrial and economic development under the broader BRI framework (1 + 2 + 3' cooperation: infrastructural development, oil and gas, and nuclear energy) (Wang, 2018).

China's Westward strategy has positioned the Islamic world at the center of China's foreign policy which has become an ardent participant and backbone of the BRI. China ought to secure its economic and energy interests in the Islamic world. Whereas the Islamic world realigns eastward (toward China) to form strategic alliances for political support and economic development (Galal, 2014). Therefore, BRI can accomplish the common goal of mutual benefits and shared development for win-win outcomes for both China and the Islamic world as China's pledges for huge infrastructural investments in transportation sectors (i.e., roads, railways, seaports, and airports) to ease free trade; energy exploration and transportation (i.e., oil and gas pipelines); electricity generation and transmission (i.e., dams and grid stations) to overcome energy shortages and telecommunication networks via fiber-optic cables to boost cyber connectivity across Afro-Eurasia regions and beyond. Resultantly, it will create a robust transportation, economic, and energy corridor between China and the Islamic world for "mutual benefits" and "win-win outcomes" (Amighini, 2017; Selmier-II, 2018). For example, China's proposed investment of US$62 billion in the China-Pakistan Economic Corridor (CPEC)—a flagship project of BRI will engender infrastructural development and create economic activities in Pakistan. In return, it will cut the 9,000 km geographical distance between China's Xinjiang and the Middle East. It will also provide an alternative trade and energy supply line to China through Gwadar port (Pakistan) and will also ensure safe access to vital energy resources (oil and gas) in the Middle East and Africa regions (Umbach, 2022).

In sum, China and the Islamic world bonded with multifaceted mutually beneficial relationships, mainly developed through the historic Silk Road and BRI which foster bilateral trade, and security cooperation via mutual learning and understanding between the two great civilizations. China and the Islamic world possess great potential for inclusive partnership as China tries to maintain its growing economic trajectory by securing unimpeded energy supplies and broadening its global political influence through the Islamic world while the Islamic world faces economic recession and battling security challenges. Particularly, the Middle East and North Africa region need an alternative global power to resolve its political disputes and infrastructural investment to strengthen regional connectivity and propel the shrinking national economies (Al-Ghwell, 2018; Scobell, 2017; Scobell & Nader, 2016; Sheikhneshin et al., 2020). Khan and Pratt (2019) argue that the Arab Islamic world is revamping its geostrategic, geo-economic, and geopolitical calculus owing to the U.S. and the West's political meddling in their internal affairs and perennial mistrust between them on the issues related to Iran's nuclear program, U.S. invasion of Afghanistan, Libya, and Syria, its avowed support for Israel over the just cause of the Palestinian people, and former U.S. President Trump's decree to concede Jerusalem as Israel's capital. The Islamic world sees China as a potential alternative global power (substitute to the U.S. and the West) to settle their political disputes and economic miseries. Therefore, it moves even closer to China as a reliable and trustworthy friend who respects state sovereignty, believes in non-interference in internal affairs, stands with the just cause of the Palestinian people, and is a "keeper of peace and stability in the Middle East" (Almedia, 2018; Chaziza, 2018; Khan et al., 2022). Conversely, healthy Sino-Islamic relations will promote China's energy interests, rebalance its security posture, and boost its economic growth. Moving westward (Islamic world) will ease China's heavily based strategic posture in East Asia and will provide more stability to its internal security in West China by creating a friendlier periphery in Central Asia and the Middle East. It will palliate the domestic threats of radical Islamization posed by the East Turkestan Islamic Movement (ETIM) and diminish the international criticism of China's alleged mistreatment of its Uyghur Muslims in Xinjiang. Finally, it will boost China's standing as a great power and will facilitate its involvement in asset-rich Islamic regions (Guzansky & Orion, 2017; Khan & Pratt, 2019).

References

Abbasi, A. R. K. (1989). China's relations with the Muslim World. *Strategic Studies*, *12*(3), 33–50. <https://www.jstor.org/stable/45182518>

Aizhu, C. (2022, May 20). China's April Saudi oil imports soar 38% over previous year, Russian oil up 4%. *Reuters*. <https://www.reuters.com/business/energy/chinas-april-saudi-oil-imports-soar-38-yr-russian-oil-up-4-2022-05-20/>

Al-Ghwell, H. (2018, June 30). Why the Arab world should build bridges with China. *Arab News*. http://www.arabnews.com/node/1330736

Ali, M. (2020). China–Pakistan economic corridor: prospects and challenges. *Contemporary South Asia*, 28(1), 100-112. <https://doi.org/10.1080/09584935.2019.1667302>

Almedia, M. (2018, July 14). China's "Marshall Plan" for the Arab world. *Arab News*. <http://www.arabnews.com/node/1338856>

Amighini, A. (2017). *China's Belt and Road: A game changer?* Edizioni Epoké.

Arkman, M. S. (2019). Turkey's middle corridor and Belt and Road Initiative: Coherent or conflicting? In *Economic Policy Research Foundation of Turkey* (Vol. N201937). <https://think-asia.org/handle/11540/11336>

Bandung Conference (Asian-African Conference). (1955). Office of the Historian, Foreign Service Institute, United States Department of State. <https://history.state.gov/milestones/1953-1960/bandung-conf>

Benabdallah, L. (2018). China's relations with Africa and the Arab World: Shared trends, different priorities. *South African Institute of International Affairs*, *67*(November), 1–14. <https://www.jstor.org/stable/resrep25989>

Bhola, P. L. (1986). *Pakistan-China relations: Search for politico-strategic relationship.* RBSA Publishers.

Bianchi, R. R. (2013). China-Middle East relations in light of Obama's pivot to the Pacific. *China Report*, *49*(1), 103–118. <https://doi.org/10.1177/0009445513479456>

Bianchi, R. R. (2019). *China and the Islamic World: How the New Silk Road is transforming global politics* (1st ed.). Oxford University Press. <https://doi.org/10.1093/oso/9780190915285.001.0001>

Blanchard, B. (2019). Saudi Arabia strikes $10 billion China deal, talks de-radicalization with Xi. *Reuters*. <https://www.reuters.com/article/us-asia-saudi-china-idUSKCN1QB15H>

Capri, A. (2017, June 21). China's growing influence on Middle East shouldn't be lost on an impulsive trump administration. *Forbes*. <https://www.forbes.com/sites/alexcapri/2017/06/21/china-obor-qatar-middle-east-america/>

Chaziza, M. (2018). China's mediation efforts in the Middle East and North Africa: Constructive conflict management. *Strategic Analysis*, *42*(1), 29–41. <https://doi.org/10.1080/09700161.2017.1418956>

Chen, J. (2011). *The emergence of China in Middle East* (Issue 271, pp. 1–8). National Defense University, Washington, DC. <https://doi.org/10.1111/j.1539-6975.2009.01318.x>

Chen, Y. (2020). Developments in China–Turkey relations: A view from China. *Critical Sociology*, *46*(4–5), 777–787. <https://doi.org/10.1177/0896920519885001>

Cooper, W. W., & Yue, P. (2015). Global oil flow and strategic geography of the Muslim World Article information. In W. W. Cooper & P. Yue (Eds.), *Challenges of the Muslim World* (1st ed., pp. 60–101). Emerald Group Publishing Limited.

de L.T. Oliveira, G., Murton, G., Rippa, A., Harlan, T., & Yang, Y. (2020). China's Belt and Road Initiative: Views from the ground. *Political Geography*, *82*(January), 102225. <https://doi.org/https://doi.org/10.1016/j.polgeo.2020.102225>

Elmagherbi, F. I. (2010). A case study of China's relations with the Arab world. *2010 2nd IEEE International Conference on Information and Financial Engineering*, 646–650. <https://doi.org/10.1109/ICIFE.2010.5609442>

Fasslabend, W. (2015). The Silk Road: A political marketing concept for world dominance. *European View, 14*(2), 293–302. <https://doi.org/10.1007/s12290-015-0381-3>

Frankel, J. D. (2016). Chinese-Islamic connections: An historical and contemporary overview. *Journal of Muslim Minority Affairs, 36*(4), 569–583. <https://doi.org/10.1080/13602004.2016.1248175>

Fulton, J. (2020). Situating Saudi Arabia in China's belt and road initiative. *Asian Politics & Policy, 12*(3), 362–383.

Galal, M. N. (2014). The China-Arab States Cooperation Forum: Achievements, challenges and prospects. *Journal of Middle Eastern and Islamic Studies (in Asia), 8*(2), 1–21. <https://doi.org/10.1080/19370679.2014.12023244>

Chinese Government. (2016). China's Arab Policy Paper. *January 13. China Daily.* <http://english.gov.cn/archive/publications/2016/01/13/content_281475271412746.htm>

Chinese Government. (2017). Xi Jinping meets with President Abdel-Fattah al-Sisi of Egypt. *September 5.* <http://ph.china-embassy.gov.cn/eng/chinew/201709/t20170907_1166388.htm>

Gernet, J. (1982). *A history of Chinese civilisation.* Cambridge University Press.

Government of Pakistan (2014). *Pakistan 2025: One Nation One Vision.* Ministry of Planning, Development and Reform, Islamabad. <https://www.pc.gov.pk/uploads/vision2025/Pakistan-Vision-2025.pdf>

Grim, B. J., & Karim, M. S. (2011). The future of the global Muslim population. Projections for 2010–2030. In *Pew Research Center.* <https://www.pewresearch.org/religion/wp-content/uploads/sites/7/2011/01/FutureGlobalMuslimPopulation-WebPDF-Feb10.pdf>

Gul, A. (2022, March 11). China-Built Fighter Jet takes its place in Pakistan Air Force. *Voice of America.* <https://www.voanews.com/a/china-built-fighter-jet-takes-its-place-in-pakistan-air-force-/6480887.html>

Guo, X., & Fidan, G. (2018, June 26). China's Belt and Road Initiative (BRI) and Turkey's Middle Corridor: "Win-Win Cooperation." *Middle East Institute.* <https://www.mei.edu/publications/chinas-belt-and-road-initiative-bri-and-turkeys-middle-corridor-win-win-cooperation>

Guzansky, Y., & Orion, A. (2017). Slowly but surely : Growing relations between Saudi Arabia and China. In *Institute for National Security Studies* (Issue 891, pp. 1–5). <http://www.jstor.com/stable/resrep08664>

Halsall, J. P., Cook, I. G., & Oberoi, R. (2022). Connecting the world: China's Belt and Road Initiative. In P. G. Figueiredo, F. J. Leandro, & Y. Li (Eds.), *Handbook of research on special economic zones as regional development enablers* (Vol. 1, pp. 1–20). IG. <https://doi.org/10.4018/978-1-7998-7619-9.ch001>

Hayoun, M. (2013). Strange Bedfellows: China's Middle Eastern Inroads. *World Affairs, 175*(5), 89–96. <http://www.jstor.org/stable/43554744>

Huang, Y. (2016). Understanding China's Belt & Road Initiative: Motivation, framework and assessment. *China Economic Review, 40*(September), 314–321. <https://doi.org/10.1016/j.chieco.2016.07.007>

Huntington, S. P. (1997). *The clash of civilizations and the remaking of world order.* Penguin Books India.

Hussain, M. (2022, April 12). China's entry into the Muslim World. *The Manila Times.* <https://www.manilatimes.net/2022/04/12/opinion/columns/chinas-entry-into-the-muslim-world/1839703>

Insinna, V., Gould, J., & Mehta, A. (2020, August 12). Congress has secretly blocked US arms sales to Turkey for nearly two years. *DefenceNews.* <https://www.defensenews.com/breaking-news/2020/08/12/congress-has-secretly-blocked-us-arms-sales-to-turkey-for-nearly-two-years/>

Jones-Leaning, M., & Pratt, D. (2012). Islam in China: From silk road to separatism. *Muslim World, 102*(2), 308–334. <https://doi.org/10.1111/j.1478-1913.2012.01399.x>

Kaplan, R. D. (2011). *Monsoon: The Indian Ocean and the future of American power.* Random House Trade Paperbacks.

Khan, M. K., & Pratt, C. B. (2019). China's Belt and Road Initiative: Its landscape (and trajectory) in the Islamic World. In A. Visvizi, M. Lytras, X. Zhang, & J. Zhao (Eds.), *Foreign business in China and opportunities for technological innovation and sustainable economics* (pp. 117–142). IGI Global. <https://doi.org/10.4018/978-1-5225-8980-8.ch006>

Khan, M. K., Sallam, M. H., Pratt, C. B., & Farid, T. (2022). Stereotyping the Chinese in Arab Nations: The effects of media use, perceived realism and Chinese-Arab relations. *The Social Science Journal.* <https://doi.org/https://doi.org/10.1080/03623319.2021.2025197>

Khan, M. K., Sandano, I. A., Pratt, C. B., & Farid, T. (2018). China's Belt and Road Initiative: A global model for an evolving approach to Sustainable Regional Development. *Sustainability, 10*(11), 4234. <https://doi.org/10.3390/su10114234>

Kliman, D., & Grace, A. (2018, June 18). China smells opportunity in the Middle East's crisis. *Foreign Policy.* <https://foreignpolicy.com/2018/06/14/china-smells-opportunity-in-the-middle-easts-crisis/>

Legrenzi, M., & Lawson, F. H. (2015). China's Gulf policy: Existing theories, new perspectives. *Middle East Policy, 22*(2), 58–71. <https://doi.org/10.1111/mepo.12128>

Lehr, D. (2018, July 21). How China is winning over the Middle East. *The Diplomat.* <https://thediplomat.com/2018/07/how-china-is-winning-over-the-middle-east/>

Li, F. (2018). The role of Islam in the development of the 'Belt and Road' initiative. *Asian Journal of Middle Eastern and Islamic Studies, 12*(1), 35–45. <https://doi.org/10.1080/25765949.2018.1439617>

Majoka, M. I., Sahibzada, H. E., & Khan, M. S. (2012). Resources of the Muslim World: A reflection on the Muslim World's resources, their development and utilization. *Journal of Islamic Thought and Civilization, 02*(01), 73–87. <https://doi.org/10.32350/jitc.21.05>

Malik, M. (2002). Dragon China's on terrorism: Assessing gains tactical and strategic losses after 11 September. *Contemporary Southeast Asia, 24*(2), 252–293. <https://www.jstor.org/stable/25798597>

Moniruzzaman, M. (2013). The rise of China and its implications for the Muslim World. *Journal of Economic Cooperation and Development, 34*(1), 1–32. <https://doi.org/10.4324/9780203127063-7>

Moniruzzaman, M. (2020, December 3). China and the Muslim world: Civilizational partnership? *CGTN,* 1–12. <https://news.cgtn.com/news/2020-12-03/China-and-the-Muslim-world-Civilizational-partnership--VTIF8i7xdK/index.htm>

Park, H. (2012). *Mapping the Chinese and Islamic Worlds: Cross-cultural exchange in pre-modern Asia* (Vol. 1). Cambridge University Press.

Pelosi, N. (2022, August 2). Nancy Pelosi: Why I'm leading a congressional delegation to Taiwan. *Washington Post.* <https://www.washingtonpost.com/opinions/2022/08/02/nancy-pelosi-taiwan-visit-op-ed/>

Pompeo. (2020). Pompeo criticizes China's "corruption, coercion" in Tokyo. October 27. *Taipei Times.* <https://www.taipeitimes.com/News/front/archives/2020/10/07/2003744729>

Reuters. (2022). Biden says he would be willing to use force to defend Taiwan. (2022, May 23). *Reuters.* <https://www.reuters.com/world/biden-says-he-would-be-willing-use-force-defend-taiwan-2022-05-23/>

Rossabi, M. (1985). China and the Islamic World. *Comparative Civilizations Review, 13*(13). <https://doi.org/10.1093/oso/9780190915285.001.0001>

Ryter, P. (2018). A personal experience in Turkey, Iran and China : The need for the ICRC to adapt in a multipolar world. *International Review of the Red Cross,* 1–11. <https://doi.org/10.1017/S1816383118000334>

Salman, M. bin. (2016, September 3). Fusing vision 2030 with Belt Road Initiative. *Arab News.* <http://www.arabnews.com/node/979346/saudi-arabia>

Scobell, A. (2017). Why the Middle East matters to China. In *China's presence in the Middle East* (pp. 9–23). Routledge.

Scobell, A., & Nader, A. (2016). China in the Middle East: The wary dragon. In *China in the Middle East: The Wary Dragon.* Rand Corporation. <https://doi.org/10.7249/rr1229>

Sekkal. (2013). Upheaval in the Arab World and China-Arab Cooperation. *China International Studies, 41*(July/August), 84–89. <https://heinonline.org/HOL/LandingPage?handle=hein.journals/chintersd41&div=8&id=&page=>

Selmier-II, W. T. (2018). The Belt and Road Initiative and the influence of Islamic economies. *Economic and Political Studies, 6*(3), 257–277. <https://doi.org/10.1080/20954816.2018.1498989>

Sheikhneshin, A. G., Vakili, B., & Amoei, H. (2020). Chinese soft power : Creating a charm image in the Islamic World. *International Journal of Political Science, 10*(2), 25–39. <https://journals.iau.ir/article_678019_d08bbb11e0d52989e877010d6e7f77ea.pdf>

Swaine, M. D. (2015). Chinese views and commentary on the "One Belt, One Road". Initiative. *China Leadership Monitor, 47,* 1–24.

Sun, D., & Xu, R. (2022). China and Egypt's comprehensive strategic partnership in the Xi-sisi era: A "role theory" prism. *Mediterranean Politics,* 1–21. <http://www.hoover.org/sites/default/files/research/docs/clm47ms.pdf>

Umbach, F. (2022, April 8). How China's Belt and Road Initiative is faring. *Geopolitical Intelligence Services.* <https://www.gisreportsonline.com/r/belt-road-initiative/>

Upadhyay, B. (2016, April 29). US "drops planned Pakistan F-16 fighter jet subsidy." *BBC News.* <https://www.bbc.com/news/world-asia-36169079>

Wang, Y. (2018, July 8). Arab countries and China are natural partners in growth. *Khaleej Times.* <https://www.khaleejtimes.com/editorials-columns/arab-countries-and-china-are-natural-partners-in-growth>

Xi, J. (2018, July 10). Xi Jinping delivers a speech at the opening ceremony of the eighth ministerial meeting of The China-Arab States Cooperation Forum. *Ministry of Foreign Affairs of People's Republic of China*. <https://www.fmprc.gov.cn/mfa_eng/zxxx_662805/t1575994.shtml>

Yi, W. (2022, March 23). China investing over $400 bn in 54 Muslim countries: Foreign Min Wang Yi. *Business Standard*. <https://www.business-standard.com/article/international/china-investing-over-400-bn-in-54-muslim-countries-foreign-min-wang-yi-122032301426_1.html>

Yu, X. (2006). *50 years of Sino-Egyptian diplomacy,|| Silk Road Stories: 50 years of diplomacy between New China and Arab Countries*. Beijing: World Affairs Press.

Zambelis, C., & Gentry, B. (2008). China through Arab eyes: American influence in the Middle East. *Parameters, 38*(1), 60–73. <https://doi.org/10.55540/0031-1723.2412>

Zhan, S. (2006). *Premier Zhou Enlai works for Sino-Egyptian and Sino-Arab Friendship. Silk Road Stories: 50 years of diplomacy between New China and Arab Countries*. World Affairs Press.

Zhu, W. (2011). On the strategic relationship between China and Islamic countries in the Middle East. *Journal of Sino-Islamic Communications, 3*(1), 1–27.

Zreik. (2021a). Academic exchange programs between China and the Arab Region: A means of cultural harmony or indirect Chinese influence? *Arab Studies Quarterly, 43*(2), 172. <https://doi.org/10.13169/arabstudquar.43.2.0172>

Zreik, M. (2021b, April 9). China-Arab relations: From Silk to friendship. *Modern Diplomacy*. <https://moderndiplomacy.eu/2021/04/09/china-arab-relations-from-silk-to-friendship/>

III

China's Belt and Road Initiative: Prospects and Challenges in the Islamic World

President Xi's signature public diplomacy initiative—the Belt and Road Initiative (BRI) underpins China's grand economic strategy and strategic foreign policy endeavors to reshape China's global image and rejuvenate the Chinese nation and reinforce China's position as an influential global (great) power and to attain a status of a developed nation by the centennial jubilee of People's Republic of China in 2049 (Halsall et al., 2022; Khan et al., 2023; Schulhof et al., 2022). It is "an ambitious, proactive, and globally driven strategic foreign policy venture" that anchors China's soft power globally and repositions the regional and global discourses on the geo-economics, geopolitics, and transnational collaboration (Khan et al., 2018; Khan & Pratt, 2019). It drives up China's diplomatic and economic strategy through lucrative financial and economic investments to magnify China's soft power and leverage its positive image across the Afro-Eurasia region and beyond (e.g., the Pacific, Latin America, and Caribbean region) (Halsall et al., 2022; Khan et al., 2018; Khan et al., 2023).

Through BRI, China aims to revive China's historical status of great power—a center of civilizations for cultural, economic, and political exchange by way of bracing the ancient Silk Road that links China with the Eastern and Western world (Kuah et al., 2021). China often outlines BRI as a "project of the century"—a win-win partnership that will make globalization more inclusive through unimpeded trade, regional connectivity, cultural cognizance, financial integration, and flow of knowledge and ideas between nations across Eurasia and African continents (de L.T. Oliveira et al., 2020; Halsall et al., 2022). Therefore, President Xi coined the BRI as a joint development initiative that follows "the principle of wide consultation, joint contribution, and shared benefits. The programs of development will be open and inclusive, not exclusive. They will be a real chorus comprising all countries along the routes, not a solo for China itself" (Xi, 2015). He emphasized that:

> "China will actively promote international cooperation through the Belt and Road Initiative. In doing so, we hope to achieve policy, infrastructure, trade, financial, and people-to-people connectivity and thus build a new platform for international cooperation to create new drivers of shared development." (Xi, 2017c, p. 61)

Landscape of BRI

President Xi's much-decorated BRI was launched during his official visit to Kazakhstan and Indonesia in September and October 2013. It is the world's largest infrastructural and development program through which China plans to invest US$8 trillion to connect China with Afro-Eurasia regions through sea and land routes (Alves & Lee, 2022; Khan et al., 2018; Khan & Pratt, 2019). It is a cornucopia of giant infrastructural, energy, economic, and communication development projects that aim to enhance regional as well as global connectivity, strengthen economic cooperation and integration, and build energy, economic, and communication corridors across South Asia, Southeast Asia, Central Asia, the Middle East, East Africa, North Africa, West Africa, and Western Europe, particularly in the landlocked economies of the Afro-Eurasia regions. It encapsulates the range of opportunities for infrastructural development and economic cooperation for mutual benefit and shared development for the poor nation-states of Afro-Eurasia regions and beyond (Khan et al., 2018; Khan & Pratt, 2019; Williams et al., 2020; Wu et al., 2020).

Initially, China launched BRI in 65 Afro-Eurasian countries to strengthen its cooperation with the participant countries in the fields of infrastructure, energy, and economy (Khan & Pratt, 2019). However, the initiative quickly grabbed the attention of the poor nation-states across the Afro-Eurasian regions and beyond (e.g., the Pacific, Latin America, and Caribbean region) to seek Chinese funding for much-needed infrastructural and economic development in their countries. China's BRI promises to uphold the principle of wide consultations, peaceful economic cooperation, inclusiveness and openness, mutual learning, joint contribution, shared development, and mutually shared benefits for all (Dunford, 2021; Khan et al., 2018; Xinhua, 2015). As a result, a total of 153 sovereign states have officially signed the Memorandum of Understandings (MoUs) with the Chinese government to join the BRI from September 2013 through April 1, 2022. The distribution of the BRI participant countries across geographical regions: South Asia (7 countries); East Asia & Pacific (25 countries); Central Asia & Europe (35 countries); the Middle East and North Africa (20 countries); Sub-Saharan Africa (47 countries); Latin America & Caribbean (19 countries). Most of those are low- and middle-income countries and belong to the underdeveloped world. The details of the BRI partner countries are in Table 1.1.

China's BRI has two vital components—the "Silk Road Economic Belt" and the "21st Century Maritime Silk Road". The "Silk Road Economic Belt" comprises six economic corridors: (a) China–Pakistan Economic Corridor (CPEC), (b) the China-Central and West Asia Economic Corridor (CCWAEC), (c) China–Mongolia–Russia Economic Corridor (CMREC), (d) China–Indochina Peninsula Economic Corridor (CIPECC), (e) New Eurasian Land Bridge (NELB), and (f) Bangladesh–China–India–Myanmar Economic Corridor (BCIMECC) (Figure 3.1). Whereas the "21st Century Maritime Silk Road" constitutes 11 sea routes that connect China with Southeast Asia, South Asia, the Middle East, East Africa, and Europe through the South China Sea, Indian Ocean, and the Mediterranean Sea (Table 3.1). It also pledges vital networks of roads, railways, seaports, energy pipelines (e.g., oil and gas), telecommunication networks (e.g., high-speed fiber optic cables, Internet of Things (IoT)), and other socio-economic developing infrastructures (e.g., dams, bridges, dry ports, economic zones, schools, hospitals, etc.,) that will enhance international cooperation, boost regional connectivity, stimulate economic activities, and strengthen transportation systems to achieve common prosperity and shared development across Afro-Eurasia regions and beyond.

China believes that the lack of regional as well as global connectivity and economic integration has severely damaged the landlocked economies of Afro-Eurasia regions (Rolland, 2017). Therefore, China should take responsibility for developing much-needed infrastructural, energy, and economic corridors between China and Afro-Eurasia regions (e.g., linking China to Asia, Africa, Europe, and

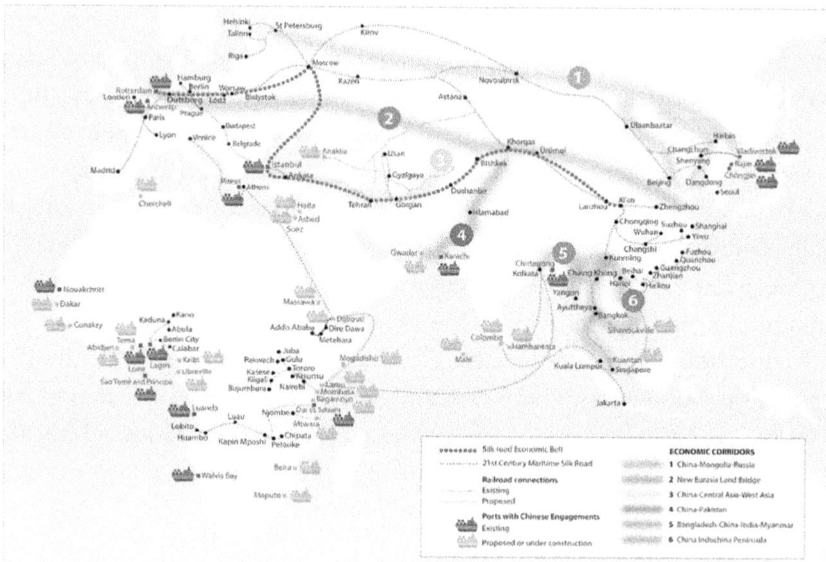

Figure 3.1: Mapping of the Infrastructural Networks and Economic Corridors of China's Belt and Road Initiative.
Source: Organization for Economic Co-operation and Development (OECD) Research, 2018

vice versa) to facilitate unimpeded trade between nation-states, nourish people to people interactions, encourage financial and economic integration, improve systematic policy coordination and regional as well as global connectivity across Afro-Eurasia regions. Subsequently, it will enhance China's political stature, diplomatic leverage, and economic influence in the Afro-Eurasia region and beyond and will facilitate and "expand cooperative interactions, create an integrated web of mutually beneficial economic, social and political ties, and ultimately lower distrust and enhance a sense of common security" (Swaine, 2015, p. 1). Scholars (e.g., Li, 2015; Rolland, 2017; Swaine, 2015; Yi, 2015) argue that the BRI has the potential to integrate Afro-Eurasian economies into the international economic governance system as it guarantees the nation-states' political choice, sovereignty, economic interest, and mutual benefits for win-win outcomes for both China and Afro-Eurasia regions.

China has ambitiously extended the scope of BRI not only geographically beyond the Afro-Eurasia regions but new elements have also been added to the BRI projects to get a more prominent leadership role in the emerging new world order and global governance (Umbach, 2022). For example, the Digital Silk Road

Table 3.1: China's 21st Century Maritime Silk Road and Its Trajectory in the Islamic World.

	Regions	Maritime Silk Routes	Islamic Countries/ Ports
1.	China–Southeast Asia	China–Vietnam, Myanmar Qinzhou–Yangpu–Zhanjiang–Gaolan Port–Yantian–Nansha–Ho Chi Minh City (Vietnam)–Singapore–Yangon (Myanmar)–Palawan (Indonesia)–Singapore–Qinzhou.	Palawan (Indonesia)
		China–Philippines Qingdao–Shanghai–Ningbo–Manila (South)–Manila (North)Qingdao.	Nil
		China–Singapore, Malaysia Newport–Dalian–Qingdao–Shanghai–Xiamen–Hong Kong–Singapore–Klang Port (Malaysia)–Penang (Malaysia)–Singapore–Hong Kong–Xingang.	Klang Port (Malaysia) Penang (Malaysia)
		China–Indonesia Shanghai–Newport–Dalian–Qingdao–Ningbo–Nansha–Jakarta (Indonesia)–Klang Port (Malaysia)–Singapore–Laem Chabang Port (Thailand)–Hong Kong-Shanghai.	Jakarta (Indonesia) Klang Port (Malaysia)
		China–Thailand, Cambodia Ningbo–Shanghai–Shekou–Sihanoukville (Cambodia)–Bangkok–Leam Chabang (Thailand)–Ningbo.	Nil
2.	China–South Asia	China–Pakistan Qingdao–Shanghai–Ningbo–Singapore–Klang Port (Malaysia)–Karachi (Pakistan)–Mundra (India)–Colombo (Sri Lanka)–Singapore–Qingdao.	Karachi (Pakistan) Klang Port (Malaysia)
		China–India, Sri Lanka Shanghai–Ningbo–Shekou–Singapore–Port Klang (Malaysia)–Nawa Shiva (India)–Pipavawa (India)–Colombo (Sri Lanka)–Port Klang–Singapore–Ho Chi Minh City (Vietnam)–Hong Kong–Shanghai.	Port Klang (Malaysia)

Continued

Table 3.1: *Continued*

	Regions	Maritime Silk Routes	Islamic Countries/ Ports
3.	China–Middle East	China–Iraq, UAE Shanghai–Ningbo–Kaohsiung–Xiamen–Shekou–Port Klang (Malaysia)–Alishan Port (UAE)–Umm Qasr (Iraq)–Port Klang–Kaohsiung–Shanghai.	Port Klang (Malaysia) Alishan Port (UAE) Umm Qasr (Iraq)
		China–Red Sea Shanghai–Ningbo–Xiamen–Chiwan–Singapore–Djibouti (East Africa)–Jeddah (Saudi Arabia)–Sudan (Sudan)–Djibouti–Port Klang–Shanghai.	Djibouti (East Africa) Jeddah (Saudi Arabia) Djibouti
4.	China–East Africa	Dalian–Tianjin–Ningbo–Nansha–Singapore–Colombo (Sri Lanka)–Mombasa (Kennedy)–Dar es Salaam (Tanzania)–Colombo (Sri Lanka)–Pasir Gudang (Malaysia)–Singapore–Shanghai–Dalian.	Dar es Salaam (Tanzania) Pasir Gudang (Malaysia)
5.	China–Europe	Qingdao–Shanghai–Ningbo–Kaohsiung–Hong Kong–Yantian–Singapore–Piraeus (Greece)–La Spezia (Italy)–Genoa (Italy)–Fos-sur-Mer (France)–Valencia (Spain)–Piraeus (Greece)–Jeddah (Saudi Arabia)–Colombo (Sri Lanka)–Singapore–Hong Kong.	Jeddah (Saudi Arabia)

Source: Xinhua Baltic International Shipping Centre Development Index Report, 2018

(DSR) was launched to improve global digital connectivity in 2015 (Ghiasy & Krishnamurthy, 2021); Polar Silk Road (PSR) to develop Arctic shipping routes, explore and develop oil, gas, and mineral resources and non-fossil energies to facilitate fishing and tourism in the Arctic region (*Reuters*, 2018); China's Internet of Things (IoT) to enhance China's role in cyberspace governance and transformation of the global economic system and social relations (Lee, 2021); and Health Silk Road (HSR) to play a global health leadership role in the global crisis of COVID-19 pandemic (Lancaster et al., 2020). It has been estimated that China's goal spending through the BRI project will reach US$3.7 trillion by 2027 which will realign the geo-economic, geopolitical, and geostrategic calculus and will have wide-ranging implications for the new world order and global governance (Umbach, 2022).

Western scholars (Alves & Lee, 2022; Blanchard, 2020; Mendez & Alden, 2021) are skeptical of the BRI's ambitious geopolitical outreach which they believe is designed strategically to advance China's status as a great power and fortify China's strategic and diplomatic position in Afro-Eurasia region and beyond. China can use BRI as a strategic tool to rewrite the world order and its normative settings (e.g., economic and political rules), even if BRI aims to improve infrastructure development and to stimulate economic activities for mutual benefits and shared development in poor Afro-Eurasia countries and beyond (Alves & Lee, 2022; Khan et al., 2023; Mogato & Petty, 2017; Shambaugh, 2013; Swaine, 2014). Western allies, particularly, the U.S. suspects that China has entwined its strategic political and economic institutions [e.g., Shanghai Cooperation Organization (SCO), Forum on China-Africa Cooperation (FOCAC), Asian Infrastructure Investment Bank (AIIB), New Development Bank (NDB), The Export-Import Bank (Exim) and the National Silk Road Fund (NSRF)] with the BRI to extricate the Western-centric political and economic orders with China-centric political and economic rules (Dunford, 2021; Yu, 2017). Therefore, former U.S. President Barack Obama warned the U.S. Congress during his State of the Union address in January 2015, as he said: "But as we speak, China wants to write the rules for the world's fastest-growing region. That would put our workers and our businesses at a disadvantage. Why would we let that happen? We should write those rules" (Obama, 2021).

While other scholars (e.g., Padilla, 2017; Scobell et al., 2018) believe that BRI is an over-ambitious global infrastructure strategy that is chiefly designed to buoy China's domestic economic growth and enhance its global economic and political influence instead of facilitating the economic development of BRI's countries, China will use BRI as an offensive mercantilist strategy to safeguard its domestic industries, particularly the manufacturing and construction industries that are afflicted with overcapacity by exploring new foreign markets in the BRI countries (Holslag, 2017). It will enhance China's commercial footprint, and expand its political, economic, and military influence in the Afro-Eurasian regions (Nagao, 2016; Shambaugh, 2013, 2015).

The United States and its Eurasian allies are also concerned about China's huge investments in the New Maritime Silk Road and financial investment in strategic seaports (e.g., Military support base in Djibouti; investment in Egyptian Suez Canal; Chittagong port, Bangladesh; Gwadar port, Pakistan; Hambantota port, Sri Lanka; and Sittwe port in Myanmar). These strategic BRI projects will enhance China's maritime capabilities and strengthen its naval power projection. It will jeopardize the freedom of navigation, international maritime security, and economic activities in the South China Sea and the Indian Ocean (Brewster, 2018; D. A. Jones & Liu, 2017; Mogato & Petty, 2017; Rahman et al., 2021). Some ASEAN countries also indicated suspicion toward the BRI's investments due to China's negative perception related to military operations in the South China Sea and regional fear of "Chinese hegemony" that might undermine their state sovereignty and impede long-term economic prosperity (Herlijanto, 2017; Yuniarto, 2019). There is a fear that China is pursuing a *"guerre de course"* (war of the chase) strategy to fortify, maintain, and operate a "balanced fleet" (e.g., surface cruises and submarines) to chase down foreign shipping in the South and East China sea. Its maritime fortification along the Western Pacific Rim of Asia is presumably aimed against Japan, South Korea, and "potentially some or all of the ASEAN bloc countries unless they cooperate with China and ship products to Europe along the OBOR [BRI] infrastructure" (D. A. Jones & Liu, 2017, p. 496). China also keeps contesting the U.S. Freedom of Navigation Operation in the South China Sea over territorial claims and is actively involved in aviation reconnaissance in the East China Sea (U.S. Navy, 2021; Held, 2017). In addition, India also sees China's investment under the auspice of BRI in the strategic seaport infrastructures in South Asia as a threat to its strategic interests and national security, as it offers China strategic advantages over India in the Indian Ocean (Joshi et al., 2017; Kaya, 2017; Panneerselvam, 2017; Rahman et al., 2021). Garlick (2018) argues that the primary aim of China's investments (CPEC plus other economic and financial investments) in Pakistan is to hedge against India by strengthening its geo-positional balancing and interminable physical footprint in the Indian Ocean region without taking a greater risk.

The Chinese government debunks those allegations and President Xi ensures the world's leaders that China will not employ outdated tactics of geopolitics through BRI. It will promote peaceful development and economic cooperation rather than military alliance and will endorse national, regional, and global development agendas among the participant countries (Alves & Lee, 2022; Bei, 2017; Lai et al., 2018; Zheng, 2017). In addition, the BRI does not pose a threat to the Western-centric political and economic order; instead, it complements the existing world order by facilitating free trade and transnational connectivity across the Afro-Eurasia region and beyond through economic corridors and infrastructural development (Huang, 2016; Khan et al., 2018; Zheng, 2005).

Scholars (e.g., Dunford, 2021; Dunford & Liu, 2019; Liu & Dunford, 2016) argue that China's rise and revitalization of the historic Silk Road have challenged and reduced the asymmetric dominance of the U.S. and its Western allies in political, economic, moral, cultural and financial domains at the global stage and therefore, the U.S. and its Western allies gauge BRI as a zero-sum game which threatens the Western dominance and global leadership in the realm of the geostrategic, geopolitical, and geo-economic domains. Although China's BRI strategy reflects its keen desire as an emerging economic power to accede to the status of a major power in a multipolar world to collectively address the aggravated issues of peace, development, and global governance in the world (Xi, 2017b), it is not seeking hegemony but a multipower world based on the principle of common values of peaceful coexistence and social harmony, including the principle of non-interference in sovereign states' internal affairs (Dunford, 2021; Liu & Dunford, 2016). Therefore, it aims to revitalize the Afro-Eurasia connectivity and transmute the Western-dominated "core-periphery" system with a more transparent, open, and balanced international system based on mutual benefit and shared development to achieve win-win outcomes for all through the BRI (Khan et al., 2018; Sun, 2021).

BRI's trajectory in the Islamic World

President Xi chose to launch its signature policy initiative—The BRI through the Islamic world due to its magnificent significance in China's future strategic ambits during his maiden visit to Kazakhstan and Indonesia in 2013. Initially, 30 Muslim countries joined BRI but now it has been extended to 48 Islamic countries and become an integral part of the entire Islamic world. The entire Islamic world (except Mayotte, West Sahara, and the Republic of Kosovo—the semi-independent states that are not officially recognized by the People's Republic of China) has joined BRI to seek Chinese investments for infrastructural and economic development (Table 1.1). The development of five out of six proposed BRI flagship economic, energy, and transportation corridors has further enlarged the strategic positioning of the Islamic world in China's future strategic framework and made it indispensable for the successful implementation of China's BRI strategy (Table 3.2). Historically, the Islamic countries are strategically located along the Silk Road and constitute a huge East-West Islamic Silk Road Corridor that extends from South Asia to Central Asia, Southeast Asia, West Asia, North Africa, and Europe. Therefore, the Islamic world has become a critical partner in China's BRI strategy (Khan & Pratt, 2019; Li, 2018; Moniruzzaman, 2021).

Table 3.2: China's BRI Economic Corridors in the Islamic World.

	Economic Corridors	Muslim Countries (*N* = 14)
1.	China-Indochina Peninsula Economic Corridor	Indonesia, Malaysia
2.	China-Central Asia-West Africa Economic Corridor	Iran, Kazakhstan, Kyrgyzstan, Kuwait, Qatar, Saudi Arabia, Tajikistan, Turkey, Uzbekistan
3.	Bangladesh-China-India-Myanmar Economic Corridor	Bangladesh,
4.	China-Pakistan Economic Corridor	Pakistan
5.	New Eurasian Land Bridge Economic Corridor	Kazakhstan,
6.	China-Mongolia-Russia Economic Corridor	Nil

The Islamic world stands at the critical juncture of recalibrating its future political and economic alliances and has embraced the BRI fervidly to revive its dwindling economy and much-need infrastructural development as Chinese financial investment guarantees political choices, state sovereignty, shared economic interests, and mutual benefits based on the shared development and win-win outcomes for all the participant countries (Khan et al., 2018; Khan & Pratt, 2019; Li, 2015; Swaine, 2015; Yi, 2015). The Islamic world views BRI as a grand opportunity to embattle the inadequate infrastructure for transnational connectivity, industrial imbalance, deficient business environment, energy crisis, and insufficient innovation capacities that hinder its effective participation in the global values chains.

China's BRI promises healthy Sino-Islamic relations and encourages people-to-people connectivity to create shared cultural understanding and a collaborative cultural basin that would promote policy coordination and intercultural dialogue between China and the Islamic world for social harmony, mutual development, and peaceful coexistence (Jia, 2017; Jin et al., 2016; Kuah et al., 2021; Shambaugh, 2015; Sheikhneshin et al., 2020; Yang et al., 2018). Therefore, the Islamic world has become an ardent participant in China's BRI.

In recent years, China has deepened its social, political, and economic engagement with Islamic countries under the auspice of the BRI and poured massive foreign direct investments into the Islamic world. China has directed its financial institutions (e.g., AIIB, NDB, Exim Bank, and NSRF) to provide requisite capital for the BRI-related infrastructural and economic development projects across the Afro-Eurasian region and beyond. Therefore, Chinese state-owned enterprises and private companies are exploring new opportunities for investments in much-needed infrastructural and economic development projects in Islamic countries. For example, China has pledged US$62 billion for CPEC—a flagship and most comprehensive project of BRI that aims to usher in a new era of economic integration and regional connectivity. It will facilitate infrastructure development and stimulate economic activities by creating more than 7 million jobs, elevating 1.1 million people out of poverty, and adding annual growth of 2.5% in domestic economic growth in Pakistan (Akhtar et al., 2021; Kanwal et al., 2020; Rafiq, 2017).

CPEC also enlists economic and strategic prospects for China as it will provide China's shortest trade and energy routes to the Middle East, North Africa, and Europe and strengthen its position in the strategic Indian Ocean through Gwadar port. The corridor also offers an alternative lifeline to China's trade and energy supply in case of tension or armed conflict in the South China Sea (Akhtar et al., 2021; Hali et al., 2014; Roy, 2019). Therefore, the multibillion-dollar projects under CPEC are mutually beneficial for China and Pakistan and can change the destiny of people and countries along CPEC through economic and infrastructure development, regional connectivity, and economic and financial integrations (Hussain, 2020; Khan et al., 2020; Zhang et al., 2018).

China has upgraded its strategic partnership with the Islamic world under the BRI framework. Relationships with many Islamic countries are elevated to the more pre-eminent level of strategic relations (i.e., comprehensive strategic partnership—Table 3.3) to enhance mutual cooperation in the fields of energy, infrastructure, hi-tech, defence, culture, trade, and economy (Chaziza, 2016; O'Connor & Donovan, 2022; Sun & Xu, 2022). For example, China has upgraded its strategic relationship with Egypt to the level of "comprehensive strategic partnership" and pledges a hefty amount of US$50 billion for the development and construction of new administrative capital in Cairo and of the new Suez Canal cooperation zone under the BRI projects in Egypt.

President Xi Jinping and Saudi Crown Prince Mohammed bin Salman Al Saud have principally agreed to jack up China-Saudi relations to a new level of "comprehensive strategic partnership" and to integrate the BRI with Saudi Arabia's Vision 2030 (Foley, 2017; Fulton, 2020; Shay, 2018). As a result, Beijing

Table 3.3: China's Strategic and Cooperative Relationship with the Islamic Countries.

Level of Relationship	Islamic Country Name	Geographical Region
All-Weather Strategic Cooperative Partnership	Pakistan	South Asia
Comprehensive Strategic Cooperative Partnership	Senegal	Sub-Saharan Africa
	Guinea	Sub-Saharan Africa
	Sierra Leone	Sub-Saharan Africa
Strategic Cooperative Partnership	Afghanistan,	South Asia
	Bangladesh	South Asia
	Brunei	Pacific
Permanent Comprehensive Strategic Partnership	Kazakhstan	Central Asia
Comprehensive Strategic Partnership	Tajikistan	Central Asia
	Azerbaijan	Central Asia
	Uzbekistan	Central Asia
	Kyrgyzstan	Central Asia
	Indonesia	East Asia
	Malaysia	East Asia
	Iran	Middle East
	Kuwait	Middle East
	United Arab Emirates	Middle East
	Saudi Arabia	Middle East
	Algeria	North Africa
	Egypt	North Africa
	Morocco	North Africa
Strategic Partnership	Comoros	Sub-Saharan Africa
	Djibouti	Sub-Saharan Africa
	Nigeria	Sub-Saharan Africa
	Jordan	Middle East
	Oman	Middle East
	Qatar	Middle East
	Iraq	Middle East
	Turkmenistan	Central Asia
	Turkey	Europe
Future-Oriented Comprehensive Friendly Cooperative Partnership	Maldives	South Asia
Comprehensive Cooperative Partnership	Guinea	Sub-Saharan Africa

and Riyadh signed a bilateral agreement of US$65 billion under the BRI framework to step up mutual cooperation in trade, economic development, space technology, renewable energy, nuclear energy, and petroleum engineering (Fulton, 2020; Shay, 2018). Chinese state-owned Railway Construction Corporation has recently completed a mega project "Haramain high-speed rail" worth US$16 billion in Saudi Arabia—the largest railway project in the Middle East that linked the two holy cities of Islam: Makkah and Madinah. It reduces the long road journey by two hours and makes it more comfortable and pleasant for more than 60 million Muslim pilgrims who travel between Makkah and Madinah to perform Hajj and Umrah (Islamic pilgrimage) every year. The project has contributed economically and religiously to the well-being of the Muslim Ummah and added positive synergy to the Sino-Islamic relationship (Khan & Pratt, 2019).

Under the BRI, China also pledges massive investments in infrastructure, energy, and economic development in other Islamic countries. For example, China is constructing an oil refinery in Oman with an investment of US$10.7 billion in the Sino-Oman industrial city that will handle 235, 000 barrels of crude oil per day (Khan et al., 2022; Kliman & Grace, 2018; Lehr, 2018). It will open a credit line of US$10 billion for Iran to support its economic growth through the state-owned CITIC group and plan to build a "Silk Road high-speed railway" between China and Iran through central Asian states that will connect China with Europe via Turkey. The freight will run from Urumqi, Xinjiang (China) to Almaty (Kazakhstan), then pass through Tashkent and Samarkand (Uzbekistan), and Ashgabat (Turkmenistan) before entering the Iranian cities of Mashhad and Tehran. It will further travel to Turkey and enter Bulgaria (Europe). The route will reduce the time and cost of freight shipping and transportation of goods between China and the Islamic world (Macauley, 2015; Osiewicz, 2018). In addition, China has promised substantial financial and economic investments in war-ridden Islamic countries such as Afghanistan, Iraq, Libya, Yemen, and Syria, to restore their destroyed infrastructure and engine their economies. For example, China pledged US$2 billion for investment in Syria under the BRI framework and US$29 million for humanitarian aid in 2017 (COAR, 2022). Therefore, China's BRI will inject new impetus into Sino-Islamic strategic relationships under President Xi's version of "the community with a shared future for mankind" and will play a crucial role in the infrastructural and economic development of the Islamic world (Kliman & Grace, 2018; Lehr, 2018).

Prospects and challenges

The Islamic world has warmly welcomed the BRI and positively received the huge Chinese financial and economic investments through BRI in infrastructure development, energy (e.g., oil and gas, electricity grids, and dams), transport (e.g., road, railways, ports), mining (e.g., exploration and drillings), information and communication technologies (e.g., fiber optics, IoT), industrial parks, urban development and development of special economic zones (SEZ) in the Islamic countries. Particularly, Chinese infrastructure projects (e.g., energy exploration, electricity generation, dams constructions, roads, railways, and ports) and pro-poor social infrastructures aid (e.g., schools, hospitals, and public transport) have enhanced China's positive image in the Islamic world (Bluhm et al., 2020; Khan et al., 2023; Maruta et al., 2020). However, the versatility of the financial and economic system, sociopolitical landscape, and diverse culture in the Islamic world both provide unique prospects and pose challenges for the successful implementation of BRI in the Islamic world.

Economic prospects and energy needs

China's robust economic growth is the major propeller of China's peaceful rise and its socio-political stability. However, China's economic growth has been facing serious challenges of macroeconomic issues and structural transformation in recent years. The economic growth has dropped down to signal-digit growth from a double-digit growth rate due to disproportion in investment-led growth, overcapacity in construction and manufacturing sectors, the disparity in regional development and connectivity, low income and inequality, and increased reliance on energy import (Aglietta & Bai, 2016; de L.T. Oliveira et al., 2020; Tekdal, 2018). Therefore, the Chinese economy is moving toward structural transformation to increase the share of domestic consumption in the GDP, increase services, high-tech, and innovation-based economic growth, exploration of new export destinations to address the overcapacity in the manufacturing and construction sectors, and increase the investment in infrastructures for regional connectivity to enhance free trade (Naughton, 2016; Pencea, 2017). Therefore, the successful implementation of the BRI will play a momentous role in China's future economic growth and its dreams of becoming a great power.

The Islamic world which constitutes 50 Muslim-majority countries is abundant in natural resources (crude oil, natural gas, and minerals) and holds the world's largest consumer market of 1.9 billion people that make up 24.1 %

of the total world population (Majoka et al., 2012; World Population Review, 2022). Most importantly, the largest chunk of the Muslim population (62 %) lives in Asia—geographically close to China (Li, 2018; Sherani, 2013). Despite the abundance of natural resources and the largest consumer market, the Islamic world struggles with the paucity of industrial skills, technological advancement, innovation, energy shortage, and modern infrastructures both in the information and communication (ICT) and transportation that hinder economic prosperity in the Islamic world (Galal, 2014; Halsall et al., 2022; Khan & Pratt, 2019; Yang, 2014).

On the other hand, China has become the world's second-largest economy. It has achieved landmark success in the fields of science and technology, industrial skills, manufacturing, engineering, innovation, ICT, and agriculture sectors. However, recently the Chinese economy has witnessed an economic slowdown after unprecedented economic growth in the last few decades due to rising macroeconomic issues, structural transformation, a growing trade war with the U.S., and a global economic slowdown. There is also an overcapacity challenge in the manufacturing and construction industries. Particularly, the construction sectors (i.e., aluminum, steel, and cement) are the largest overcapacity industries in China (de L.T. Oliveira et al., 2020; Fasslabend, 2015; Huang, 2016; Swaine, 2015). Therefore, China thrives on new strategies under the BRI to find new consumer markets and lucrative investment avenues to relieve the overabundance of manufacturing and construction industries, enhance its trade, sell its innovative technologies, and invest its surplus capital in infrastructure development projects abroad to reboot its economic growth and attain more sustainable socio-economic growth. Therefore, the Islamic world is the best potential foreign market of 1.9 billion people and a rewarding place for China's hefty investments in infrastructure development and to utilize its overabundance of resources (e.g., economic, technological, and material) for mutual benefits and shared development (e.g., infrastructure development, technological advancement, industrial and agricultural development) under the BRI. It will realize mutual goals; *First*, it will help the Islamic world to modernize its transportation infrastructures like motorways, highways, railways, airports, and seaports to improve its regional connectivity; develop energy sectors, like exploration and drilling of oil, gas, and minerals, and build vibrant energy infrastructures like pipelines, dams, electricity lines, and grid stations; and facilitate industrial and economic development through technology transfer and develop free economic zones under BRI framework. *Second*, it will provide China access to the huge Islamic consumer market and an abundance of national resources to address its overabundance issue in the construction and manufacturing sectors as well as to fulfill its future energy needs (Amighini, 2017; Selmier-II, 2018). The raison d'être for such a win-win outcome is fivefold.

First, China's strategic "Westward March" (mainly toward Islamic countries) is envisioned in BRI's grand strategy that aims to expand China's outreach through the western border to grasp energy-rich Central Asian states and the Middle East via CCWAEC and CPEC and eventually reach to Europe through inland routes and railways. The Westward approach shows the pivotal shift in China's economic development strategy to correct and rebalance what "tended to be a lopsided eastward overemphasis in terms of economic development and national security protection" (Scobell & Nader, 2016, p. 73). This strategy opens new avenues of potential trade and economic cooperation with the Islamic countries in Central Asia, South Asia, Southeast Asia, the Middle East, North Africa, and Europe and it also eludes the U.S. westward containment strategy, bloc politics, and strategic alliance with South Korea and Japan to expand U.S.-led economic sphere of influence and subdue China's strategic influence in East Asia. The Westward push will further globalize and integrate China's economy with Afro-Eurasian states and will facilitate the realization of China's dream of becoming a global power (great power) in the long term as compared to China's Eastward overemphasis that might stimulate a potential conflict with the U.S. and its Eastern allies and also reduce China's role in Asia (Ferdinand, 2016). Beijing's Westward drive toward the Islamic world is also legitimized in the BRI framework that argues for building a harmonious society (i.e., Afro-Eurasian society) of common destiny and a shared future where everybody can live a happy life (Khan et al., 2018; Xi, 2017a). Meanwhile, the Islamic world is recalibrating its economic and political calculus and tilting eastward to strengthen its relationship with China for economic and financial investments and political support for its lingering regional disputes (Galal, 2014).

The BRI has the potential to accomplish the common agenda of both China's economic growth and the Islamic world's thirst for financial and economic investments in infrastructure development i.e., building transportation networks (i.e., highways, motorways, railways, bridges, tunnels, dry ports, seaports, and airports) to ease regional connectivity and fasten free trade; strengthen energy sectors through exploration, drilling, generation, transmission and transportation (i.e., oil, coal, electricity, grid station and gas pipelines) to subdued energy crisis; and bridge the communication linkages through fiber-optic cables and IoT. This will create an affluent economic and energy corridor between China and the Islamic world and will equally contribute to the shared development and mutual benefits with win-win outcomes

(Amighini, 2017; Hu, 2019; Khan & Pratt, 2019; Selmier-II, 2018). For example, CCWAEC and CPEC—two crucial BRI flagship economic and energy corridors can stir up the economic growth, infrastructure development, and energy interests of both China and the Islamic world. Scholars (e.g., Fulton, 2016; Jinbo, 2019) argue that CCWAEC is central to China's energy supply lines (oil and gas) and sustainable economic growth as it connects China to the energy-rich Islamic countries in Central Asia, Persian Gulf, Arabian Peninsula, and the Mediterranean coast. China's oil and gas exports mainly came from the Islamic countries in Central Asia, the Persian Gulf, and the Middle East. Similarly, the CPEC, another BRI flagship project of US$62 billion in Pakistan has already started playing a critical role in developing energy and transportation infrastructure and stimulating economic activities in Pakistan. It also provides China with an alternative energy and trade route through Xinjiang to the Middle East, North Africa, and Europe and reduced transportation distance of up to 9,000 km for China to access the Middle East's vital energy resources. It also paves the way for China to export its goods to the Middle East, Persian Gulf, North Africa, and Europe through the Gwadar seaport to boost its declining economic growth. In addition, CCWAEC and CPEC will also play a crucial role in the socio-economic development and national integration of China's less-developed western regions which are left behind in socio-economic development compared to South China regions due to geographical distance and natural disadvantages particularly the Muslim-populated areas—Xinjiang, Ningxia, Gansu, and Qinghai, etc., (Tekdal, 2018). Recently, China has built the world's largest dry port (Khorgos) and Khorgos gateway in the Central Asian Islamic country, Kazakhstan, to accelerate economic activities, trade, and energy supplies from Central Asia, West Asia, and Europe via railway link. The Khorgos gateway has strategic importance as it provides a strategic juncture between CCWAEC and NELB economic corridors. It started from Urumqi (Xinjiang, China), and runs through Kazakhstan (Bishkek and Samarkand), Turkmenistan, Iran (Tehran), and Turkey (Istanbul and Ankara) where it takes Northeast to links Europe via Bulgaria, Moldova, Romania, and Ukraine to Russia (Moscow). From Moscow, it turned westward to connect Belarus and Poland to Germany and passed through the Netherlands, France, Belgium, and Switzerland to reach Venice. Therefore, the Khorgos gateway has strategic importance in BRI as it will handle 15–30 million tons of freight from Eurasia per year and will expand Chinese economic influence and international cooperation from Central Asia to the Persian Gulf and Europe (Fasslabend, 2015; Sági & Engelberth, 2018; Selmier-II, 2018).

Second, as stated above, the Islamic world is full of natural resources, particularly oil, and gas, as it possesses 75% of the world's proven oil reserves and 42–55% of the world's natural gas reservoirs (Cooper & Yue, 2015; Majoka et al., 2012). The Middle East region alone contributes more than 42% of crude oil and 26 % of natural gas to the world's oil and gas supply chain and holds more than 65% of the world's proven oil resources and 51% of the world's total natural gas reserves (Khan & Pratt, 2019). Islamic countries like Saudi Arabia, Iraq, Iran, Kuwait, United Arab Emirates, and Qatar are among the world's largest oil and gas suppliers and an engine of the world's economic growth, energy security, social development, and human prosperity. China heavily relies on Islamic countries (e.g., Saudi Arabia, Iran, and Iraq) for their petroleum products to sustain China's economic growth and social development (Chen, 2011; Cooper & Yue, 2015; Khan & Pratt, 2019; Majoka et al., 2012).

In recent years, China's energy demands have increased meteorically and it has become the world's largest crude oil importer (10.8 million barrels per day [bpd]) surpassing the U.S. crude import demand of 7.9 million bpd in 2017 (Barron, 2018; Reuters, 2022). China's oil consumption showed a steady rise from 0.2 million bpd in December 1965 to 14.2 million bpd in December 2020. There is an average increase in oil consumption of 2.9 million bpd in 56 years (CEIC, 2020b). China's domestic oil resources are scarce and, therefore, the Chinese economy deeply depends on imported oil as it grows, its oil import demand also rose from 1.404 thousand bpd in 1980 to 10.8 million bpd in May 2022, showing an average increase of 1.21 million bpd in 40 years (CEIC, 2020a; *Reuters*, 2022).

Beijing can explore and even secure its future access to the vital oil resources in the energy-rich Islamic countries under the BRI framework by pledging infrastructural investments, technical cooperation, and extending innovative technologies in the exploration, development, and transportation of petroleum products and natural gas as a trustworthy partner in the Islamic world (Kamel, 2018; Khan & Pratt, 2019; Li, 2018; Selmier-II, 2018). Many of the oil-rich Islamic countries are still under-explored due to scarce financial resources, lack of technical expertise, mechanical equipment, and industrial standards in petroleum engineering (e.g., exploration, drilling, extraction, refinement, and transportation). Therefore, the BRI energy-related projects in the Islamic world, particularly, huge investments in oil and gas sectors in the Persian Gulf, Central Asian states, the Middle East, and African countries will play a central role in satisfying China's future energy needs and provide safe and secure energy supply routes from Persian Gulf, Central Asia, the Middle East, and African countries.

Third, the Islamic world possesses a multitrillion-dollar Islamic economic market of 1.9 billion people that accumulated funds worth US$5.5 trillion in 2019. The funds are available in the form of OIC sovereign wealth funds worth US$3.2 trillion and "dry powder" (unutilized capital) funds worth US$3.2 trillion for wider regional investment and food security supply chain. Therefore, the Islamic economic market offers massive economic prospects for China's BRI projects. In addition, the Islamic economic market is growing steadily and valued at US$5.7 trillion in 2021. It is predicted that the Islamic economic market will achieve an accumulated wealth of US$7.8 trillion by 2025. The market is driven by eight main sectors: Islamic banking and finance; tourism and travel; media and recreation; pharmaceutical; fashion; cosmetic and Islamic fintech, providing ample opportunities for China to invest in those fast-growing sectors under the auspice of BRI in the Islamic world. (Table 3.4).

Fourth, Islamic banking and finance (IBF) is the major driver behind the steady growth of the Islamic economic market in 2021. Currently, more than 1000 international institutions are offering Islamic finance and banking services in more than 75 countries (Baydoun et al., 2021) and its accumulative value has reached US$3.6 trillion in 2021. It will further increase up to US$4.9 trillion by 2025 (Table 3.4). The Islamic world is progressively adhering to the IBF system and the Sukuk Islamic bonds (based on risk-sharing and real asset financing)

Table 3.4: An Existing and Estimated Size of Islamic Economy Market in U.S. Billion Dollars.

	Islamic Economy Exited Size		Islamic Economy Estimated Size	
	2019	2021	2024	2025
Islamic Banking and Finance	$2,880	$3,600	$3,690	$4,900
Halal Food	$1,170	$1,270	$1,380	$1,670
Tourism and Travel	$194	$102	$208	$189
Fashion	$277	$295	$311	$375
Media and Recreation	$222	$231	$270	$308
Pharmaceutical	$94	$100	$105	$129
Islamic Fintech	-	$49	$108	$128
Cosmetics	$66	$70	$76	$93
Total	$4,903	$5,717	$6,148	$7,792

Source: State of the Global Islamic Economy Reports, 2020–2022 (DinarStandard, 2022)

have provided an alternative source of funding to governments and corporations. A total worth of US$1.35 trillion of Sukuk Islamic bonds has already been issued for wider regional development from 1990 through 2020. Islamic countries such as Saudi Arabia, United Arab Emirates (UAE), Qatar, Kuwait, Bahrain, Oman, and Malaysia, have great potential and are the major contributors to Sukuk Islamic bonds. For example, Saudi Arabia issued US$113.9 billion worth of Sukuk bonds compared with Western bonds that were worth US$64.2 billion between 2017 through 2020. Therefore, China can use Sukuk Islamic bonds to bridge the funding gap related to BRI infrastructure development projects that need US$49 trillion by 2030. According to the World Bank, Asia's infrastructure development under BRI alone will require US$22.6 trillion by 2030 (US$1.7 trillion per year). China's engagement in Africa needs an additional US$38 billion for infrastructural development and US$37 billion per year for operations and maintenance of BRI infrastructure (Baydoun et al., 2021; Li, 2018; Townsend, 2018). China's massive investment in infrastructural development across Afro-Eurasia regions and beyond needs financial and macroeconomic stability. China can secure substantial fund inflow and financial stability for BRI-related projects through IBF which is grounded in the principle of asset-based financing and risk-sharing. It will mitigate risk management and deject the credit booms (Al-Jarhi, 2017; Bo et al., 2016). China can link up financial institutions (e.g., AIIB, NDB, The Exim Bank, and NSRF) "with Islamic financial products, using such a setup for risk management in BRI-related projects in the Islamic world" (Khan & Pratt, 2019, p. 127).

The IBF has expanded globally and successfully integrated into the international financial system (Ahmad et al., 2019; Novikov et al., 2020). Islamic finance like Sukuk Islamic bond has earned a good reputation in financing and bankrolling infrastructural projects which contributed significantly to the economic growth in many countries. This is also evident from increased global interest and demand for Sukuk Islamic bonds in the international market. Many Western and non-Islamic countries have allowed the IBF to operate in their respective jurisdictions. For example, the U.K. has fully adopted the IBF system and recently issued Sukuk Islamic bonds in the international market to raise government revenue for socio-economic development. Similarly, Germany, Japan, and many other non-Islamic countries have opened full-fledged Islamic banking and started offering Islamic banking products (e.g., Sukuk, Takaful-Islamic insurance certificates) (Djafri et al., 2021; Laldin & Djafri, 2019). China is new to the IBF system, but it has started efforts toward facilitating Islamic financing in infrastructural development projects. For example, AIIB signed a MoU with the Islamic Development Bank (IDB—a multilateral Islamic bank that focuses on IBF) to jointly finance infrastructural projects in Africa and other underdeveloped regions in 2016. Other Chinese banks such as the Industrial Commercial Bank of China (ICBC), also signed a MoU with the Qatar National Bank (QNB) to invest capital in the IBF in the Islamic world. AIIB has also planned to use Hong Kong as a launch of paid-for Sukuk Islamic bonds to strengthen financial integration with the Islamic world and explore new investors or investment opportunities in the Islamic world. The IDB has already shown interest in issuing Sukuk Islamic bonds through AIIB which will extend its global economic influence and will bring Islamic investment in the BRI projects (Bo et al., 2016; Djafri et al., 2021; Sarker et al., 2019). Subsequently, IBF industries have shown rapid growth in Hong Kong and investment in Sukuk Islamic bonds has increased from US$1.1 trillion in 2013 to US$1.6 trillion in 2018. The Hong Kong government invested US$4.7 billion for five years in Sukuk Islamic bonds in September 2014. Therefore, Hong Kong has the potential to become a door for Islamic financing in mainland China and generate substantial capital for BRI-related projects to bridge the funding gap (Li, 2018).

Fifth, halal food is the second largest part of the fast-growing Islamic economic market which constitutes 19% of the international food market. Muslims living around the world consume halal food worth US$1.13 trillion annually (DinarStandard, 2022). The halal food industry is expected to achieve growth worth US$3.7 trillion by 2025 (Table 3.4). China hosts more than 23 million Muslim population, scattered across China but largely concentrated in the relatively less developed western parts of China (i.e., Xinjiang, Ningxia, Gansu, and Qinghai)—relatively close to the Islamic world both culturally and geographically. In addition, China's unprecedented economic growth, scientific development, and potent manufacturing industries have also attracted huge numbers of Islamic enterprises, Muslim traders, businessmen and women, international students, and workers to China and created a huge market for halal food products' consumption in China.

Both China and the Islamic world can capitalize on this huge opportunity to find new venues for halal food trade under the BRI framework. Particularly, China can utilize this opportunity to facilitate its Muslim population living in less developed and historically disadvantaged areas to export their halal products to the Islamic world which will not only bring socio-economic prosperity to China's Muslim areas but will also increase people-to-people contacts and enhance the political and economic relationship between China and Islamic world. China has already realized the socio-economic output of this vast opportunity and established the International Halal Certificate Service Center and China-Malaysia Halal E-commercial Center in the Muslim-populated area, Ningxia to meet the standards of halal food and to catch up with the halal food market for mutual benefits and win-win outcomes.

There are some other potential areas of the Islamic economic market where China can invest and earn valuable financial capital. For example, the tourism and travel sectors have shown US$102 billion growth in 2021 and are expected to attain an annual growth worth US$189 billion by 2025. Similarly, fashion sectors are expected to generate US$375 billion annual capital by 2025, the media and recreation industry will reach US$308 billion, the pharmaceutical industry is expected US$129 billion growth, Islamic fintech is estimated at US$129 billion and cosmetics will grow up to US$93 billion by 2025 (Table 3.4). China can explore new opportunities in those fast-growing sectors in the Islamic economic market to invigorate its slowdown economic growth under the BRI framework.

Strategic and political advantages

BRI carries both geopolitical and geostrategic recompenses for China and the Islamic world. *First*, the Islamic world is a major political bloc comprised of 50 Muslim countries that are strategically located across Afro-Eurasian contentions. A quarter of the world's population (1.9 billion) adheres to the Islamic faith and more importantly, 62% of the Muslim population lives in China's closed neighborhood which galvanizes its strategic and political importance for China's dream of global leadership (Li, 2018; Majoka et al., 2012; Sherani, 2013; World Population Review, 2022). The Islamic world also runs and controls global political and economic institutions like the Organization of Islamic Cooperation (OIC), The Islamic Development Bank (IDB), the Gulf Cooperation Council (GCC), and the Organization of the Petroleum Exporting Countries (OPEC) which further mesmerize its significance in the global politics and economy. OIC is the world's second-largest intergovernmental organization after the United Nations and holds membership of 57 sovereign countries across four continents—Asia, Europe, Africa, and South America. It is considered the collective voice of the Muslim Ummah and the Islamic world. The IDB is a global Islamic financial institution of 57 member states that provides Islamic finance for global infrastructure development projects. It can provide crucial Islamic finances for the BRI projects and facilitate "Sharia-compliant ways" for the core BRI projects in the Islamic countries across Afro-Eurasian regions and beyond. GCC is another powerful regional, political, economic, and intergovernmental organization of six major Gulf counties (Saudi Arabia, UAE, Bahrain, Kuwait, Oman, and Qatar)—the major players in the Middle East's political and economic affairs. In addition, the Islamic world is a major stakeholder in OPEC that controls and influences the entire world's energy supply chains and petroleum prices in the global market. Therefore, BRI can pave the way for Sino-Islamic strategic collaboration through those political and economic institutions and can leverage China's political and economic power on the global stage.

Second, China's westward approach toward Islamic countries is pivotal for its economic development and national security. It will rebalance China's relations with the U.S., avoid unnecessary confrontation in East Asia, and even provide an opportunity for cooperative relations in West Asia, particularly in the Middle East to ensure security and stability in the region (Ferdinand, 2016). China and the U.S. are in continuous rivalry and indulge themselves in a zero-sum game in East Asia. Moreover, U.S. policies and strategic alliances with China's rivals—India, Japan, and Austria, are posing serious challenges to China's strategic interests and prospects for global leadership. In the past, U.S. hegemony and unilateral actions in the Middle East have curtailed China's ability to play an influential role in the region and jeopardized its access to vital petroleum resources. Therefore, the BRI can provide impetus to China's westward push and pave the way for making new strategic alliances with the Islamic world while grabbing the economic and trading opportunities in West Asia, Central Asia, Africa, and Europe (Aoyama, 2016; Chen, 2011; Khan & Pratt, 2019; Sági & Engelberth, 2018; Scobell & Nader, 2016).

Third, the U.S. invasion and abrupt withdrawal from Afghanistan, Iraq, Syria, and Libya have routed the U.S. decline in global supremacy and created a vacuum of global leadership. It has also fueled new conflicts and instigated new threats in the Middle East. Therefore, China has moved faster to establish a "comprehensive strategic partnership" with the Islamic world, particularly with Saudi Arabia, Pakistan, Iran, UAE, Egypt, Indonesia, Malaysia, Kazakhstan, Tajikistan, Uzbekistan, Azerbaijan, Kuwait, Algeria, and Morocco under the BRI to avoid wider spectrum of threats to its strategic interests and to strengthen the political and economic relationship with the Islamic world (O'Connor & Donovan, 2022). Even though China witnessed an unprecedented rise in economic and military stature, its strategic alliances with the Islamic world and its political support will be pivotal for its case for global leadership and great power (Khan et al., 2018; Malik, 2002). Therefore, BRI can synergize the existing relations to a new level of strategic, political, economic, and military alliances through a comprehensive strategic partnership between China and the Islamic world.

Fourth, the U.S. hegemonic policies, and continuous political and military interventions (e.g., the Israel-Palestine issue, the Afghan war, the Iraq war, the Syria war, and the Libya war) in domestic and national affairs of the sovereign Islamic countries have displeased the Islamic leadership. Thus, the Islamic world is in search of an alternative power to address its lingering political issues and kick-start the strained economies. China's peaceful rise and unprecedented economic growth have made it a new alternative to the U.S. in the Islamic world that guarantees non-interference in the country's internal affairs, and its national sovereignty. China has political leverage as a permanent member of the United Nations Security Council (UNSC) to settle political disputes among the Islamic countries due to its neutral stance and friendly relationship with the Islamic world (Elmagherbi, 2010; Hayoun, 2013; Li, 2018; Sheikhneshin et al., 2020; Zambelis & Gentry, 2008; Zhu, 2010). In addition, China has earned great appreciation in the Islamic world for its staunch support of the just cause of the Palestinian and Kashmiri peoples and its strong denouncement of U.S. interference, invasion, and occupation of sovereign Islamic countries. Therefore, King Abdullah bin Abdulaziz Al Saud of Saudi Arabia described China as a close and trustworthy friend of the Islamic world that "always stands on the side of truth and justice, always on the side of the just cause of the Palestinian people and the Arab people" (Khan et al., 2022; Zhu, 2010). Recently, China's mediated peace agreement between two adversarial Islamic powers: Saudi Arabia and Iran displays the Islamic countries' trust in China as a dependable friend and potential alternative to the U.S. to settle their lingering disputes. The peace deal harbingers China's new leading role in Middle East Politics—hitherto seized by global superpowers like the U.S. and Russia. It also signals that China is keen to strengthen its diplomatic clout to match its economic footprint in the Islamic world. Therefore, under the auspice of the BRI, China can capitalize on this responsiveness and fill the vacuum of distrust between the U.S. and the Islamic world to enhance its political and economic leverage and stature as an emerging great power in the Islamic world.

Fifth, China's problematic image abroad poses a "strategic threat" to China's dream of rejuvenation into a new global power (Ramo, 2004, 2007). It is often considered a "major issue" and a challenge to China's peaceful rise, and its role in global governance and leadership (Hayden, 2012; Khan et al., 2023; Ramo, 2007). China's poor global image and growing unpopularity hurt its strategic, economic, political, and diplomatic interests and pose challenges to smoothly accomplishing strategic goals in democratic countries "where politicians know how much their voters now dislike China" (Kurlantzick, 2022a, p. 2, 2022b).

China's poor image also undermines its efforts to resuscitate its "once-effective soft power campaign" and decreases its ability to present a positive image through state media, diplomatic channels, Confucius Institutes, and other available tools of soft power projection. Therefore, China devoted sufficient resources to enhance its positive image abroad but Western media steadily disparage China's role in international politics and the new world order due to its exponential expansionism abroad, an abridgment of the freedom of speech, and alleged human rights violations (Armony, 2012; Ezell, 2021; Hayden, 2012; Kurlantzick, 2007). China's flimsy political image abroad made it vulnerable, particularly in the West, therefore, China needs to strengthen its positive image to counter the Western media's evolving propaganda of the "China threat" in international media (Corkin, 2014; Li, 2008).

China has earned a global reputation for its robust economic growth and poverty elevation efforts for uplifting the socio-economic standards of more than 800 million people in a short time (The World Bank, 2022), and its competitive favorability advantage compared to the U.S. has improved but its positive and favorable image is still largely contested in many countries e.g., Japan Australia, Vietnam, U.S., South Korea, Sweden, Spain, Turkey, Egypt, Jordan, and Lebanon, where more than 50% of the population have a negative perception about China (Khan et al., 2022; Pew Research Center, 2017; Xie & Page, 2013). The public perception of China in some Islamic countries like Turkey, Egypt, Lebanon, Saudi Arabia, and Jordan, is also negative and even hostile in some instances (Al-Sudairi, 2013; Khan et al., 2023). Therefore, China can utilize BRI projects as public diplomacy tools to improve its favorable image and positive public perception in the Islamic world.

Political and security challenges

The Islamic world is entangled with complex political and security challenges due to political scuffles, extremism, terrorism, wars, and regional, religious, and ethnic conflicts that might hamper the smooth completion of BRI-related projects in the Islamic world. Islamic countries like Afghanistan, Iraq, Libya, Yemen, Syria, and Sudan are in a state of war while countries like Pakistan, Turkey, Egypt, and Saudi Arabia have been suffering from the brunt of religious extremism, terrorism, and political instability. For example, terrorist groups have repeatedly targeted Chinese citizens and BRI projects related to CPEC in Pakistan in the last few years (Akhtar et al., 2021; Chaudary, 2022; E. Hussain, 2018). Apart from a few Islamic countries (e.g., Malaysia, Qatar, and the UAE), the larger part of the Islamic world is embroiled in political and security crises. There is also sectarian cleavage and rivalry between Saudi-led Sunni Muslim countries and Iran-led Sharia Muslim countries that might further complicate the political conditions for China to implement its BRI projects in the Islamic world.

The perception of mistreatment of Uyghur Muslims in China's Xinjiang is still a major issue between China and the Islamic world (Kelemen & Turcsányi, 2020) and it can trickle the negative spillover on Sino-Islamic relations that might hurtle the BRI projects in the Islamic world. Particularly, Turkey has shown great concern and displeasure over China's alleged clampdown on Uyghur Muslims in Xinjiang due to their Turkic origins. Turkish President Tayyab Erdogan strongly condemned China's crackdown on Uyghur Muslims during ethnic violence in 2009, describing it as "a kind of genocide (BBC News, 2009). Protest in support of Uyghur Muslim rights in Xinjiang has also been witnessed in a few other Islamic countries (e.g. Turkey, Malaysia, Kazakhstan, and Indonesia) in recent years (Al-Jazeera, 2022; Ezell, 2021). Iranian religious clerics, the public, and the media also disparage the role of the Chinese government in handling the Xinjiang Muslim issues (Singh, 2021b) and China's vote in support of a U.N. Security Council Resolution that levied economic sanctions on Iran in 2010 (Chen, 2011). China has also been criticized by the Islamic and Western media for its alleged confinement of Uyghur Muslims in "re-ëducation" camps (Clarke, 2015; Ezell, 2021). Though China defends its action as deradicalization efforts to curtail the growing extremism and radicalism in Xinjiang (Benabdallah, 2018; Dabashi, 2018; Page et al., 2018), the anger in a few Islamic countries is on the rise where more than 50% of the population holds an unfavorable opinion about China, mainly in four key Islamic countries (Egypt, Turkey, Jordan, and Lebanon) (Pew Research Center, 2017; Xie & Page, 2013). The negative public perception of China and criticisms of Chinese policies toward the Uyghur Muslims in Xinjiang in the Islamic world carry significant reputational, political, and economic costs for China in the Islamic world. Therefore, China should use the BRI projects as public diplomacy initiatives to dispel this negative public perception and present itself as a trustworthy and close comrade of the major Islamic countries such as Saudi Arabia, Pakistan, Turkey, Egypt, and Indonesia (Benabdallah, 2018).

Collision of strategic interests

The smooth execution of BRI-related projects in the Islamic world is also entangled with the regional and global collision of interests. Regional forces in South Asia, particularly India strongly criticize and disavow the implementation of

CPEC in Pakistan and termed it against the national security and territorial integrity of India as it runs through the disputed territory of Kashmir. India connects BRI with the "string of pearls" strategy in South Asia that aims to link strategic dots through Hambantota (Sri Lanka) and Gwadar deep seaports (Pakistan) to marginalize India's geopolitical and strategic influence in the Indian Ocean Region and tactically jeopardize Indian future naval ambitions and prospects of great regional power (Brewster, 2018; Panneerselvam, 2017; Rahman et al., 2021; Suryanarayana, 2021).

Under the auspice of the BRI, China has also stepped up its political, economic, and security engagements and enhanced its "comprehensive strategic partnership" with the Middle Eastern countries in recent years. Its prominence has increased manifold and its fast-growing regional influence, and political, diplomatic, economic, and security-related activities are seriously posing challenges to the U.S. national interests and political hegemony in the region (Singh, 2021a). For example, the late King Abdullah of Saudi Arabia chose China as his first foreign country to visit after becoming the ruler in 2006, even though the U.S. was a key ally and security partner of the kingdom in the Middle East.

In recent years, the perception of Washington's role as a security partner or an ally in the Middle East has decreased and countries like Saudi Arabia are moving away from the U.S. ambit of influence and tilting toward China to establish a new strategic alliance for economic development, national security, and regional stability. Therefore, China's growing influence under the BRI in the Middle East can engender a clash of economic, political, and strategic interests between China and the U.S. and regional powers. For example, a former Chinese diplomat, Sun Bigan noted that the scrimmage between China and the U.S. will escalate over the political and economic influence and oil trade in the Middle East, and "Bilateral quarrels and clashes are unavoidable" in the future (Khan & Pratt, 2019; The Daily Star, 2009).

China still upholds a low profile and emphasizes more on economic incentives and energy-related activities in the Middle East. The regional countries are dragging China to play a more prominent and active role in settling the political disputes and security conflicts in the region. Khan and Pratt (2019) argue that China's deep involvement in economic and energy-related activities under the BRI projects in the Middle East will open for political exploitation in the future to gain support over certain critical issues like the pro-long Arabs-Israel conflict over the independent state of Palestine by the Arab countries. Such assumption is evident from the opinion of Arab League Secretary-General Amr Musa who once said: "If you protect my interests, I will protect yours. If you take a position that does not reflect that will, I will take a similar position" (Chen, 2011, p. 6; Haghirian & Zaccara, 2022).

China's growing friendship with Iran has also annoyed the U.S. which is steadily trying to snub Iran over its nuclear program. Iran has become China's major trading partner and crude oil supplier. Therefore, China opposes the strict punitive action against Iran over the nuclear issue and supports constructive engagement to resolve this issue through dialogue. For example, China opposed the strong-worded UNSC resolution against Iran in 2010. It supported only the feeblest form of economic sanction that undermines the effectiveness of the U.S. plan to deflate the Iranian economy and compel Iranian leadership to throw away its nuclear program (Khan & Pratt, 2019).

The Islamic world is divided into two sectarian lines—Sunni and Shia blocs. Particularly, the intra-faith divide is palpable in the Middle East. Saudi Arabia leads the Sunni bloc (e.g., UAE, Bahrain, Qatar, Kuwait, Yemen, and Oman) and Iran guides the Shia bloc (Lebanon, Iraq, Syria, and Yemen [Houthis]). Historically, Saudi Arabia and Iran are opponents and support rival groups to safeguard their political, economic, and strategic interests in the Middle East. For example, Saudi Arabia and Iran have been supporting rival groups in the civil war in Yemen since 2010. Saudi Arabia firmly supported President Abdrabbuh Mansur Hadi (a Sunni leader) and even established a regional military alliance to physically support and strengthen his position in Yemen. While Iran is consistently supporting Houthis (Shia anti-government militia) to maintain their power in Yemen. There are other regional issues where both countries hold significantly different positions, and a collision of strategic interest is visible on the issue of Iran's nuclear program, the Iraq war, and Iranian military support for Bashar al Asad (a Shia leader) in the Syrian war. Even though China maintains a careful balance between these regional rivals to safeguard its economic, political, and strategic interests in the region, fast-changing regional, political, and economic dynamics may brush the bubble of this balance and sabotage the smooth implementation of BRI-related projects in the Middle East (Moonakal, 2022). In addition, China's friendly relations with Israel will be closely watched and can be exploited for economic or political favors by the Arab countries (Ferdinand, 2016).

Some regional powers in the Islamic world have also shown concerns about the geopolitical and geostrategic disadvantages of the BRI projects. For example, some strategic analysts in Egypt are concerned that China's hefty investment in the Suez Canal region will undermine Egyptian sovereignty and regional stability in the future (Al-Khair, 2021). There is concern that China will use the Suez Canal region as a supporting base to connect its strewn bases in Africa and regulate naval frigates in the Black Sea (Al-Khair, 2021; Khan et al., 2023; Sun & Xu, 2022). Other regional issues may also lead to the collision of strategic and geopolitical interests between China and the Islamic world. For example, the Egyptian-Turkish conflict over Libya and the Eastern Mediterranean gas fields. In addition, the Egyptian government has serious reservations about the Chinese investment in the construction of the "Ethiopian Renaissance Dam" which may jeopardize their water security and national interests in the long run (Selim & Moaaz, 2021; Khan et al., 2023).

Financial distress, debt trap, and local resentment

The "Great Recession" that turned into a global financial crisis during 2007–2009 severely damaged the lending capacities of Western countries and West-led financial institutions (e.g., International Monetary Fund [IMF], and the Paris Club). In the meantime, China emerged as a new creditor for the low- and middle-income economies due to its unprecedented economic growth and to drive its "go global" policy. Particularly, after the inauguration of China's much-celebrated BRI, China's investments and capital outflow have increased manifold and it has become the biggest lender globally superseding, the annual lending of IMF, Paris Club, and the World Bank. Resultantly, Chinese loans to low- and middle-income economies have quadrupled in the last decade and raised from US$40 billion in 2010 to US$170 billion by 2020 (Wang, 2022). The critics argue that Chinese generous lending to the low- and middle-income economies in South Asia, East Asia, Central Asia, and Africa is a "Debt Trap" to exploit those countries for political and economic gains (Carmody, 2020; Risberg, 2019). The takeover of Sri Lanka's strategic Hambantota port in lieu of US$8 billion debt by a Chinese state-owned company is often cited as an example of China's debt trap strategy (Chaziza, 2021; Risberg, 2019; Wang, 2022). However, the claim about "debt trap diplomacy" is largely unjustified. For example, Carmody (2020) argues that the rapid increase in Chinese debt in Africa is the result of their growing dependence on China for economic and infrastructural development. China did not imply the debt trap intentionally rather the upsurge in overseas borrowing is both outcome and vector of development in Africa.

However, the financial debt distress in the low-and middle-income countries has been amplified due to the economic shocks of the pandemic (COVID-19) and the Russia-Ukraine war. According to the IMF report (2022), among 76 low-and-middle-income countries, 44 are at "high risk" of or in debt distress, and the other 20 are on the brink of high-risk threshold due to continuous stagflation, depleting foreign reserves, and mounting budget deficit in 2022 (Chabert et al., 2022). A majority of those countries are official partners in China's BRI. In addition, the Center for Global Development (CGD) report (2017) indicates that 23 BRI countries are facing a "quite high" risk of financial debt distress; and eight of them—Kyrgyzstan, Tajikistan, the Maldives, Pakistan, Laos, Montenegro, Djibouti, and Mongolia will face difficulty to repay Chinese debt in time (Khan & Pratt, 2019; Ming, 2018). China's BRI partner—Sri Lanka has already defaulted on its sovereign debt (Hoskins, 2022).

China's BRI largely targets the low-and middle-income countries in the Afro-Eurasian region and beyond which are confronting acute financial distress. Therefore, China's investment in modern infrastructure in many Islamic countries will not be sustainable and will increase its financial debt distress (Carmody, 2020). For example, China pledges to invest US$50 billion in Egypt's new capital infrastructure in Cairo under the BRI which will further aggravate the already financially distressed economy of Egypt. Egypt owes US$137.85 billion in sovereign debt to multilateral creditors in June 2020 and its debt to China has increased from US$4.7 billion in 2017 to US$7.5 billion in 2020 (Elleithy, 2021; Hurley et al., 2019). Similarly, the Malaysian government deserted the multibillion-dollar high-speed rail project between Singapore and Malaysia to "avoid being declared bankrupt" (Shukry & Park, 2018). China's all-weather strategic partner and a major collaborator in the BRI—Pakistan, is on the verge of an economic collapse due to the rapid increase in the volume of foreign debt, sinking of foreign reserves, and growing trade deficit (Khabar, 2022). According to the World Bank International Debt Statistics (2022) and CGS (2017), Pakistan witnessed a rapid increase in international borrowing in the fiscal year 2019–2020 and is facing a "high risk" of debt distress or in debt distress. China pledges US$62 billion in investment in CPEC-related projects in Pakistan and 80 percent of those investments will be in form of Chinese loans (Ming, 2018). Therefore, the former Pakistani Prime Minister Imran Khan decided to review and reevaluate some major CPEC projects and put them on hold in the quest for compelling evidence to proceed carefully while keeping in mind the tottering national economy (Anderlini et al., 2018; Kiani, 2019). The World Bank International Debt Statistics (2022) also revealed that China's massive investments in large infrastructural projects and extractive industries under the BRI resulted in a sharp increase in Chinese debt up to US$170 billion in the "low- and middle-income countries" at the end of 2020. The highest increase in Chinese debt was witnessed in Sub-Saharan Africa, where 45% of the total regional debt was owed to China in 2020. Chinese debt in South Asia also increased from US$4.7 billion in 2011 to US$36.3 billion in 2020, and China has become a single largest bilateral creditor to Pakistan, Sri Lanka and the Maldives (The World Bank, 2022). Therefore, Islamic countries likes, Pakistan, Bangladesh, Maldives, Nigeria, Uzbekistan, Egypt, Guinea-Bissau, Burkina Faso, Kosovo, Niger, Yemen, Iraq, Syria, Libya, and Afghanistan etc., will struggle to pay back China's loans in the future.

Under the auspice of the BRI, China's trade deficit with the Islamic world has sharply increased in recent years. For example, the Egyptian economy witnessed a record trade deficit of US$11.2 billion with China in 2019, making it the signal largest contributor to the trade deficit of the Egyptian economy (Selim & Moaaz, 2021; D. Sun & Xu, 2022). The influx of cheap Chinese products into the Islamic market has also stimulated fear and resentment in local industries and some countries have imposed anti-dumping duties to protect their local industries (Khan & Pratt, 2019; Zhu, 2010). For example, Pakistan imposed 24% anti-dumping duties on Chinese steel to protect its local steel industry in 2018 (ANI, 2018). There are also strong apprehensions of local industries and entrepreneurs about the establishment of free economic zones under the BRI framework which they believe will further squeeze the financial space and opportunities for local investors and will open the door for Chinese businesses to take over the local manufacturing, domestic production and affect the country export capacity. Besides, some other major issues are workplace practices, hiring patterns, an influx of Chinese labor and employment incentives, etc., (Feng & Liang, 2018; Zambelis & Gentry, 2008).

Religious and cultural gaps

The historic Silk Road paved friendly relations between China and the Islamic world and integrated the two great civilizations by facilitating trade and cultural exchange between them (Li, 2018; Park, 2012; Zhu, 2010). However, there is a wide religious and cultural gap between China and the Islamic world that can hurt the trade relations and strategic partnership between China and the Islamic world. Historically, Islamic countries are tied with the Islamic financial system that prohibits certain kinds of financial transactions and economic engagements. For example, the Islamic financial system prohibits *riba* (fixed interest) on any financial transaction and instead argues for a fair and competitive profit-and-loss-based financial engagement (risk-sharing). Financial transactions and engagements based on fixed interest are strictly forbidden (haram) in the Islamic banking and financial system. Islam encourages investors to become partners in financial contracts based on the principle of profit and risk sharing instead of lending or borrowing on fixed interest or profits (Mohieldin, 2012). Another communal aspect of the Islamic financial and banking system is the deduction of *zakat* (a religious obligatory 2.5% tax levied on the net worth of wealthy Muslim people and the total assets of a company). Islam also prohibits investment in trade and business related to drugs, alcohol, gambling, and other unlawful religious, ethical, and social activities. Although, non-Muslim are exempt from certain activities (e.g., drinking alcohols and paying zakat), the regulations and practices in different Islamic countries and communities are different. The Sunni and Shia Islamic countries imply different Islamic banking and financial systems in their respective countries (Chu & Muneeza, 2019; Khan, 2015; Rethel, 2011). Therefore, China needs a cautious approach in executing financial engagements with the Islamic world and should adhere to the principles of the Islamic financial system in the BRI's projects.

The Islamic world strictly follows the Islamic principles, rules, regulations, and practices enshrined in the Islamic Sharia—the holy book Quran and hadith (practices and sayings of Prophet Muhammad) while China is a secular country where a majority of people are non-religious (atheist or agnostic) and do not adhere to religious code of conduct and practices (Noack, 2015).

Therefore, China should employ a well-thought-out strategy and pragmatic approach to securing commercial incentives and grabbing economic opportunities in the Islamic world while dealing with religiously and culturally sensitive projects under the BRI framework. Such projects can either: enhance China's image and reputation in the Islamic world or stimulate resentment and contribute to a negative image of China in the Islamic world. For example, China's construction of "the Haramain high-speed rail" between the two holy cities of Islam, Makkah and Madinah in Saudi Arabia has largely been welcomed and contributed positively to China's image in the Islamic world (Khan & Pratt, 2019). However, the construction of the "Grand Mosque of Algiers" by China State Construction Engineering Corporation prompted anger and resentment in Algeria and raised serious questions about China's involvement in the construction of a religious warship place—the grand mosque in Algiers: (a) "Can we entrust an atheist enterprise from an atheist state that represses its own Uyghur minority in Xinjiang [in China's far West region] to construct a mosque here in Algeria?" (b) "What glory and what blessings will we get from this project—constructing a mosque as an act of faith that will reinforce the oppression of our Uyghur brothers at the cost of a billion dollars?"(Hayoun, 2013, p. 96). These kinds of sentiments, if associated with BRI projects, will pollute the public mindset, and will generate nefarious impressions about China in the Islamic world.

Conclusion

Since the decline of the U.S. prominence in global politics and economy, the Islamic world has started to recalibrate its political, economic, and strategic calculus and gradually moved away from the (perceived) U.S. hegemonic influence. At the same time, China under the auspice of the BRI desires to reconfigure its geostrategic, geopolitical, and geoeconomic stature on a global scale. The rising tension in the South China Sea, and the U.S.' consistent efforts to curtail China's political, economic, and strategic influence in SouthEast Asia are nudging China westward mainly toward the Islamic world for new political, economic, and strategic alliances. The Islamic world can entrust China with worthy strategic, political, and economic capital as Islamic countries control the strategic points on the global maritime and land routes across the globe, hold strong political power blocs, and are full of vital natural resources (e.g., oil, gas, minerals) and possess plentiful opportunities for trade and investment in industries, microfinance, and infrastructure development. At the same time, the Islamic world witnessed unprecedented resentment against the U.S.'s unjust policies toward the Islamic world, its hegemonic behavior in political disputes (e.g., recognition of Jerusalem as Israeli capital against the collective will of the Islamic world), political meddling, and invasion of the sovereign Islamic countries (e.g., Afghanistan, Iraq, Syria, and Libya). Therefore, the Islamic world is tilting eastward and pondering China as an alternative power to the U.S. for political and economic support in resolving their political disputes, refurbishing their teetering economies, modernizing their dilapidated infrastructure, and increasing economic growth to elevate poverty in their countries.

The Islamic leadership has started viewing China as the best possible choice for the Islamic world against the U.S. repressive policies in the Middle East and North Africa (MENA) region and to gear up economic development. The Islamic world considers Sino-Islamic cooperation under the BRI framework as a win-win situation for both China and the Islamic world that can fulfill the common desire for mutual benefits and shared development while keeping the state sovereignty, political choice, strategic and political interest intact (Khan et al., 2023; Khan & Pratt, 2019; Li, 2015; Yi, 2015). The smooth execution of China's BRI will strengthen the new strategic, political, and economic alliance between China and the Islamic world. It will enhance China's global political and economic stature, facilitate its access to vibrant energy resources, and provide new destinations for exports and businesses in the Islamic world. To the Islamic world, participating fully in BRI will hinder and resist the perceived U.S. hegemony in the internal affairs of the Islamic world.

China's deep involvement in the Islamic world under the BRI can engender a backlash due to massive financial debt, trade deficit, and religious and cultural gaps (e.g., the Uyghur Muslim issue in Xinjiang). There are also considerable risks of unintended collision of strategic interests in different regions and unconscious export of terrorism in China. A majority of low-and-middle-income Islamic countries are overburdened with financial debt distress and Islamic countries like Kyrgyzstan, Tajikistan, Pakistan, Maldives, and Djibouti are at quite "high risk" of debt distress. There is an argument that these countries will struggle to pay back Chinese debts in time in the future (Khan & Pratt, 2019; Ming, 2018; The World Bank, 2022). China's deep affinity toward Africa and strategic partnership with the Middle Eastern countries under the BRI can also yield calamitous knock-on effects for China's national security and extremist ideologies from war-torn countries in Africa (e.g., Sudan, Somalia, Libya), Asia (e.g., Afghanistan and Pakistan) and the Middle East (e.g., Iraq, Syria, Yemen, and Egypt) can transfer into Chinese Muslim communities and refuel "East Turkmenistan" issues in Xinjiang (Luft, 2016).

Under the auspice of the BRI, China's engagement in the Afro-Eurasian region has intensified and its growing economic and political influence in Africa, and the Middle East, its tenacious support of Iran, and its strategic alliance with Pakistan have challenged the strategic interests of the U.S. in Africa and the Middles East and India's strategic interests in Asia. Therefore, China's growing BRI engagement in the Islamic world can engender new conflicts of interest among three rival countries—China, the U.S., and India over regional economic and political influence and their strategic interests in Asia, Africa, and the Middle East (Rahman et al., 2021; Sun & Zoubir, 2018; Suryanarayana, 2021).

References

Aglietta, M., & Bai, G. (2016). *China's 13th Five-Year Plan. In pursuit of a"Moderately Prosperous Society"*. <https://ideas.repec.org/p/cii/cepipb/2016-12.html>

Ahmad, W. M. W., Hanifa, M. H., & Hyo, K. C. (2019). Are non-Muslims willing to patronize Islamic financial services? *Journal of Islamic Marketing, 10*(3), 743–753. <https://doi.org/10.1108/JIMA-01-2017-0007>

Akhtar, N., Khan, H. U., Jan, M. A., Pratt, C. B., & Jianfu, M. (2021). Exploring the determinants of the China-Pakistan economic corridor and its impact on local communities. *SAGE Open, 11*(4). <https://doi.org/10.1177/21582440211057127>

Al-Jarhi, M. A. (2017). An economic theory of Islamic finance. *ISRA International Journal of Islamic Finance, 9*(2), 117–132. <https://doi.org/10.1108/IJIF-07-2017-0007>

Al-Jazeera. (2022, January 23). Uighurs in Turkey call for boycott of Beijing Winter Olympics. *Al-Jazeera English*. <https://www.aljazeera.com/news/2022/1/23/uighurs-in-turkey-call-for-boycott-of-beijing-winter-olympics>

Al-Khair, W. A. (2021, December 10). Chinese investment in Egypt comes at high price, analysts warn. *Al-Mashareq*. <https://almashareq.com/en_GB/articles/cnmi_am/features/2021/12/10/feature-01>

Al-Sudairi, M. T. (2013). China in the eyes of the Saudi Media. *Gulf Research Center, February*(February), 1–38. <https://www.ictsd.org/sites/default/files/downloads/2013/04/china-in-the-eyes-of-the-saudi-media.pdf>

Alves, A. C., & Lee, S. H. (2022). China's BRI developmental agency in its own words: A content analysis of key policy documents. *World Development, 150*, 105715. <https://doi.org/10.1016/j.worlddev.2021.105715>

Amighini, A. (2017). *China's Belt and Road: A game changer?* Edizioni Epoké.

Anderlini, J., Sender, H., & Bokhari, F. (2018, September). Pakistan rethinks its role in Xi's Belt and Road plan. *Financial Times*. <https://www.ft.com/content/d4a3e7f8-b282-11e8-99ca-68cf89602132>

ANI. (2018, June 28). Pakistan imposes 24% anti-dumping duty on Chinese steel. *WION*. <https://www.wionews.com/business-%26-economy/pakistan-imposes-24-anti-dumping-duty-on-chinese-steel-147673>

Aoyama, R. (2016). "One Belt, One Road": China's new global strategy. *Journal of Contemporary East Asia Studies, 5*(2), 3–22. <https://doi.org/10.1080/24761028.2016.11869094>

Armony, A. C. (2012). A view from Afar: How Colombia sees China. *The China Quarterly, 209*, 178–197. <https://doi.org/10.1017/S0305741011001536>

Barron, J. (2018, February 5). China surpassed the United States as the world's largest crude oil importer in 2017. *The U.S. Energy Information Administration*. <https://www.eia.gov/todayinenergy/detail.php?id=34812>

Baydoun, N., Aziz Anwar, S., & Sohail, M. S. (2021). The perceived determinants of Islamic finance for China's Belt and Road initiative. *Journal of Transnational Management, 26*(1), 18–38. <https://doi.org/10.1080/15475778.2021.1880880>

BBC News. (2009, July 10). Turkey attacks China "genocide." *BBC News*.

Bei, J. (2017). Economic globalization 3.0 and the concept of interconnection under the Belt and Road Initiative. *China Economist, 12*(2), 2–21. <https://www.proquest.com/openview/30d494a8ce126f40dab6b23cab730e39/1?pq-origsite=gscholar&cbl=1806366>

Benabdallah, L. (2018). China's relations with Africa and the Arab World: Shared trends, different priorities. *South African Institute of International Affairs, 67*(November), 1–14. <https://www.jstor.org/stable/resrep25989>

Blanchard, J.-M. F. (2020). Problematic prognostications about China's Maritime Silk Road Initiative (MSRI): Lessons from Africa and the Middle East. *Journal of Contemporary China, 29*(122), 159–174. <https://doi.org/10.1080/10670564.2019.1637565>

Bluhm, R., Dreher, A., Fuchs, A., Parks, B., Strange, A., & Tierney, M. J. (2020). Connective financing: Chinese infrastructure projects and the diffusion of economic activity in developing countries. *CESifo Working Paper No. 8344*, 1–54. <https://doi.org/10.2139/ssrn.3623679>

Bo, D., Ali, E. R. A. E., & Saiti, B. (2016). Sukuk issuance in China: Trends and positive expectations. *International Review of Management and Marketing, 6*(4), 1020–1025. <https://dergipark.org.tr/tr/download/article-file/367439>

Brewster, D. (2018). *India and China at sea: Competition for naval dominance in the Indian Ocean.* Oxford University Press.

Carmody, P. (2020). Dependence not debt-trap diplomacy. *Area Development and Policy, 5*(1), 23–31. <https://doi.org/10.1080/23792949.2019.1702471>

CEIC. (2020a). *China crude oil: Imports.* <https://www.ceicdata.com/en/indicator/china/crude-oil-imports>

CEIC. (2020b). *China oil consumption (1965–2020).* <https://www.ceicdata.com/en/indicator/china/oil-consumption>

Chabert, G., Cerisola, M., & Hakura, D. (2022, April 7). Restructuring debt of poorer nations requires more efficient coordination. *IMF.* <https://blogs.imf.org/2022/04/07/restructuring-debt-of-poorer-nations-requires-more-efficient-coordination/>

Chaudary, K. M. (2022, May 17). Pakistan says it foiled suspected attack against Chinese citizens. *Al-Jazeera.* <https://www.aljazeera.com/news/2022/5/17/pakistan-says-it-foiled-suspected-attack-against-chinese-citizens>

Chaziza, M. (2016). Comprehensive strategic partnership: A new stage in China-Egypt Relations. *Middle East Review of International Affairs, 20*(3), 41–51. <https://www.proquest.com/openview/1457e4966613369ec6fe3a6476acbaca/1?pq-origsite=gscholar&cbl=54955>

Chaziza, M. (2021). China's economic relations with Mauritania in the age of the belt and road initiative. *Journal for Interdisciplinary Middle Eastern Studies, 7*(1), 65–86. <https://doi.org/10.26351/JIMES/7-1/3>

Chen, J. (2011). *The emergence of China in Middle East* (Issue 271, pp. 1–8). National Defense University, Washington, DC. <https://doi.org/10.1111/j.1539-6975.2009.01318.x>

Chu, J., & Muneeza, A. (2019). Belt and Road Initiative and Islamic financing: The case in public private partnership infrastructure financing. *International Journal of Management and Applied Research, 6*(1), 24–40. <https://doi.org/10.18646/2056.61.19-002>

Clarke, M. (2015). China and The Uyghurs: The "Palestinization" of Xinjiang? *Middle East Policy, 22*(3), 127–146. <https://doi.org/10.1111/mepo.12148>

COAR. (2022, July 11). China in Syria: Aid and trade now, influence and industry later? *COAR.* <https://coar-global.org/2022/07/11/china-in-syria-aid-and-trade-now-influence-and-industry-later/>

Cooper, W. W., & Yue, P. (2015). Global oil flow and strategic geography of the Muslim World Article information. In W. W. Cooper & P. Yue (Eds.), *Challenges of the Muslim World* (1st ed., pp. 60–101). Emerald Group Publishing Limited.

Corkin, L. J. (2014). China's rising soft power: The role of rhetoric in constructing China-Africa relations. *Revista Brasileira de Politica Internacional, 57,* 49–72. <https://doi.org/10.1590/0034-7329201400204>

Dabashi, H. (2018, December 22). Muslim cleansing: A global pandemic? *Al-Arabiya English.* <https://www.aljazeera.com/opinions/2018/12/22/muslim-cleansing-a-global-pandemic>

de L.T. Oliveira, G., Murton, G., Rippa, A., Harlan, T., & Yang, Y. (2020). China's Belt and Road Initiative: Views from the ground. *Political Geography, 82*(January), 102225. < https://doi.org/10.1016/j.polgeo.2020.102225>

DinarStandard. (2022). *State of the global Islamic economy report 2022.* <https://salaamgateway.com/specialcoverage/SGIE22>

Djafri, F., Laldin, M. A., & Laallam, A. (2021). The global perspective of Islamic Finance and the potential for China to tap into the Islamic Finance Market. *Journal of Islamic Business and Management (JIBM), 11*(01), 14–28. <https://doi.org/10.26501/jibm/2021.1101-002>

Dunford, M. (2021). China's Belt and Road Initiative and its implications for global development. *Acta Via Serica, 6*(1), 91–118. <https://doi.org/10.22679/avs.2021.6.1.004>

Dunford, M., & Liu, W. (2019). Chinese perspectives on the Belt and Road Initiative. *Cambridge Journal of Regions, Economy and Society, 12*(1), 145–167. <https://doi.org/10.1093/cjres/rsy032>

Elleithy, A. (2021, October 23). Despite reaching all-time high, Egypt's external debt is within safe levels. *Al-Monitor.* <https://www.al-monitor.com/originals/2021/10/despite-reaching-all-time-high-egypts-external-debt-within-safe-levels>

Elmagherbi, F. I. (2010). A case study of China's relations with the Arab world. *2010 2nd IEEE International Conference on Information and Financial Engineering*, 646–650. <https://doi.org/10.1109/ICIFE.2010.5609442>

Ezell, C. (2021). Human Rights abuses in Xinjiang: Perspectives and responses from the Islamic World and the Middle East. In *Center for Open Science.* SocArXiv. <https://doi.org/10.31219/osf.io/mk7q6>

Fasslabend, W. (2015). The Silk Road: A political marketing concept for world dominance. *European View, 14*(2), 293–302. <https://doi.org/10.1007/s12290-015-0381-3>

Feng, D. H., & Liang, H. (2018). Understanding the issues surrounding the Belt and Road Initiative (BRI). *China and the World: Ancient and Modern Silk Road, 1*(03). <https://doi.org/10.1142/S2591729318500219>

Ferdinand, P. (2016). Westward ho—The China dream and "one belt, one road": Chinese foreign policy under Xi Jinping. *International Affairs, 92*(4), 941–957. <https://doi.org/10.1111/1468-2346.12660>

Foley, S. (2017). When oil is not enough: Sino-Saudi relations and vision 2030. *Asian Journal of Middle Eastern and Islamic Studies, 11*(1), 107–120. <https://doi.org/10.1080/25765949.2017.12023296>

Fulton, J. (2020). China-Saudi Arabia relations through the "1+ 2+ 3" Cooperation pattern. *Asian Journal of Middle Eastern and Islamic Studies, 14*(4), 516–527. <https://doi.org/10.1080/25765949.2020.1841991>

Fulton, J. (2016). An analysis of two corridors in China's One Belt, One Road Initiative: China-Pakistan and China Central-West Asia. *Proceedings of International Conference on Inter-Regional Connectivity: South Asia and Central Asia*, 43–49. <https://www.academia.edu/34492093/An_Analysis_of_Two_Corridors_In_Chinas_One_Belt_One_Road_Initiative_China_Pakistan_and_China_Central_West_Asia>

Galal, M. N. (2014). The China-Arab States Cooperation Forum: Achievements, challenges and prospects. *Journal of Middle Eastern and Islamic Studies (in Asia), 8*(2), 1–21. <https://doi.org/10.1080/19370679.2014.12023244>

Garlick, J. (2018). Deconstructing the China-Pakistan economic corridor: Pipe dreams versus geopolitical realities. *Journal of Contemporary China, 27*(112), 519–533. <https://doi.org/10.1080/10670564.2018.1433483>

Ghiasy, R., & Krishnamurthy, R. (2021, April 13). China's Digital Silk Road and the global digital order. *The Di.* <https://thediplomat.com/2021/04/chinas-digital-silk-road-and-the->global-digital-order/

Haghirian, M., & Zaccara, L. (Eds.). (2022). *China's economic and political presence in the Middle East and South Asia.* Taylor & Francis.

Hali, S. M., Shukui, D. T., & Iqbal, S. (2014). One Belt and One Road: Impact on China-Pakistan economic corridor. *Strategic Studies, 34*(4), 147–164. <https://www.jstor.org/stable/48527479>

Halsall, J. P., Cook, I. G., & Oberoi, R. (2022). Connecting the World: China's Belt and Road Initiative. In P. G. Figueiredo, F. J. Leandro, & Y. Li (Eds.), *Handbook of research on special economic zones as regional development enablers* (Vol. 1, pp. 1–20). IG. <https://doi.org/10.4018/978-1-7998-7619-9.ch001>

Hayden, C. (2012). *The rhetoric of soft power: Public diplomacy in global contexts.* Lexington Books.

Hayoun, M. (2013). Strange Bedfellows: China's Middle Eastern Inroads. *World Affairs, 175*(5), 89–96. <http://www.jstor.org/stable/43554744>

Held, A. (2017, May 19). Chinese Su-30 fighter jets intercept US WC-135 Constant Phoenix plane over East China Sea. *National Public Radio.* <https://www.npr.org/sections/thetwo-way/2017/05/19/529107132/chinese-fighter-jets->buzz-u-s-air-force-plane-over-east-china-sea

Herlijanto, J. (2017). *Public perceptions of China in Indonesia: The Indonesia national survey.* ISEAS-Yusof Ishak Institute.

Holslag, J. (2017). How China's New Silk Road threatens European Trade. *International Spectator, 52*(1), 46–60. <https://doi.org/10.1080/03932729.2017.1261517>

Hoskins, P. (2022, May 20). *Sri Lanka defaults on debt for first time in its history.* <https://www.bbc.com/news/business-61505842>

Hu, B. (2019). Belt and Road Initiative: Five years on implementation and reflection. *Global Journal of Emerging Market Economies, 11*(1–2), 1–10. <https://doi.org/10.1177/0974910119871377>

Huang, Y. (2016). Understanding China's Belt & Road Initiative: Motivation, framework and assessment. *China Economic Review, 40*(September), 314–321. <https://doi.org/10.1016/j.chieco.2016.07.007>

Hurley, J., Morris, S., & Portelance, G. (2019). Examining the debt implications of the Belt and Road Initiative from a policy perspective. *Journal of Infrastructure, Policy and Development, 3*(1), 139–175. <https://doi.org/10.24294/jipd.v3i1.1123>

Hussain, E. (2018). CPEC: Governance and security challenges—Implications for the Belt and Road Initiative. *Chinese Political Science Review, 0123456789.* <https://doi.org/10.1007/s41111-018-0109-z>

Hussain, E. (2020). CPEC and the Belt and Road Initiative: Economic implications for the Greater Middle East. *Asian Journal of Middle Eastern and Islamic Studies, 14*(1), 35–50.

Jia, W. (2017). Now, globalization with Chinese characteristics. *YaleGlobal Online*, June. <http://yaleglobal.yale.edu/content/now-globalization-chinese-characteristics>

Jin, X., Li, D. D., & Wu, S. (2016). How will China shape the world economy? *China Economic Review, 40*, 272–280. <https://doi.org/10.1016/j.chieco.2016.07.006>

Jinbo, W. (2019). The China–Central Asia–West Asia economic corridor. In C. Fang & P. Nolan (Eds.), *Routledge handbook of the Belt and Road.* Routledge. <https://www.routledgehandbooks.com/citation?doi=10.4324/9780429203039-38>

Jones, D. A., & Liu, H. (2017). Management of Chinese foreign direct investment: "One Belt, One Road" Across Eurasia to Africa and Europe amidst maritime tensions in the South China Sea Region. *International Relations and Diplomacy, 5*(8), 486–500. <https://doi.org/10.17265/2328-2134/2017.08.003>

Joshi, M., Abidi, S., & Rai, A. (2017). The eco-politics of CPEC and India. *Available at SSRN 2982942*, 1–5. <https://papers.ssrn.com/sol3/papers.cfm?abstract_id=2982942>

Kamel, M. S. (2018). Cambridge review of International Affairs China's Belt and Road Initiative : Implications for the Middle East. *Cambridge Review of International Affairs, 7571*, 1–19. <https://doi.org/10.1080/09557571.2018.1480592>

Kanwal, S., Pitafi, A. H., Malik, M. Y., Khan, N. A., & Rashid, R. M. (2020). Local Pakistani citizens' benefits and attitudes toward China–Pakistan economic corridor projects. *Sage Open, 10*(3), 2158244020942759.

Kaya, T. Ö. (2017). Sino-Indian strategic rivalry in the Indian Ocean Region. *Insan ve Toplum, 7*(2), 155. <https://doi.org/10.12658/human.society.7.14.M0223>

Kelemen, B., & Turcsányi, R. Q. (2020). It's the politics, stupid: China's relations with Muslim countries on the background of Xinjiang crackdown. *Asian Ethnicity, 21*(2), 223–243. <https://doi.org/10.1080/14631369.2019.1677145>

Khabar, I. (2022, May 27). Pakistan's economic condition continues to deteriorate due to "deep debt." *The Economic Times.* <https://economictimes.indiatimes.com/news/international/world-news/pakistans-economic-condition-continues-to-deteriorate-due-to-deep-debt/articleshow/91841819.cms>

Khan, F. (2015). *Islamic Banking in Pakistan: Shariah-compliant Finance and the quest to make Pakistan more Islamic.* Routledge.

Khan, M. K., & Pratt, C. B. (2019). China's Belt and Road Initiative: Its landscape (and trajectory) in the Islamic World. In A. Visvizi, M. Lytras, X. Zhang, & J. Zhao (Eds.), *Foreign business in China and opportunities for technological innovation and sustainable economics* (pp. 117–142). IGI Global. <https://doi.org/10.4018/978-1-5225-8980-8.ch006>

Khan, M. K., Pratt, C. B., & Akhtar, N. (2023). China's public diplomacy for image making in Islamic North Africa: Frames of the Belt and Road Initiative in Daily News Egypt. In: A. A. Anani-Bossman, T. E. Mudzanani, C. B. Pratt, I. A. Blankson (Eds.), *Public relations management in Africa Volume 1.* Cham: Palgrave Macmillan. <https://doi.org/10.1007/978-3-031-26704-8_5>

Khan, M. K., Sallam, M. H., Pratt, C. B., & Farid, T. (2022). Stereotyping the Chinese in Arab Nations: The effects of media use, perceived realism and Chinese-Arab Relations. *The Social Science Journal.* <https://doi.org/10.1080/03623319.2021.2025197>

Khan, M. K., Sandano, I. A., Pratt, C. B., & Farid, T. (2018). China's Belt and Road Initiative: A global model for an evolving approach to Sustainable Regional Development. *Sustainability, 10*(11), 4234. <https://doi.org/10.3390/su10114234>

Khan, Z., Changgang, G., & Afzaal, M. (2020). China-Pakistan economic corridor at the cross intersection of China, Central Asia and South Asia: Opportunities for regional economic growth. *The Chinese Economy, 53*(2), 200–215. <https://doi.org/10.1080/10971475.2019.1688005>

Kiani, K. (2019, January 14). Govt puts major CPEC power project on hold. *Dawn*. <https://www.dawn.com/news/1457449>

Kliman, D., & Grace, A. (2018, June 18). China smells opportunity in the Middle East's Crisis. *Foreign Policy*. <https://foreignpolicy.com/2018/06/14/china-smells-opportunity-in-the-middle-easts-crisis/>

Kuah, K. E., Rezaei, S., & Zhang, Z. (2021). Negotiating cultural and socio-economic flows in the era of Belt and Road Initiatives: An introductory overview. *Asian Journal of Social Science, 49*(4), 183–187. <https://doi.org/10.1016/j.ajss.2021.09.010>

Kurlantzick, J. (2007). *Charm offensive: How China's soft power is transforming the world.* Yale University Press.

Kurlantzick, J. (2022a). *China's collapsing global image: How Beijing's unpopularity is undermining its strategic, economic, and diplomatic goals* (Issue July, pp. 1–38). Council on Foreign Relations. <https://www.cfr.org/report/chinas-collapsing-global-image>

Kurlantzick, J. (2022b, July 22). China's poor global image is undermining its strategic goals. *The Diplomat*. <https://thediplomat.com/2022/07/chinas-poor-global-image-is-undermining-its-strategic-goals/>

Lai, T. L., Tang, J., & Yin, H. (2018). Spatial economics in the era of One Belt One Road and counter-globalization. *Modern Economy, 09*(01), 61–66. <https://doi.org/10.4236/me.2018.91004>

Laldin, M. A., & Djafri, F. (2019). Islamic finance in the digital world: Opportunities and challenges (Kewangan Islam dalam Dunia Digital: Peluang dan Cabaran). *Journal of Islam in Asia (E-ISSN 2289-8077), 16*(3), 283–299. <https://doi.org/10.31436/jia.v16i3.853>

Lancaster, K., Rubin, M., & Rapp-Hooper, M. (2020, April 10). Mapping China's Health Silk Road. *Council on Foreign Relations*. <https://www.cfr.org/blog/mapping-chinas-health-silk-road>

Lee, J. (2021, June 24). No Title. *Mercator Institute for China Studies*. <https://merics.org/en/report/connection-everything-china-and-internet-things>

Lehr, D. (2018, July 21). How China is winning over the Middle East. *The Diplomat*. <https://thediplomat.com/2018/07/how-china-is-winning-over-the-middle-east/>

Li, F. (2018). The role of Islam in the development of the "Belt and Road" Initiative. *Asian Journal of Middle Eastern and Islamic Studies, 12*(1), 35–45. <https://doi.org/10.1080/25765949.2018.1439617>

Li, M. (2008). *Soft power in Chinese discourse : Popularity and prospect.* <http://hdl.handle.net/10220/4552>

Li, M. (2015). China's "One Belt, One Road" Initiative : New round of opening up? In *RSIS Commentaries* (Issue 050, pp. 1–2). Nanyang Technological University. <https://www.rsis.edu.sg/wp-content/uploads/2015/04/CMS_Bulletin0015.pdf>

Liu, W., & Dunford, M. (2016). Inclusive globalization: unpacking China's Belt and Road Initiative. *Area Development and Policy, 1*(3), 323–340. <https://doi.org/10.1080/23792949.2016.1232598>

Luft, G. (2016, January 26). China's new grand strategy for the Middle East. *Foreign Policy*. <https://foreignpolicy.com/2016/01/26/chinas-new-middle-east-grand-strategy-iran-saudi-arabia-oil-xi-jinping/>

Macauley, R. (2015, November 23). China wants to build a high-speed rail link to a newly open Iran. *Quartz*. <https://qz.com/557009/chinas-next-big-idea-is-a-high-speed-railway-to-iran/>

Majoka, M. I., Sahibzada, H. E., & Khan, M. S. (2012). Resources of the Muslim World: A reflection on the Muslim World's resources, their development and utilization. *Journal of Islamic Thought and Civilization*, *02*(01), 73–87. <https://doi.org/10.32350/jitc.21.05>

Malik, M. (2002). Dragon China's on terrorism: Assessing gains tactical and strategic losses after 11 September. *Contemporary Southeast Asia*, *24*(2), 252–293. <https://www.jstor.org/stable/25798597>

Maruta, A. A., Banerjee, R., & Cavoli, T. (2020). Foreign aid, institutional quality and economic growth: Evidence from the developing world. *Economic Modelling*, *89*(July), 444–463. <https://doi.org/10.1016/j.econmod.2019.11.008>

Mendez, A., & Alden, C. (2021). China in Panama: From peripheral diplomacy to grand strategy. *Geopolitics*, *26*(3), 838–860. <https://doi.org/10.1080/14650045.2019.1657413>

Ming, C. (2018, March 5). China's mammoth Belt and Road Initiative could increase debt risk for 8 countries. *CNBC*. <https://www.cnbc.com/2018/03/05/chinas-belt-and-road-initiative-raises-debt-risks-in-8-nations.html>

Mogato, M., & Petty, M. (2017, April 27). Push for South China Sea code stirs ASEAN suspicions about Beijing's endgame. *Reuters*. <https://www.reuters.com/article/us-southchinasea-asean-analysis-idUSKBN17T0A5>

Mohieldin, M. (2012). *Realizing the potential of Islamic finance* (Vol. 77, Issue March). Washington, DC: World Bank.

Moniruzzaman, M. (2021, January 14). A confluence of interests: China and Muslim countries have plenty of reasons to develop an engaging partnership. *Daily China*, 24. <http://irep.iium.edu.my/id/eprint/88535>

Moonakal, N. A. (2022, July 9). The impact and implications of China's growing influence in the Middle East. *The Diplomat*. <https://thediplomat.com/2022/07/the-impact-and-implications-of-chinas-growing-influence-in-the-middle-east/>

Nagao, H. (2016). *China's soft power investment in African nations* [University of Kansas]. <https://kuscholarworks.ku.edu/handle/1808/21880>

Naughton, B. (2016). Restructuring and reform: China 2016. In I. Day & J. Simo (Eds.), *Structural change in China: Implications for Australia World* (pp. 55–78). Reserve Bank of Australia. <https://www.rba.gov.au/publications/confs/2016/pdf/rba-conference-volume-2016-naughton.pdf>

Noack, R. (2015). Map: These are the world's least religious countries. April 14. *The Washington Post*. <https://www.washingtonpost.com/news/worldviews/wp/2015/04/14/map-these-are-the-worlds-least-religious-countries/>

Novikov, V., Britikova, E., Yarushkina, E., & Kovalenko, L. (2020). Islamic banking in the global financial system: Current situation and global environment. *5th International Conference on Economics, Management, Law and Education (EMLE 2019)*, 138–143. <https://doi.org/10.2991/aebmr.k.191225.025>

Obama, B. (2021). *Barack Obama Selected Speeches*. Canterbury Classics. San Diego. CA.

O'Connor, T., & Donovan, S. (2022, February 16). With world's eyes on Beijing, here's how China Ranks relations across Globe. *Newsweek*. <https://www.newsweek.com/worlds-eyes-beijing-heres-how-china-ranks-relations-across-globe-1679183>

Osiewicz, P. (2018). The Belt and Road Initiative (BRI): Implications for Iran-China relations. *Przeglad Strategiczny*, *11*(September), 221–232. <https://doi.org/10.14746/ps.2018.1.16>

Padilla, T. (2017, June 9). Analysis: China to shape international trade via Belt and Road. *The Journal of Commerce*. <https://www.joc.com/international-trade-news/infrastructure-news/china-infrastructure-news/analysis-china-shape-international-trade-belt-and-road_20170609.html>

Page, J., Dou, E., & Shah, S. (2018, September 27). China's Muslim Detention Camps Spark Protests in Islamic World. *The Wall Street Journal*. <https://www.wsj.com/articles/chinas-detentions-of-muslims-trigger-protests-in-islamic-world-1538040605>

Panneerselvam, P. (2017). Maritime component of China–Pakistan Economic corridor (CPEC): India–China competition in the Arabian Sea. *Maritime Affairs: Journal of the National Maritime Foundation of India*, *13*(2), 37–49. <https://doi.org/10.1080/09733159.2017.1412577>

Park, H. (2012). *Mapping the Chinese and Islamic Worlds: Cross-Cultural exchange in Pre-modern Asia* (Vol. 1). Cambridge University Press.

Pencea, S. (2017). A look into the complexities of the One Belt, One Road Strategy. *Global Economic Observer*, *5*(1), 142–158. <https://search.proquest.com/docview/1906364588?accountid=12834>

Pew Research Center. (2017). *China image: Do you have a favorable or unfavorable view of China?* <http://www.pewglobal.org/database/indicator/24/survey/17/response/Unfavorable/>

Rafiq, A. (2017, October 24). China's $62 Billion Bet on Pakistan. *Foreign Affairs*. <https://www.foreignaffairs.com/articles/china/2017-10-24/chinas-62-billion-bet-pakistan>

Rahman, Z. U., Khan, A., Lifang, W., & Hussain, I. (2021). The geopolitics of the CPEC and Indian Ocean: Security implication for India. *Australian Journal of Maritime and Ocean Affairs*, *13*(2), 122–145. <https://doi.org/10.1080/18366503.2021.1875807>

Ramo, J. C. (2004). *The Beijing Consensus*. Foreign Policy Centre London.

Ramo, J. C. (2007). *Brand China*. Foreign Policy Centre.

Rethel, L. (2011). Whose legitimacy? Islamic finance and the global financial order. *Review of International Political Economy*, *18*(1), 75–98. <https://doi.org/10.1080/09692290902983999>

Reuters. (2018, January 26). China unveils vision for "Polar Silk Road" across Arctic. *Reuters*. <https://www.reuters.com/article/us-china-arctic-idUSKBN1FF0J8>

Reuters. (2022, June 20). China's imports of Russian crude oil hit record high. *CNN*. <https://edition.cnn.com/2022/06/20/energy/china-russia-oil-imports-record>

Risberg, P. (2019). The Give-and-Take of BRI in Africa. *New Perspectives in Foreign Policy*, *17*, 43–47. < https://csis-website-prod.s3.amazonaws.com/s3fs-public/NewPerspectives_APRIL2019_Risberg.pdf>

Rolland, N. (2017). China's "Belt and Road Initiative": Underwhelming or game-changer? *The Washington Quarterly, 40*(1), 127–142. <https://doi.org/10.1080/0163660X.2017.1302743>

Roy, N. (2019). China-Pakistan economic corridor–Is it the road to the future? *Asian Affairs, 50*(2), 268–282. <https://doi.org/10.1080/03068374.2019.1614767>

Sági, J., & Engelberth, I. (2018). The Belt and Road Initiative—A way forward to China's expansion. *Contemporary Chinese Political Economy and Strategic Relations, 4*(1), 9–37. <https://www.proquest.com/openview/b6f1042cf0208648afb040c2a60ac0b6/1?pq-origsite=gscholar&cbl=2042768>

Sarker, M. N. I., Khatun, M. N., & Alam, G. M. M. (2019). Islamic banking and finance: Potential approach for economic sustainability in China. *Journal of Islamic Marketing, 11*(6), 1725–1741. <https://doi.org/10.1108/JIMA-04-2019-0076>

Schulhof, V., van Vuuren, D., & Kirchherr, J. (2022). The Belt and Road Initiative (BRI): What will it look like in the future? *Technological Forecasting and Social Change, 175*(October), 121306. <https://doi.org/10.1016/j.techfore.2021.121306>

Scobell, A., Lin, B., Shatz, H. J., Hanauer, L., Johnson, M., Chase, M. S., Cevallos, A. S., Rasmussen, I. W., Chan, A., & Strong, A. (2018). *At the dawn of belt and road: China in the developing world.* Rand Corporation. <https://www.rand.org/pubs/research_reports/RR2273.html>

Scobell, A., & Nader, A. (2016). China in the Middle East: The Wary Dragon. In *China in the Middle East: The Wary Dragon.* Rand Corporation. <https://doi.org/10.7249/rr1229>

Selim, G. M., & Moaaz, R. S. (2021). Sino-Egyptian relations post-2013: The dynamics and challenges of an emerging strategic partnership. *Arab Studies Quarterly, 43*(4), 349–370. <https://doi.org/10.13169/arabstudquar.43.4.0349>

Selmier-II, W. T. (2018). The Belt and Road Initiative and the influence of Islamic economies. *Economic and Political Studies, 6*(3), 257–277. <https://doi.org/10.1080/20954816.2018.1498989>

Shambaugh, D. (2013). *China goes global: The partial power.* Oxford University Press.

Shambaugh, D. (2015). China's soft-power push: The search for respect. *Foreign Affairs, 94*(4), 99–107. <https://www.jstor.org/stable/24483821>

Shay, S. (2018). Saudi Arabia and the "nuclearization" of the Middle East. *Institute for Policy and Strategy, March.* <https://www.runi.ac.il/media/bnbddxrh/shaul_shay18_03_18.pdf>

Sheikhneshin, A. G., Vakili, B., & Amoei, H. (2020). Chinese soft power : Creating a charm image in the Islamic World. *International Journal of Political Science, 10*(2), 25–39. <https://journals.iau.ir/article_678019_d08bbb11e0d52989e877010d6e7f77ea.pdf>

Sherani, S. (2013, August 12). Economies of the ummah. *Dawn.* <https://www.dawn.com/news/1035026>

Shukry, A., & Park, K. (2018, May 28). Malaysia scraps Multibillion-Dollar High-Speed Rail Project to Singapore. *Bloomberg.* <https://www.bloomberg.com/news/articles/2018-05-28/mahathir-to-scrap-malaysia-singapore-high-speed-rail-project>

Singh, M. K. (2021a). China and the United States in the Middle East: Between dependency and rivalry. In A. Farhadi & A. J. Masys (Eds.), *The great power competition Volume 1* (pp. 369–395). Springer.

Singh, R. (2021b). Critical discourse analysis of Iran-China relations through Football Headlines. *English Linguistics Research, 10*(2), 1. <https://doi.org/10.5430/elr.v10n2p1>

Sun, D. (2021). China and the Islamic World: How the New Silk Road is transforming global politics By Robert R. Bianchi. *Journal of Islamic Studies, 32*(3), 441–444. <https://doi.org/10.1093/jis/etab026>

Sun, D., & Xu, R. (2022). China and Egypt's comprehensive strategic partnership in the Xi-sisi era: A "role theory" prism. *Mediterranean Politics, 00*(00), 1–21. <https://doi.org/10.1080/13629395.2022.2035139>

Sun, D., & Zoubir, Y. (2018). China's participation in conflict resolution in the Middle East and North Africa: A case of quasi-mediation diplomacy? *Journal of Contemporary China, 27*(110), 224–243. <https://doi.org/10.1080/10670564.2018.1389019>

Suryanarayana, P. S. (2021). *The elusive tipping point: China–India ties for a new order.* World Scientific.

Swaine, M. D. (2014). Chinese views and commentary on periphery diplomacy. *China Leadership Monitor, 44*(1). <https://www.hoover.org/sites/default/files/research/docs/clm44ms.pdf>

Swaine, M. D. (2015). Chinese views and commentary on the "One Belt, One Road" Initiative. *China Leadership Monitor, 47,* 1–24. <http://www.hoover.org/sites/default/files/research/docs/clm47ms.pdf>

Tekdal, V. (2018). China's Belt and Road Initiative: At the crossroads of challenges and ambitions. *Pacific Review, 31*(3), 373–390. <https://doi.org/10.1080/09512748.2017.1391864>

The Daily Star. (2009, October 1). What will China's rising influence mean for the Middle East region? *The Daily Star.* <http://www1.dailystar.com.lb/Opinion/Editorial/2009/Oct-01/119578-what-will-chinas-rising-influence-mean-for-the-middle-east-region.ashx>

The World Bank. (2022). *International Debt Statistics 2022.* https://openknowledge.worldbank.org/handle/10986/36289

The World Bank (2022, April 1). Lifting 800 Million People Out of Poverty – New Report Looks at Lessons from China's Experience. <https://www.worldbank.org/en/news/press-release/2022/04/01/lifting-800-million-people-out-of-poverty-new-report-looks-at-lessons-from-china-s-experience>

Townsend, S. (2018, October 30). Islamic banking key to financing China's Belt and Road. *The National Business.* <https://www.thenationalnews.com/business/banking/islamic-banking-key-to-financing-china-s-belt-and-road-1.786098>

Umbach, F. (2022, April 8). How China's Belt and Road Initiative is faring. *Geopolitical Intelligence Services.* <https://www.gisreportsonline.com/r/belt-road-initiative/>

US Navy. (2021, February 16). 7th Fleet destroyer conducts freedom of navigation operation in South China Sea. *U.S. Navy Office of Information.* <https://www.navy.mil/Press-Office/News-Stories/Article/2505124/7th-fleet-destroyer-conducts-freedom-of-navigation-operation-in-south-china-sea/>

Wang, K. (2022, January 6). China: Is it burdening poor countries with unsustainable debt? *BBC News.* <https://www.bbc.com/news/59585507>

Williams, J., Robinson, C., & Bouzarovski, S. (2020). China's Belt and Road Initiative and the emerging geographies of global urbanisation. *The Geographical Journal, 186*(1), 128–140. <https://doi.org/10.1111/geoj.12332>

World Population Review. (2022). *Muslim majority countries 2022.* https://worldpopulationreview.com/country-rankings/muslim-majority-countries

Wu, Z., Hou, G., & Xin, B. (2020). Has the Belt and Road Initiative brought new opportunities to countries along the routes to participate in global value chains? *SAGE Open*, *10*(1). <https://doi.org/10.1177/2158244020902088>

Xi, J. (2015). Asia's new future: Towards a community of common destiny. *Boao Forum for Asia Annual Conference 2015*. <http://english.boaoforum.org/u/cms/www2/201503/25112018qw3q.pdf>

Xi, J. (2017a, January 18). Work together to build a community of shared future for mankind. *Xinhua*. <http://news.xinhuanet.com/english/2017-01/19/c_135994707.htm>

Xi, J. (2017b, May 14). President Xi's speech at opening of Belt and Road forum. *Xinhua*. <http://news.xinhuanet.com/english/2017-05/14/c_136282982.htm>

Xi, J. (2017c, October 18). Secure a decisive victory in building a moderately prosperous society in all respects and strive for the great success of socialism with Chinese Characteristics for a new era. *Xinhua*, 1–66. <http://www.xinhuanet.com/english/download/Xi_Jinping's_report_at_19th_CPC_National_Congress.pdf>

Xie, T., & Page, B. I. (2013). What affects China's national image? A cross-national study of public opinion. *Journal of Contemporary China*, *22*(83), 850–867. <https://doi.org/10.1080/10670564.2013.782130>

Xinhua. (2015, March 30). Vision and actions on jointly building Silk Road Economic Belt and 21st-Century Maritime Silk Road. *Xinhua*. <https://eng.yidaiyilu.gov.cn/qwyw/qwfb/1084.htm>

Yang, D., Jiang, L., & Ng, A. K. Y. (2018). One Belt one Road, but several routes: A case study of new emerging trade corridors connecting the Far East to Europe. *Transportation Research Part A: Policy and Practice*, *117*(July 2017), 190–204. <https://doi.org/10.1016/j.tra.2018.08.001>

Yang, F. (2014). Invigorating Sino-Arab relations by One Belt and One Road Strategy. *Journal of Middle Eastern and Islamic Studies (in Asia)*, 1–26.

Yi, H. (2015, March 20). China's One Belt/One Road' policy is open to all nations. *Executive Intelligence Review*. <http://schillerinstitute.org/economy/phys_econ/2015/27-29_EIR12-one_belt_one_road.html>

Yu, H. (2017). Motivation behind China's "One Belt, One Road" Initiatives and establishment of the Asian infrastructure investment bank. *Journal of Contemporary China*, *26*(105), 353–368. <https://doi.org/10.1080/10670564.2016.1245894>

Yuniarto, P. R. (2019). Intercultural gaps between Indonesia and China on the Belt and Road Initiative: Causes and remedies. *China Quarterly of International Strategic Studies*, *5*(3), 395–416. <https://doi.org/10.1142/S2377740019500234>

Zambelis, C., & Gentry, B. (2008). China through Arab eyes: American influence in the Middle East. *Parameters*, *38*(1), 60–73. <https://doi.org/10.55540/0031-1723.2412>

Zhang, R., Shi, G., Wang, Y., Zhao, S., Ahmad, S., Zhang, X., & Deng, Q. (2018). Social impact assessment of investment activities in the China–Pakistan economic corridor. *Impact Assessment and Project Appraisal*, *36*(4), 331–347. <https://doi.org/10.1080/14615517.2018.1465227>

Zheng, B. (2005). China's "peaceful rise" to great-power status. *Foreign Affairs*, 18–24. <https://www.foreignaffairs.com/articles/asia/2005-09-01/chinas-peaceful-rise-great-power-status>

Zheng, B. (2017). China's "One Belt, One Road" plan marks the next phase of globalization. *New Perspectives Quarterly, 34*(3), 27–30. <https://doi.org/10.1111/npqu.12090>

Zhu, W. (2010). On the strategic relationship between China and Islamic countries in the Middle East. *Journal of Middle Eastern and Islamic Studies (in Asia), 4*(3), 1–27. <https://doi.org/10.1080/19370679.2010.12023159>

IV Framing National Image: China's Global Image Making in Media

National/Country image

National image and country image are interchangeable terms that are widely used in communication disciplines (Han & Wang, 2015; Luther, 2002). Boulding (1959) was the first who offer a classical definition of national image (Castano et al., 2016). According to Boulding (1959), a national image is a "cognitive, affective, and evaluative structure of a nation" that is constructed in an international environment. Kunczik ([1997] 2016, p. 46) argues that national image is a "cognitive representation that a person holds of a given country, what a person believes to be true about a nation and its people". It is integrated cognitive schemas that simplify the individual's view of the global environment and help them to evaluate the country's behavior in international relations (Anholt, 2011; Castano et al., 2016; White, 2012).

A country's image is formed through the individual's subjective interpretation of events, subjective judgments, and associations and it thereby contains cognitive, affective, and behavioral dimensions (Boulding, 1959; Buhmann, 2016; Herz & Arnegger, 2017; Lala et al., 2009; Roth & Diamantopoulos, 2009). The cognitive dimension of a country's image is based on the perceived competence and competitiveness of a country and can be measured at the following three levels: (a) functional country image; (b) normative country image; and (c) aesthetic country image (Buhmann, 2016). A country's functional image dimension is based on the individual's beliefs about the country's competencies and its competitiveness with another country concerning its political organization and national economy. It specifically refers to the individual's judgment about a country's state of the economy, and its commerce; the competitiveness of a country's education system, its labor market, products, and services as well as the effectiveness and competence of its political system, performance and contribution in research, innovations, and technology. The normative image dimension is based on the individual's beliefs about the integrity of a country and is particularly attributed to its norms and values. This dimension comprises the individual's judgment of the country's social and environmental performance and compliance of its related responsibilities. The aesthetic dimension of a country's image is based on the individual's beliefs about the aesthetics of the country's culture and its scenic places. This dimension comprises of a country's traditions, public culture, and territory and is based on the individual's judgment and attraction to the country's culture, traditions, and beauty of its landscapes.

The affective image of a country is based on the individual's emotions, affections, fascinations, and degree of affinity toward a country (Buhmann, 2016; Herz & Arnegger, 2017; Lala et al., 2009; Roth & Diamantopoulos, 2009). Whereas, a behavioral dimension of a country's image is based on the individual's intentions to visit the country or invest in the country, purchase or recommend a product or service from the country. It also includes the willingness to meet people and learn more about the country (Buhmann, 2016; Herz & Arnegger, 2017; Roth & Diamantopoulos, 2009). Martin and Eroglu (1993, p. 193) argue that country image is "the total of all descriptive, inferential and informational beliefs one has about a particular country". It is "the sum of beliefs and impressions people hold about places. Images represent a simplification of numerous associations and pieces of information connected with a place. They are a product of the mind trying to process and pick out essential information from huge amounts of data about a place" (Kotler & Gertner, 2002, p. 251).

National image constitutes a complex historical process that involves social and political realities, diplomatic relations, global politics, economic stature as well as media representation, and popular culture (Etzioni, 1962; Peng, 2004). It is connected with all beliefs, impressions, perceptions, attitudes, and behaviors that people hold about a country by assessing and evaluating all the related concepts, e.g., culture, history, tourism, geography, politics, economy, science and technology, and international relations (Carneiro & Faria, 2016; Roth &

Diamantopoulos, 2009; Zhang et al., 2018). Li and Chitty (2009) noted that the national image constitutes two frames: public frames that are presented in media about the country's image in which media evaluate and present reports about foreign countries while private frames are held in the public's minds as perceived national image and represent public opinion about foreign countries. Hu (2011) argues that national image is a product of a person's knowledge about a given country and it is based on personal experiences, social learning, societal relations, booklore, and knowledge acquired from the media. Hu breaks down national image into three different understandings; *First*, national image is a relatively stable assessment of a foreign audience about a country. *Second*, national image is a public perception or opinion about a sovereign country's behavior, appearance, and its public on the international stage. *Third,* national image is the collective assumption (assessment, evaluation, and conviction) of the foreign and domestic audience about a country's behavior (actual activities) and its outcome (Hartig, 2016).

National image is not a state-owned universally recognized property but a compendium of others' perceptions and even a country's same behavior may not receive equivalent responses in different countries (Mercer, 2010). However, national image is not a constant phenomenon. Rather it is an adaptable construct that might change over time, depending on the country's behavior on the international stage. Particularly, when a country fails to fit the normative expectations of the audiences, they may readjust or even reject that particular country's behavior and alter their perception of the country's image (Anholt, 2011). A country's image formation is a continuous process that involves construction, deconstruction, modification, and even reconstruction of an individual's perception of a country's image depending on the media information, acquired knowledge, personal skills, and intrinsic factors, like education, cultural background, occupation and predisposition (Muhoho-Minni & Lubbe, 2017).

In contrast, others (Herz & Arnegger, 2017; Rothbart & John, 1993) argue that the country image is a stable construct that has been constructed into the individual's mental schema for years. It constitutes the individual's solid perception and stable attitude toward that country. Therefore, a single advertisement of a country or a new stimulus might not transform an individual's entire country's image perception; rather it can add a new perspective to an already existing country's image perception. Researchers argue that national image is part of a country's soft power and it reflects its political and economic stature in the international arena (Nye, 2005; Wang, 2006; White, 2012).

National image is also used as an interchangeable term for national branding (Zhang & Meadows III, 2012), and national stereotypes (Huang & Leung, 2005), and it is often associated with international perception, public diplomacy, and international relations (Fong & Chia, 2017). Kaneva (2011) notes that there are three different facets of nation branding (image building): economic, political, and cultural. The economic perspective is purely functional and directed to build and uphold a country's competitive gains for economic development and to ensure a favorable public perception of a country to compete with other nations effectively for trade, investment, products and services, cultural heritages, tourism, governance and public's immigration (Anholt, 2006, 2011). The political approach of nation branding is often deployed by smaller nations to fortify their political and economic footprint and to grow their leverage against powerful countries (Volcic, 2008; Volcic & Andrejevic, 2011). The cultural approach is employed to construct a given national identity, explore social power relations, and expand agenda-setting (Kaneva, 2011).

Media and national image

In recent decades, the national image has become a mediated construct in the public's mind that is defined as the "mental network of affective and cognitive associations connected to the country" (Verlegh, 2001, p. 25). Hanan (2006, p. 8) argues that a country's image is "a representation of a country's positive or negative standing in media, in terms of historical, political, economic, military, diplomatic and religious context". In addition, the way the media carries the country's image in its mainstream content shapes public understanding of the country's image (Rivenburgh, 1992). Media often frame a country's image through specific language use including the use of value-loaded words, sentences, phrases, metaphors, and adjectives to support or oppose the domestic, regional, and global policies of that country (Hanan, 2006). Therefore, public perception of a country's image largely develops through the reading of media text and can be assessed in terms of media discourses about the economic, political, diplomatic, military, and religious relationship with other countries in the context of the changing domestic, regional, and global scenarios and its effects on individual's thoughts, feeling and behavior about that country (Saleem, 2007). Scholars argue that the news media possess soft power which is the fundamental component of image formation (Melissen, 2005; Nye, 2005). Therefore, media is often rated as the number one competitor in international image formation because "most of us gather our impressions of our countries and societies from the media" (Galtung & Ruge, 1965, p. 65).

Mass media is a vital and strongest force in disseminating, shaping, and constructing the national image of a country (Archetti, 2012; Kunczik, 2016; Seo, 2011; Soroka, 2003). Wood (2017) notes that due to globalization and the proliferation of new media technologies, everything from consumer goods to a country's economic performance has become associated with its image. Therefore, media portrayal of a country's image influences target audiences in the host country and builds a kind of relational paradigm that in the future may determine the country's engagement and relationship with the host country (Szondi, 2010; Wang, 2008a). The country's image shapes the "hard geopolitical realities that nations face as they engage with the rest of the world" (Coe & Neumann, 2011, p. 139).

Mass media is considered the central tool of public diplomacy and national image branding that influences foreign public opinion about a particular country's image (Gilboa, 2008; Mogensen, 2015; J. Wang, 2006; Yuan, 2017). Scholars (McCombs, 2014; Shaw & Martin, 1992) argue that media representation of a country's image can affect public opinion as they found a positive correlation between the salience of an issue's portrayal in news media and the public. Other studies have also shown strong effects of a mass-mediated national image on public opinion formation about foreign countries (Mcnelly & Izcaray, 1986; Semetko et al., 1992; Wanta et al., 2004).

Media contribute greatly to people's perception of other countries because most of the information about other countries that are out of our reach comes from the mass media (Cho & Lacy, 2000; McCombs, 2014; Saleem, 2007). People have fewer chances to travel internationally. Therefore, media play a decisive role in constructing their audiences' perception of the national image. Media frame events within an ideological, cultural, and political context—generating images of the world as pictures in our heads to fabricate our conceptualization of "us" and "them" (Kellner, 1995). Lippmann (1922) rightfully argues that our understanding of the world's public affairs largely comes from the media's constructed pictures in our heads, as the world remains "out of reach, out of sight and out of mind" for a larger population of the world. Our knowledge about the world is mainly shaped by news media reports, particularly in the current mediated environment, where media priorities strongly influence public priorities and the media's agenda predominantly inflicts upon the public minds (McCombs, 2014). Wanta, Golan, and Lee's (2004) study of national poll data and content analysis of newscasts in the United States indicates that the U.S. media coverage of a particular country significantly influences the U.S. public perception and its importance to U.S. foreign policy. They found that countries that receive higher media coverage are considered more important to the United States by the respondents. Similarly, Brewer, Graf, and Willnat's study (2003) on the US citizen perception and media portrayal of Iran, Libya, Colombia, and Mexico found that the respondents used the media's frame of reference while answering questions related to those particular countries. Thus, U.S. newspaper stories play a significant role in shaping the U.S. public perception of these countries as well as cultivating support for U.S. foreign policy.

Media has the power to inspire the formation of a foreign country's national image. As a major source of information, it sets the agenda for public consumption and sways their perception of a country in a particular direction (Brewer et al., 2003; Nisbet et al., 2004; Wanta et al., 2004; J. Zhang & Cameron, 2003). Kunczik (2016) argues that the national image of certain countries, whether right or wrong is fundamentally formed through very complex communication processes that involve various information sources—but the television and radio international broadcasts, newspapers, news services (news agencies), books are perhaps the most powerful image shapers in a newly mediated world. Scholars also note that framing, priming, and agenda-setting play central roles in a country's image formation. For example, a study (Nisbet et al., 2004) on the media influence on the U.S. image perception in the Middle East indicates that attention to the news media coverage significantly contributes to anti-U.S. sentiments in the Middle East. However, the relationship between anti-U.S. sentiments and Arab transnational media is significantly mediated by the political identification and type of news channel (Nisbet & Myers, 2011). Other studies (Al-Kandari, 2010; Willnat et al., 2006) also note the similar effects of news media on public perception of the U.S. and its foreign policies.

Herman and Chomsky (1984) in their classic work—" *Manufacturing Consent: The Political Economy of Mass Media*" argue that the U.S. government uses the mass media "propaganda model" to construct the image of different countries according to their interests. For example, they illustrated that the American media used a propaganda model to frame the images of three countries (i.e., Guatemala, El Salvador, and Nicaragua) based on the U.S. foreign policies toward those countries. Guatemala and El Salvador were framed positively due to their alliance with the U.S., while Nicaragua was famed negatively due to its dissentient view. Therefore, a country needs to build communicative power within the international communication environment if it wishes to build and guard its national image (Peng, 2017).

The national image of a country is not essentially hinged on its actual performance, capabilities, or capacity of national power, but is largely shaped by the media portrayal in front of foreign audiences (Duan, 2007; Kunczik, 2016; Peng, 2017). Peng (2017) argues that a country's national image functions on three levels: the substantial image (real image), the mediated image (media-constructed image), and the perceived image (the audience's perceived image). The substantial image is the real image—representing the country's reality, performance, capabilities, and capacities in the field of politics (political stature and influence), economy (economic growth and strength), culture (culture prestige and strength), national unity (national solidarity and integration) and progress (social development and living standards). It is an original and primitive image of a national country that provides a basis for the interpretation of mediated and audience's perceived image in the international environment.

The mediated image of a country involves a systematic process of using mediated texts (including all forms: text, image, graphics, audio, and video) to construct a country's national image through the synthesis of the different facets of a country's overall national power (includes, nation strength, performance, capabilities, and capacities). Although this synthesis emerges from social reality, it does not equate with the reality of a country and is largely based on the contested international mediated environment. Therefore, international communicative powers play pivotal roles in shaping and constructing a country's national image based on their interests related to that country (Adoni & Mane, 1984). Based on those interests, media in different countries use different mechanisms to construct and portray a country's national image based on their interest in a different part of the world. For example, during the Tibetan unrest in 2008, the U.S. media, particularly CNN, allegedly used biased reporting to undermine China's national image within the international community. CNN's coverage of the Afghanistan War and Iraq War also shows that the media plays an important role in the image construction of a nation or a country. During the Iraq war, CNN framed the U.S. invasion of Iraq as "savers", "liberators", and not "invaders", who came to save the Iraqi people from Saddam Hussein's tyranny and enslavement. Thus, a country-mediated image is not a simple mirror of its real image but a purposefully constructed image that aims to extend its international power and performance on a global scale (Duan, 2007; Peng, 2017).

Lastly, the audience's perception of a country's image is a public perception of a country that is mainly built through media transmissions of stereotypes about a nation or a country. The audience's perception of a country's image is largely subjective—based on vicariously learned beliefs, values, and behaviors from media in the absence of direct interaction and knowledge about a foreign country or its public (Bandura, 2009; Brewer et al., 2003). The international audience mainly sees and hears about a foreign country from domestic and international news media and, therefore, their impression, attitudes, and stereotypes about a country are largely rooted in media messages (Brewer et al., 2003; Fullerton & Kendrick, 2017). Khan et al. (2022, p. 2) argue that "stereotypes, particularly in their commonly sordid, negative form, are an acknowledged barrier to effective social communication, to globalization, and to cross-cultural engagement". It stimulates the false and immoral representation of social reality and leads to overgeneralization and oversimplification of a belief about a nation or a country (Seiter, 1986; Snyder & Miene, 2013). Stereotypes also conduit a false and biased public opinion toward a country, and therefore, can affect a country's international image and its citizen performance on a global scale (Khan et al., 2022; McAndrew et al., 2000). For example, the Western media's stereotyping of China as the "sick man of East Asia" or the "real sick man of Asia" has widely distorted China's international image and its reputation despite China's remarkable global achievement in the field of engineering, innovation, science and technology, sports (e.g., Beijing Olympics, 2008, 2022), and socio-economic developments in recent years. Similarly, during the COVID-19 pandemic, Western media portrayal of coronavirus as the "Chinese virus", "the China virus", "the Wuhan virus"; and the COVID-19 pandemic as "the Belt & Road Initiative pandemic" and "Chinese virus pandemonium" has not only reinforced the pre-existed stereotypes about China in the West, it also exacerbates the racial discrimination against Chinese and vandalizes China's international image and reputation on the global scale (Jia & Lu, 2021; The Pew Research Center, 2022; Wen et al., 2020). Therefore, Chinese scholars (Wang, 2008b; Xie & Page, 2013) believe that international media often use and adopt "Orientalist" stereotypes to present a negative and biased perspective on China to the world.

The international media through framing, discourses, and presentation of specific topics (agenda setting) construct the specific realities that shape society's image of a country. The media process of selection, omission, and emphasis on certain subject areas contributes to the construction of a national image that can have disastrous effects on the social, economic, and political relations with those countries. Particularly the deployment of one-sided discourse and adoption of uncritical and un-reflected patterns of argumentation from the media environment in which it operates may cultivate a sense of antagonism or friendship toward other nations that can exacerbate the distrust, diminish mutual understandings, and contribute to the conflict in the international relations. Therefore, while covering international issues, countries, or regions, media should present a wide range of subject areas and adopt a plurality of argumentations to facilitate the audience's perception of the "Other" (Richter & Gebauer, 2011). A country's socio-cultural diversity and differences can also generate a misperception of a country's national image. Therefore, media practitioners should also consider the sociocultural background of the audience while crafting a national image construction process (Peng, 2017).

Framing the national image

In the new digital environment, media framing plays a pivotal role in shaping a country's image (Adoni & Mane, 1984). Therefore, framing theory is widely used as a theoretical foundation in a country's image-building research to assess the role of news media framing in a foreign country's image-building processes (Armony, 2012; Han & Wang, 2014; Li & Chitty, 2009; Saleem, 2007; Schatz & Levine, 2010). Media possess the power to shape public perception by framing issues, identities, and systems. It connects scattered, unrelated events and information into compact packages to build a strategic narrative that might shape the behavior of local and international audiences about a country (Miskimmon et al., 2014). Scholars argue that frames and narratives can play a crucial role in building a country's image in international relations and engender empathic feelings and information-seeking behavior in the audiences that might change their attitudes and behavior (Oliver et al., 2012). Mass media used value-laden words, phrases, metaphors, sentences, adverbs, and adjectives to support or reject that country's policies or strategies on various domestic or international issues (Hanan, 2006). Thus, a foreign country's image in media indicates to what extent that specific country is framed as a friend and ally in foreign relations (Yu & Riffe, 1989).

Media hold power through framing to develop our understanding of an issue through reorientation and reconceptualization of our thoughts in precise directions (Chong & Druckman, 2007a, 2007b). Media frames organize our collective experiences and give us an understanding of the occurrences around us to guide our actions. Therefore, Goffman (1974) labeled frames as "schemas"—cognitive structures that construct our reality and structure our understanding of how the world functions (Kaufman et al., 2003; Sweetser & Fauconnier, 1996). Some scholars (Gamson & Modigliani, 1987, p. 143; 1989; Gitlin, 1980, p. 7; Tuchman, 1978, p. 193) argue that frames worked as "interpretive packages" that "organize everyday reality" and "provide meaning to an unfolding strip of events" through a process of "selection, emphasis, and exclusion". This process of selection, emphasis, and exclusion results in the promotion of certain aspects of reality and the omission of others. It redefines the limits of debates and confines the range of discussions to guide the audience's perception in a particular direction (Kahneman & Tversky, 1984; Khan et al., 2021; Martin & Oshagan, 1997). Therefore, media framing plays a pivotal role in a country's image formation (Adoni & Mane, 1984).

A country's image is also impeded by certain journalistic routines such as newsroom routines, journalistic practices, and news values that influence the journalist's decisions and selection of news items that lead to the advancement of certain ideas about a country. The editor's decision about the selection of a news agency copy, and how to fill the page, where to place the news stories, how to present juicy stories to the readers consciously develop frames of mind about a country that could provoke the reorientation of the audience's thoughts about a country (Chong & Druckman, 2007b, 2007a; Entman, 1993). News organizations deliberately focus on some aspects of a country and omit others to cultivate a homogenous point of view to support the status quo or to reinforce the country's positive or negative image in the contested media environment (Reese & Buckalew, 1995; Watkins, 2001). Entman (2003) argues that media through the framing process regulates the prominence of an issue by highlighting some aspects and ignoring others—deliberately articulating the discourse that supports one side while opposing the other. Cappella and Jamieson (1997, p. 39) noted that frame is "the way the story is written or produced," in the press by employing specific headlines, word choices, images, rhetorical devices, narrative forms, etc. Some scholars term the frame as an "outcome of newsgathering routines" through which journalists disseminate information about events and issues from the perspectives of the political and economic elites' values (Hackett, 1984; Reese & Buckalew, 1995).

Media frames provide structure to the news flow to control the boundaries of debate into specific categories that define and promote some ideas in and others out to occlude the relevant ideas in a network through an active process (Reese, 2007). Frames condense and simplify the debate to produce "cognitive cues" that facilitate people to understand and evaluate the situation to perform accordingly (Benford & Snow, 2000; Chong & Druckman, 2007b; King, 2017; Reese, 2001). It offers an ideological and conceptual framework to the individual for assessing an event by ascribing one primary or dominant meaning in place of another (Reese et al., 2001) and, therefore, it works as a strategic resource for an individual or a group of individuals who construct and exercise it for examining the dormant structure of the text, such as reasoning devices: problem definition, moral evaluation and specific keywords that set the concept of a primary frame (Reese, 2009). Reese (2001, p. 11) argues that "[f]rames are organizing principles that are socially shared and persistent over time, that work symbolically to meaningfully structure the social world".

Entman et al. (2009) argue that framing is a strategic tool used by elite communicators to exercise power to convince the target audiences to accept their interpretation that suits their aims or goals. They argue that people often have no personal experience in dealing with an issue and seek information from the media portrayal. Therefore, political elites use framing as a strategy to shape public understanding and discourses to attain their interest and gain advantages, mainly to advance their future course of action (Benford & Snow, 2000; Snow & Benford, 2000).

Framing offers an explicit meaning to an event and, therefore, propagandists and policymakers use framing as a strategic tool to seek and arouse the desired level of public support for their policies and interests (Callaghan & Schnell, 2005; Druckman & Nelson, 2003).

Certain complex issues have multiple perspectives and, therefore, involve a complicated process of conceptualization and value considerations. Framing facilitates those complicated processes peculiarly by reorienting people's thinking and reconstructing the value consideration of an issue for them (Chong & Druckman, 2007b). Navasky argues that a foreign country's image "is based largely on journalism that makes up our national mind" about a particular society or a country (cited in Zelizer & Allan, 2011, p. 1). There are also shreds of evidence that the greater salience and attributes of a foreign country in news media influence our understanding and perception. For example, studies on U.S. media framing of foreign countries indicate a strong correlation between the negative portrayal of a foreign country's image and negative U.S. public perception of that foreign country. Scholars argue that frequent U.S. news media coverage of a particular foreign country increases its perception of worth to U.S. interests (Besova & Cooley, 2009; Wanta et al., 2004; Zhang & Meadows III, 2012). These potent effects of media coverage on public opinion demonstrate that it would be unwise to ignore the role of news media in the formation of a favorable country's image abroad as public opinion is the only superpower left on this planet (Anholt, 2010). Therefore, this study uses framing theory as a theoretical framework to analyze China's image construction, interpretation, and dissemination in the Islamic world.

China's image framing (Construction) in News Media

China's economic growth, political rise, and military modernization have engendered a wide range of debates in the global media. Its burgeoning political and economic weight has attracted the global media spotlight and China's international news coverage has increased manifold in recent years (Sparks, 2010). Peng's (2004) study of the U.S. news media (*The New York Times* and *Los Angeles Times*) reveals a significant increase in China-related news coverage in the U.S. news media between 1992 through 2001. A similar trend is reported in Zhang's (2010) study of European transnational news media outlets—*The Economist, International Herald Tribune*, and *The Financial Times* that indicate a noticeable increase in China-related news between 2002 through 2005. However, China-related international news coverage still lags behind the U.S. and the U.K. in the so-called prestigious global press comparatively (Chen & Gunster, 2019). For example, Cohen's (2011) study of China's coverage in international media in 17 countries on four continents such as Chile and Brazil in South America; the U.S. and Canada in North America; Israel and Egypt in the Middle East; China, Hong Kong, Taiwan, Singapore, and Japan in the Far East; and Germany, Poland, Italy, Belgium, Switzerland, and Portugal in Europe also indicates that China's prominence in global news coverage has increased, but it is still notably lower than its deserved share of coverage compared to its gigantic size and importance in the world's affairs. The study further reveals that the U.S. and some European countries still enjoy more prominence in news coverage over China in these countries.

The international news coverage of China is not only insufficient but also largely unidimensional. It focuses more on political issues (human rights violations, political suppression, anti-communist framing, etc.,) and pays little attention to its social, cultural, and economic achievements (Lams, 2016; Willnat & Luo, 2011). In contrast, China's representation on social media platforms—Facebook, Twitter, Reddit, YouTube, Digg, WordPress, Topix, Technorati, NowPublic, and CNN iReport indicates a more diverse, positive, and neutral coverage of China in terms of technology (innovative China), culture (Fascinating China) and economy (rising economic power). However, it uncritically repeats the stereotypical representation of China's social, political, ethnic, and religious images from international mainstream media (Xiang, 2013). Similarly, Richter and Gebauer's (2011) discourse analysis of China's narrative representation in German news media during 2008 illustrates that China is represented in stereotypical reinforced manners both positively (e.g., "attractive growth market" and "interesting manufacturing location") and negatively (e.g., "supporter of rogue states" and a "cheap producer") in Germany, but it is represented in a broader range of topics as compared to the other regions. For example, Chinese cultural frame received "unusual" weightage (9.2% of the total coverage), yet the important facets of China's social transformation like education, science and technology, and social issues were totally ignored. China's reporting is dominated by the media logic—focusing more on negative news, violence, and conflict. The conflict-laden core media agenda indicates Germany's self-positioning to China in terms of ideological competition and the underlying rationale for topic selection and tilt toward themes of freedom, liberalism, and democracy to compare China with the West. China's "national image created by books and the media to date has fluctuated between the poles of excessive (historical) exuberance and reveling in the country's exotic aspects on one hand, and the construction of a disconcerting and in some respects threatening adversary to our social order on the other" (Richter & Gebauer, 2011, p. 2). Wilke and Achatzi (2011) argue that China's negative political image framing in leading German newspapers overshadowed its positive economic contribution frames between 1986 through 2006 and even a single political act, event, or occasion provokes strong German media criticism of China, particularly the Chinese government conduct regarding Tibet and its reaction to Dalai Lama's reception in Germany. China's alleged human rights violations, copyright infringement, internet censorship, and its position on the issue of global climate change also received sharp criticism in the German press.

Lam's (2016) study of China framing in the non-English elite print media in Belgium and the Netherlands revealed that China coverage in the elite Dutch and French language media in Belgium and Netherlands witnessed a substantial increase but the patterns of negative sentiments about China remained identical as a Western established discourse—Eurocentric approach to the freedom of expression, human rights, rule of law, and democracy, etc. More than half of the entire corpus (58.7%) recorded negative assessments of China, and every fourth article presented China in a "very negative" manner. Only 16.1% of the articles portray China's positive image, whereas 20% were recorded as neutral. The media coverage focused more on the political and economic frames whereas social issues received little attention. Education, science, and technology were ignored.

Chinese scholars believe that the Western media is more hostile and critical of China's peaceful rise and even did not appreciate its unprecedented social and economic development; instead, they reported on China's image negatively (Gao et al., 2016; Hartig, 2015; Wang, 2008a). The U.S. media has been unswervingly spreading "China threat" narratives on a global scale since the early 1990s,

(Liu & Yang, 2015; Yang & Liu, 2012). For example, Liu and Yang's (2015) longitudinal analysis of the "China threat" discourse in U.S. print media such as *The Washington Post, The New York Times, The Wall Street Journal, The Chicago Tribune,* and *The Los Angeles Times* between 1992 and 2006 indicate that the U.S. print media framed China in three different potential threat scenarios: (a) political and ideological threat to Western and U.S. global interests between 1992 and 1994; (b) strategic and military threat between 1995 and 2005; and (c) economic threats between (1992 and 2006). Others (e.g., Liss, 2003; Wanta et al., 2004) argue that the U.S. electronic and print media predominantly portray China's national image negatively and frame China as an "aggressive, brutal, and dangerous place"; and ascribe it as a potential threat to the U.S. democratic values and long-term national interests.

The Sino-phobic discourses and "Yellow Peril" motif have increased and gained centrality in the Western and U.S. media discourses (Lams, 2016; Ono & Pham, 2009; Ono & Yang Jiao, 2008; Ooi & D'Arcangelis, 2018; Richter & Gebauer, 2011). China has been reported as a strategic, ideological, and economic threat to the developed and developing worlds in Western media and policy discussions (Broomfield, 2003). Peng (2004) argues that the U.S. news media's hostility toward China is based on political (anti-China) and ideological (anti-communist) perspectives, and therefore, since the early 2000s, the U.S. media has been depicting China as a strategic, economic, and military threat to the U.S. global leadership (Yang & Liu, 2012). Ooi and D'Arcangelis's (2018) study of China's image construction in the U.S. media and government policy documents revealed that the U.S. perceives China as a potential enemy and an emerging threat to the U.S. global hegemony. Therefore, the U.S. media employs political rhetoric and the Orientalist tropes of "Othering" to justify the U.S. policies against China and to keep it in line. Edward Said (1979, 2016) in his seminal work *Orientalism* argues that Western discourses are strategically employed to maintain flexible superiority in relations with the Orient without ever losing the ascendancy. Therefore, Western media often deploys ethnocentric framing—a biased and negative "representation of the Other" to encourage social exclusion and oppression. Riggins (1997) argues that Western media's implicit use of language, word choice, and political values create a division of "Us vs. Them" and play a vital role in a wide array of cultural settings. The "rhetoric of Othering" not only alienates the Other, referring to people, not one of us or my people but also exacerbates prejudice against them.

China's image framing in the Western Media

Historically, China's national image has swirled between positive and negative perceptions in the Western world, predominantly influenced by the political relations between China and the West during the so-called "different ages" (Cao, 2014; Zhang & Wu, 2017). Issacs's (1980/2015) model of China's chronological image evolution trajectory in the Western media noted that China's image formation can be divided into six stages between the 18th Century and the mid of 19th Century: (a) Age of Respect (18th Century); (b) Age of Contempt (1840–1905); (c) Age of Benevolence (1905–1937); (d) Age of Admiration (1937–1944); (e) Age of Disenchantment (1944–1949); and (f) Age of Hostility (1949–1957). Mosher (1992) classifies China's post-independence (1949) image into four categories in the Western world: (a) Age of Hostility (1949–1972); (b) Second Age of Admiration (1972–1977); (c) Second Age of Disenchantment (1977–1980); (d) Second Age of Benevolence (1980–1989). Cao (2014) argues that China's image portrayals in Western media can be further classified into two categories after 1879: (a) Third Age of Disenchantment (1989–2001) and (b) Age of Uncertainty (2002—to date)—a diverse and mixed representation of China's image based on experiences and knowledge of the media's producers about China and not entirely on media's positive or negative orientations. For example, in recent years, Western media portrays China's contradictory images as "the last of the great civilizations", a romanticized Orient with unique "moral order being sustained by virtue, ritual, and reverence for ancestors" and the West finds it necessary to learn something from China. On the other hand, it employs anti-China frames, as "the last great Communist tyranny" which misleads the international community and whose peaceful rise is to be countered (Cao, 2014, p. 184). China's conflicting image representation in the Western media is also evident from other studies (Chen & Gunster, 2019; Lejin Zhang & Wu, 2017) that admire China's economic role in the global economy, on the one hand, and anti-China framing, on the other hand, such as authoritarian state, geopolitical and obstructive force in the region.

Ying (2004) divides China's image in international media into four categories: (a) horrible stage (1950–1972), under the influence of the Cold War mentality, when international media presented China as a "horrible" communist state; (b) respect stage (1972–1979) when China and the U.S. established diplomatic relations and China's image of the horrible and evil country changed in international media; (c) glorifying stage (1979–1989) when China was depicted as a legendary and romantic nation; (d) demonizing stage (1989–2000) when China was presented as an alleged human rights violator and a threat to the world. Lee's (2002) study of *The New York Times'* coverage of China-related policy found three "ideological packages": (a) containment, (b) engagement, and (c) globalization between 1990 through 2000. The containment frame indicates the use of trade privileges to scold China for its meager human rights record. The engagement frame indicates the attachment of modest and attainable human rights situations to trade, and the globalization frame to bring China into the international organization ambit to increase U.S. trade and handle China's human rights problems. These three ideological packages, even though representing different strategic variations in long-term U.S. foreign policy, contribute to the same theme of "peaceful evolution". Scholars (Cao, 2014; Isaacs, 2015; Lee, 2002; Mosher, 1992; Lejin Zhang & Wu, 2017) argue that the fluctuation of China's global image construction in the Western media is largely influenced by its global relationship and change in its image construction is directly related to the change in global geopolitical shift and its relations with the Western world.

China is framed unjustly in the U.S. media due to a lack of understanding of the distant land and unfamiliar culture and the U.S. media framing of friend and foe aligning the editorial policy with changing U.S. foreign policy toward China (Mann, 1999). China was framed as a "little blue ante" or "automatons" between the 1950s and 1960s. The media frame changed into more friendly discourses during the 1970s when Nixon tried to establish diplomatic relations with China to counteract the growing Russian influence in the region. The U.S. media frame dramatically changed and focused more on the Chinese as virtuous, entertaining, and cute and portrayed their countless qualities even under communism. However, the U.S. media frame changed into China's "going capitalist" during the 1980s and a more aggressive frame of "repressive China" after the dissolution of the Soviet Union during most of the 1990s (Graber, 2000; Mann, 1999; Saleem, 2007). Yu and Riffe's (1989) study of three U.S. news magazines (*U.S News & World Report, Times,* and *Newsweek*) from 1949 through 1976 indicates that the U.S. media framing of China and Chinese leadership (Mao and Chiang) was largely influenced by the U.S. foreign interests and the government foreign policy of friend or foe. For example, the U.S. media framed China and its leader Mao as "semi-ally", and an inevitable force during the cold war era but presented it negatively during the years of hostility between the U.S. and China.

Scholars noted that China's image in the Western media is projected either selectively or negatively (Peng, 2004; Willnat & Luo, 2011; Xiang, 2013; Zhang & Cameron, 2003; Zhong & Zhang, 2016). For example, Zhong and Zhang's

(2016) content analysis of China's rhetoric and Western news media's interpretation of the "China Dream" campaign revealed that Western media not only negatively reported China's dream but also made oppositional readings in contrast to the original meaning assigned by the Chinese government. Peng (2004) noted that reporting of China-related news increased in the *New York Times* and *Los Angeles Times* from 1992 to 2001 but the overall tone of the news stories was negative and hostile. Particularly, the media's political and ideological frames related to China were unfavorable. Similarly, another study (Zhang, 2010) found an increase in China-related economic and political news coverage in European transnational news media (*Financial Times, The Economist,* and *The International Herald Tribune*) between 1979 and 2005. Wang and Shoemaker's (2011) content analysis of U.S. newspapers: *New York Times, The Washington Post,* and *USA Today* between 1979 and 2007 suggested that China's political freedom was found to positively associate with positive media coverage and with favorable American opinion. Whereas, public relations contact between U.S. and China also produced favorable media coverage of China in the U.S. The study conducted by Yang and Liu (2012) on "China threat" coverage by the *Wall Street Journal, The Washington Post, New York Times, The Los Angeles Times,* and *The Chicago Tribune* indicated China's image fluctuation between China's military power, economic influence, and political/ideological difference during 1992–2006.

Chinese scholars largely agreed that there may be different trends in reporting China's image in international media since 1949, but Western media systematically skewed and "maliciously distorted" the account of Chinese realities and did not project the real and objective accounts of Chinese events and realities to the world because of the difference in ideology, news practices, and national interests (Xiang, 2013; Xiguang, 1996).

China's handling of the COVID-19 pandemic also received cynical criticism in the Western media. The Western media labeled China as a "real sick man of Asia"; describing coronavirus as a "Chinese virus", "the China virus", and "the Wuhan virus"; and the COVID-19 pandemic as "the Belt & Road Initiative pandemic" and "Chinese virus pandemonium" to exacerbate racial discrimination against Chinese and to tarnish China's global image (Jia & Lu, 2021; Wen et al., 2020). Jia and Lu (2021) argue that the U.S. mainstream news media (*The Washington Post, Wall Street Journal, The New York Times,* and *Foreign Policy* Magazine) not only used the inherited anti-China frames but also strategically and ideologically employed rhetorical devices—naming, shaming, blaming, and taming to contain China's peaceful rise and tar its global image during the early COVID-19 pandemic news coverage between December 2019 through July 2020.

They argue that the U.S. media intentionally coordinated with former President Trump's slanderous campaign against China to support the biased attribution of China as "the real sick man of Asia" to be contained, to be isolated, or to be confined and tarnish its global image. The reason behind this coordinated effort was to curtail China's economic and political growth, eliminate China's threat (strategic competitiveness) to the U.S. supremacy or hegemony, cut off China's foreign trade, businesses, and international exchanges and divert them to the U.S. under the Trump's "America First" doctrine (Jia & Lu, 2021).

Chen and Gunster's (2019) study of China's image framing in alternative public spaces in British Colombia, Canada reveals that China's image is brushed with two contradictions. On the one hand, Canadian media frame China as a global front-runner in renewable energy and a major partner in global climate arbitrations. But on the other hand, it is framed as a powerful foreign country that unfairly affects Canada's energy infrastructure and economic policies and decisions. However, the negative image frames are more prominent than the positive discourses, and China as a country is categorized by widespread corruption, political suppression, and the maltreatment of its people. The Chinese government is framed as a belligerent expansionist that wants to expand its overseas influence and position Canada as its key victim. This political rhetoric, anti-China, and anti-communist framing are also evident in the Canadian mainstream media (Chen & Gunster, 2019).

China's image in international media is gradually changing with the transformation of the geopolitical and geo-economic landscape. Cao (2014) noted that China's global relations and geopolitical shifts have transformed China's image in the West. Particularly, the negative image of China in the Western media significantly changed after China's successful hosting of the Beijing Olympic Games (Guo et al., 2015). But, still, China-related discourses in Western media are often fearful, negative, and hostile e.g., China threat argument, China's economic domination, China's military buildup in the South China Sea (Mogato & Petty, 2017; Yang & Liu, 2012; Yee & Storey, 2013). Western media often report negative news related to China's alleged human rights violations, environmental pollution, climate change, freedom of expression, social justice, trade, urban development, etc. (Armony, 2012; Ding, 2011; Shambaugh, 2013, 2015; Xu, 2014). However, Ding (2011) noted that the negative image projection of China in Western media is not a sole outcome of Western bias toward China; it is also the outcome of the China's own "problematic political credibility, reviving popular nationalism, and some missteps in its foreign policies" (pp. 302–304). He argues that China as an authoritarian regime lacks democratic governance and political credibility ("efficient governance, respect for democracy and human rights, and responsible international behavior"); and China's local issues like environmental degradation, human rights violations, and social injustices are seriously undermining its credibility and national image even in friendly countries e.g., in Africa and Latin America (Huang, 2018). Other scholars (Huang & Leung, 2005; Leung & Huang, 2007; Liang, 2002) argue that China's negative coverage in the Western media is the result of China's actions and policies rather than the biases of foreign journalists. For example, Huang and Leung (2005) noted that during the Western media coverage of the SARS epidemic in China and Vietnam, both countries received significantly different treatments. Though the Western press traditionally employs anti-communist frames while covering the epidemic in both China and Vietnam, Vietnam received more praise from the Western media due to its open communication strategy and collaboration with World Health Organization (WHO). On the other hand, the Chinese government received sharp Western criticism for covering up the initial outbreak during the SARS epidemic. Therefore, the Western media's negative representation of China was a result of China's handling of the SARS epidemic rather than Western media bias toward China (Willnat & Luo, 2011). Jia and Lu (2021) also noted that China's expulsion of the U.S. correspondents of *The New York Times, The Washington Post,* and *Wall Street Journal* from China in retaliation for the same actions by the U.S. government against Chinese journalists in the U.S. also adversely affected China's image and exacerbated more biased news coverage in those media outlets in the absence of in-place U.S. journalists and lack of firsthand information about China during the Trump era.

A unidimensional (political focus) or two-dimensional (economic and political foci) coverage of China in the Western press also contributes to the neglect of the image of Chinese society in transformation. For example, the analysis of Dutch and Belgian presses indicates that the image of Chinese society in transformation sinks into the flood of other stories on political and economic issues related to Western audiences (De Swert & Wouters, 2011; Lams, 2016). Western media while covering China, persistently focused on political containment, human rights, and economic trade, leaving the other dimension of Chinese society unattended (Willnat & Luo, 2011). Sparks (2010) argues that the newspaper (media) audience also plays a central role in the press coverage of China. For example, populist newspapers in Britain such as the *Daily Express* and *The Sun* use more negative and dramatized frames related to China's negative aspects while the elite press such as the *Times* uses more in-depth and less polarized frames of China for their relatively wealthy and well-educated readers/audiences. China's news coverage at the national and local levels also varies in the Canadian press as the national Canadian Broadcasting Corporation (CBC) accentuates more on the negative political stories related to China, while *Ming Pao*—a Chinese language newspaper and *Toronto Star* (Canada's English newspaper) focus more on business and culture-related reporting to present China's comprehensive image in Canada (Goodrum et al., 2011).

Interestingly, the Western (particularly the U.S. journalists) and Chinese media experts held opposing opinions about China's coverage in the Western media and the journalistic divide is evident that the former perceive China's reporting in the U.S. media as balanced and objective, and the latter as biased and ideologically driven (Zhang & Cameron, 2003). Xiang (2013) argues that Western media and journalists view China as politically and culturally inferior to the West, and therefore, demonizing and distorting bias of Western media arose from Western ideology, national interests, and differences in news practices. Another challenge for the U.S. journalist is the misunderstanding of China's complex history, culture, and politics, and therefore, anti-China frames sprang from the "inherent tensions" that ascend from both Chinese national rhetoric as well as the Western anti-communist ideology (Peng, 2004; Zhong & Zhang, 2016). However, apart from ideological and political discourses in Western media, China's economic growth and rich culture have started to contribute positively to its favorable image projection in Western news media (Aukia et al., 2017; Wu, 2008).

China's image framing in African and Islamic News Media

China's image in African and Islamic news media, however, presents another perspective, in which China's "peaceful rise" and its economic engagement in Africa and the Islamic world have garnered favorable perceptions in both regions (Cheng, 2016; Nassanga & Makara, 2016). China's positive perceptions prevail in both the elite circles and at the grassroots level. Nassanga and Makara (2016) argue that China is largely portrayed as a benevolent nation in Africa. African media often use positive and neutral frames to cover China-related news and criticisms of China are much lesser than the Western media (Geerts et al., 2014). However, there is considerable coverage of China's low-quality products, lack of transparency in procurements, and marginalization of local companies (Nassanga & Makara, 2016). Wekesa (2013) argues that China's image in East

Africa is predominantly positive, though the marginal difference between positive and negative framing is not too wide. However, China's coverage in South Africa represents a relatively balanced view and it is "neither starkly positive nor starkly negative but cautiously optimistic"(Zhang et al., 2016). Another study (Hirvensalo, 2012) found a similar pattern in the media coverage of China's aid and cooperation in African countries. Both the governments and the people in Africa perceived China's investment as mutually beneficial. Therefore, the media coverage of China is overwhelmingly positive in Africa. Although some problems occasionally arose from low-quality products, lack of transparency in procurements, marginalization of local companies, illegal timber export, illegal fishing as well as illegal cutting, it did not affect the bilateral relations and positive perception of China's presence in Africa (Ilhéu, 2010; Nassanga & Makara, 2016; Wekesa, 2013).

China also received positive limelight in the Islamic news media as a majority of the people hold a positive disposition toward China in the Islamic world. China's unfolding political and economic engagements in the Islamic world are well received. The Islamic leadership started to perceive China as a close reliable political and economic ally – and a viable substitute for the U.S. in the Middle East. In recent years, the Islamic world has exhibited strong discontent with the U.S. hegemonic policies and its meddling in the internal affairs of sovereign Islamic countries and, therefore, the Islamic countries start to recalibrate their economic and political calculus—moving away from the U.S. periphery of influence to realign with China for economic and political advantages (Al-Ghwell, 2018; Cheng, 2016; Khan & Pratt, 2019; Lehr, 2018; Zambelis & Gentry, 2008). The Islamic news media also follow the non-Western narrative of China and praise its unprecedented economic development and political rise in a short time. Therefore, it often used a positive and neutral tone to report China-related news. But there is also negative media coverage of China's poor quality products, made-in-China brands, the Uyghur Muslim issues in Xinjiang, and lack of religious and moral codes (Al-Sudairi, 2013; Khan et al., 2022, 2023; Khan & Pratt, 2019; Zambelis & Gentry, 2008).

China's image in Malaysia provides a classical example of how foreign policy and diplomatic relation affects the country's image construction in news media. Historically, China's image in Malaysia was shaped (framed) as an expansionist communist state that posed a threat to Malaysia in the pre-1974 (non-diplomatic relations) period. However, China's image was reshaped and adjusted as a major trading partner and friendly country after China and Malaysia established diplomatic relations in 1974. China's image has become more favorable in Malaysia after the end of the Cold War when trade, tourism, and educational exchanges between the two countries increased. China's image shaping (negative) and reshaping(positive) is the outcome of Malaysia's historical experiences and can only be understood in the context of the Cold War, colonialism, and nationalism. Today, Malaysia does not consider China as a security threat but instead as a major trading partner and a potential market for Malaysian exports (Hing, 2015).

China's image in Iran also evolves under the umbrella of strategic, political, and economic relations between the two countries. Singh (2021) argues that news media and elites present a much rosier image of China in Iran due to strong economic and political ties between the two nations. However, there are some concerns about China in the Iranian press regarding the plight of Uyghur Muslims, Chinese low-quality products, growing Chinese dominance in the Iranian economy, and public perception of dependence on China as submission of Iranian power to China and past glory (Jin, 2016; Singh, 2021).

The BRI has momentously reshaped China's public diplomacy efforts and its positive image promotion in the Islamic world. China's huge investment under the BRI framework has not only enhanced China's soft power but also improved its positive image framing in the Islamic news media. For example, the study of China's BRI and soft power framing in Pakistani news media indicates that the local English news media endorses China's goodwill through positive framing of its culture, diplomatic relations, and economic investment of US$62 billion through CPEC—a flagship project of the BRI in Pakistan (Ittefaq et al., 2021). Another study (Afzaal et al., 2019) on CPEC coverage in Pakistani press indicates that Pakistani media is packed with positive and friendly framing of China-Pakistan relations as a "brotherhood" and bonding as an "iron-clad bond", but a few intricacies and sensitivities do exist in media coverage related to some CPEC and BRI projects (Afzaal et al., 2019; Khan et al., 2020).

References

Adoni, H., & Mane, S. (1984). Media and the social construction of reality: Toward an integration of theory and research. *Communication Research, 11*(3), 323–340. <https://doi.org/10.1177/009365084011003001>

Afzaal, M., Hu, K., Ilyas Chishti, M., & Khan, Z. (2019). Examining Pakistani news media discourses about China–Pakistan Economic Corridor: A corpus-based critical discourse analysis. *Cogent Social Sciences, 5*(1), 1683940. <https://doi.org/10.1080/23311886.2019.1683940>

Al-Ghwell, H. (2018, June 30). Why the Arab world should build bridges with China. *Arab News*. <http://www.arabnews.com/node/1330736>

Al-Kandari, A. A. J. (2010). Arab news networks and conspiracy theories about America: A political gratification study. *Journal of Arab & Muslim Media Research, 3*(1–2), 59–76. <https://doi.org/10.1386/jammr.3.1-2.59_1>

Al-Sudairi, M. T. (2013). China in the eyes of the Saudi Media. *Gulf Research Center, February*(February), 1–38. <https://www.ictsd.org/sites/default/files/downloads/2013/04/china-in-the-eyes-of-the-saudi-media.pdf>

Anholt, S. (2006). Public diplomacy and place branding: Where's the link? *Place Branding, 2*(4), 271–275. <https://doi.org/10.1057/palgrave.pb.6000040>

Anholt, S. (2010). *Definitions of place branding–Working towards a resolution*. Springer.

Anholt, S. (2011). Beyond the nation brand: The role of image and identity in International relations. In A. Pike (Ed.), *Brands and branding geographies*. Edward Elgar Publishing.

Archetti, C. (2012). The impact of new media on diplomatic practice: An evolutionary model of change. *The Hague Journal of Diplomacy, 7*(2), 181–206. <https://doi.org/10.1163/187119112X625538>

Armony, A. C. (2012). A view from Afar: How Colombia sees China. *The China Quarterly, 209*, 178–197. <https://doi.org/10.1017/S0305741011001536>

Aukia, J., Heimonen, J., Pahikkala, T., & Salakoski, T. (2017). Automated quantification of Reuters news using a receiver operating characteristic curve analysis: The Western media image of China. *Global Media and China, 2*(3–4), 251–268. <https://doi.org/10.1177/2059436418754890>

Bandura, A. (2009). Social cognitive theory of mass communication. *Media Effects: Advances in Theory and Research, 3*(3), 121–153. <https://doi.org/10.1207/S1532785XMEP0303_03>

Benford, R. D., & Snow, D. A. (2000). Framing processes and social movements : An overview and assessment. *Annual Review Sociologic, 26*, 611–639. <https://doi.org/10.1146/annurev.soc.26.1.611>

Besova, A. A., & Cooley, S. C. (2009). Foreign news and public opinion: Attribute agenda-setting theory revisited. *Ecquid Novi African Journalism Studies, 30*(2), 219–242. <https://doi.org/10.3368/ajs.30.2.219>

Boulding, K. E. (1959). National images and international systems. *Journal of Conflict Resolution, 3*(2), 120–131. <https://www.jstor.org/stable/173107>

Brewer, P. R., Graf, J., & Willnat, L. (2003). Priming or framing: Media influence on attitudes toward foreign countries. *Gazette (Leiden, Netherlands), 65*(6), 493–508. <https://doi.org/10.1177/0016549203065006005>

Broomfield, E. V. (2003). Perceptions of danger: The China threat theory. *Journal of Contemporary China, 12*(35), 265–284. <https://doi.org/10.1080/1067056022000054605>

Buhmann, A. (2016). *Measuring country image: Theory, method, and effects* (1st ed.). Springer VS Wiesbaden. <https://doi.org/10.1007/978-3-658-15407-3>

Callaghan, K., & Schnell, F. (2005). *Framing American politics*. University of Pittsburgh Press.

Cao, Q. (2014). *China under Western Gaze: Representing China in the British Television Documentaries 1980–2000*. World Scientific.

Cappella, J. N., & Jamieson, K. H. (1997). *Spiral of cynicism: The press and the public good*. Oxford University Press.

Carneiro, J., & Faria, F. (2016). Quest for purposefully designed conceptualization of the country-of-origin image construct. *Journal of Business Research, 69*(10), 4411–4420. <https://doi.org/10.1016/j.jbusres.2015.12.075>

Castano, E., Bonacossa, A., & Gries, P. (2016). National images as integrated schemas: Subliminal primes of image attributes shape foreign policy preferences. *Political Psychology, 37*(3), 351–366. <https://www.jstor.org/stable/44132822>

Chen, S., & Gunster, S. (2019). China as Janus: The framing of China by British Columbia's alternative public sphere. *Chinese Journal of Communication, 12*(4), 431–448. <https://doi.org/10.1080/17544750.2018.1530686>

Cheng, J. Y. S. (2016). China's relations with the Gulf Cooperation Council States: Multilevel diplomacy in a divided Arab World. *The China Review, 16*(1), 35–64. <https://www.jstor.org/stable/43709960>

Cho, H., & Lacy, S. (2000). International conflict coverage in Japanese local daily newspapers. *Journalism & Mass Communication Quarterly, 77*(4), 830–845. <https://doi.org/10.1177/107769900007700407>

Chong, D., & Druckman, J. N. (2007a). A theory of framing and opinion formation in competitive elite environments. *Journal of Communication, 57*(1), 99–118. <https://doi.org/10.1111/j.1460-2466.2006.00331.x>

Chong, D., & Druckman, J. N. (2007b). Framing theory. *Annual Review of Political Science, 10*, 103–126. <https://doi.org/10.1146/annurev.polisci.10.072805.103054>

Coe, K., & Neumann, R. (2011). International identity in theory and practice: The case of the modern American presidency. *Communication Monographs, 78*(2), 139–161. <https://doi.org/10.1080/03637751.2011.564641>

Cohen, A. A. (2011). Covering China: Inside and out. *Chinese Journal of Communication, 4*(3), 251–254. <https://doi.org/10.1080/17544750.2011.594551>

De Swert, K., & Wouters, R. (2011). The coverage of China in Belgian television news: A case study on the impact of foreign correspondents on news content. *Chinese Journal of Communication, 4*(3), 331–347. <https://doi.org/10.1080/17544750.2011.594561>

Ding, S. (2011). Branding a rising China: An analysis of Beijing's national image management in the age of China's rise. *Journal of Asian and African Studies, 46*(3), 293–306. <https://doi.org/10.1177/0021909611405830>

Druckman, J. N., & Nelson, K. R. (2003). Framing and deliberation: How citizens' conversations limit elite influence. *American Journal of Political Science, 47*(4), 729–745. <https://doi.org/10.2307/3186130>

Duan, P. (2007). *"Guojia Xingxiang Jiangou Zhong de Chuanbo Celue" (Development strategies and construction of national image).* Beijing: Communication University of China Press.

Entman, R. M. (1993). Framing: Toward clarification of a fractured paradigm. *Journal of Communication, 43*(4), 51–58. <https://doi.org/10.1111/j.1460-2466.1993.tb01304.x>

Entman, R. M. (2003). Cascading activation: Contesting the White House's frame after 9/11. *Political Communication, 20*(4), 415–342. <https://doi.org/10.1080/10584600390244176>

Entman, R. M., Matthes, J., & Pellicano, L. (2009). Nature, sources, and effects of news framing. In K. Wahl-Jorgensen & T. Hanitzsch (Eds.), *The handbook of journalism studies* (pp. 175–190). Routledge.

Etzioni, A. (1962). International prestige, competition and peaceful coexistence. *European Journal of Sociology/Archives Européennes de Sociologie*, *3*(1), 21–41. <https://www.jstor.org/stable/23988202>

Fong, Y. L., & Chia, T. Y. (2017). Framing diplomatic relations. *China Report*, *53*(4), 467–489. <https://doi.org/10.1177/0009445517727925>

Fullerton, J. A., & Kendrick, A. (2017). The model of country concept explained. In J. A. Fullerton & A. Kendrick (Eds.), *Shaping international public opinion: A model for nation branding and public diplomacy*. Peter Lang Incorporated, International Academic Publishers.

Galtung, J., & Ruge, M. H. (1965). The structure of foreign news: The presentation of the Congo, Cuba and Cyprus crises in four Norwegian newspapers. *Journal of Peace Research*, *2*(1), 64–90. <https://doi.org/10.1177/002234336500200104>

Gamson, W. A., & Modigliani, A. (1987). The changing culture of affirmative action. In R. G. Braungart & M. M. Braungart (Eds.), *Research in political sociology* (pp. 137–177). Greenwich, CT: JAI Press.

Gamson, W. A., & Modigliani, A. (1989). Media discourse and public opinion on nuclear power: A constructionist approach. *American Journal of Sociology*, *95*(1), 1–37. <https://www.jstor.org/stable/2780405>

Gao, J., Ingram, C., & Kee, P. (2016). *Global media and public diplomacy in Sino-Western relations*. Routledge.

Geerts, S., Xinwa, N., & Rossouw, D. (2014). *Africans' perceptions of Chinese Business in Africa: A survey* (1st ed.). Globethics.net/Ethics Institute of South Africa.

Gilboa, E. (2008). Searching for a theory of public diplomacy. *The Annals of the American Academy of Political and Social Science*, *616*(1), 55–77. <https://doi.org/10.1177/0002716207312l>

Gitlin, T. (1980). *The whole world is watching: Mass media in the making & unmaking of the new left*. University of California Press.

Goffman, E. (1974). *Frame analysis: An essay on the organizatin of experience*. New York: Harper & Row.

Goodrum, A. A., Godo, E., & Hayter, A. (2011). Canadian media coverage of Chinese news: A cross-platform comparison at the national, local, and hyper-local levels. *Chinese Journal of Communication*, *4*(3), 311–330. <https://doi.org/10.1080/17544750.2011.594557>

Graber, D. A. (Ed.). (2000). *Media power in politics* (4th ed.). University of Illinois at Chicago.

Guo, Q., Wang, H., Yu, T., Tang, X., Chen, R., & Li, P. (2015). A study on Chinese National Image under the background of Beijing Olympic Games. *International English Education Research*, *8*, 5–11. <http://en.cnki.com.cn/Article_en/CJFDTOTAL-TYKX200908002.htm>

Hackett, R. A. (1984). Decline of a paradigm? Bias and objectivity in news media studies. *Critical Studies in Mass Communication*, *1*(3), 229–259. <https://doi.org/10.1080/15295038409360036>

Han, G. (Kevin), & Wang, X. (2015). From product-country image to national image: "Made In China" and integrated valence framing effects. *International Journal of Strategic Communication*, *9*(1), 62–77. <https://doi.org/10.1080/1553118X.2014.960082>

Han, G. K., & Wang, X. C. (2014). Analysis finds U.S. Newspapers use six frames for " Made in China ". *Newspaper Research Journal*, *35*(2), 6–24. <https://doi.org/10.1177/073953291403500202>

Hanan, M. A. (2006). *The media-foreign policy relationship: Pakistan's media image and United States Foreign Policy*. ProQuest.

Hartig, F. (2015). *Chinese public diplomacy: The rise of the Confucius Institute*. Routledge.

Hartig, F. (2016). How China understands public diplomacy: The importance of national image for national interests. *International Studies Review*, *18*(4), 655–680. <https://doi.org/10.1093/isr/viw007>

Herman, E. S., & Chomsky, N. (1984). *Manufacturing consent: The political economy of the mass media*. New York: Pantheon Books.

Herz, M., & Arnegger, J. (2017). Country image formation, stability, and change: A longitudinal assessment of consumers' image of Azerbaijan. *Journal of Travel & Tourism Marketing*, *34*(9), 1169–1183. <https://doi.org/10.1080/10548408.2017.1326364>

Hing, L. K. (2015). Images and the shaping of Malaysia's China Policy: 1957–1974. *International Journal of China Studies*, *6*(2), 107–127. <https://icsum.org.my/wp-content/uploads/2020/02/lee.pdf>

Hirvensalo, K. (2012). *Narrative bias and China's foreign assistance to Africa* [Universtiy of Helsinki]. <https://helda.helsinki.fi/bitstream/handle/10138/37217/gradu_kmhirvensalo.pdf?sequence=2>

Huang, H. (2018). *China's image in the Belt and Road Initiative : Case study of Pakistan and India* [Lund University]. <https://lup.lub.lu.se/student-papers/search/publication/8960031>

Huang, Y., & Leung, C. C. M. (2005). Western-Led press coverage of Mainland China and Vietnam during the SARS crisis: Reassessing the concept of "Media representation of the other." *Asian Journal of Communication*, *15*(3), 302–318. <https://doi.org/10.1080/01292980500261621>

Ilhéu, F. (2010). *The role of China in the Portuguese speaking African countries: The case of Mozambique* [ISEG-CEsA]. <https://cesa.rc.iseg.ulisboa.pt/RePEc/cav/cavwpp/wp84.pdf>

Isaacs, H. R. (2015). *Scratches on our minds: American images of China and India*. Routledge.

Ittefaq, M., Ahmed, Z. S., & Martínez Pantoja, Y. I. (2021). China's Belt and Road Initiative and soft power in Pakistan: An examination of the local English-language Press. *Place Branding and Public Diplomacy*, 1–14. <https://doi.org/10.1057/s41254-021-00212-8>

Jia, W., & Lu, F. (2021). US Media's coverage of China's handling of COVID-19: Playing the role of the fourth branch of government or the fourth estate? *Global Media and China*, *6*(1), 8–23. <https://doi.org/10.1177/2059436421994003>

Jin, W. (2016). Selective engagement: China's Middle East Policy after the Arab Spring. *Strategic Assessment – A Multidisciplinary Journal on National Security*, *19*(2), 105. <https://strategicassessment.inss.org.il/en/articles/selective-engagement-chinas-middle-east-policy-after-the-arab-spring/>

Kahneman, D., & Tversky, A. (1984). Choices, values, and frames. *American Psychologist*, *39*(4), 341. <https://doi.org/10.1037/0003-066X.39.4.341>

Kaneva, N. (2011). Nation branding: Toward an agenda for critical research. *International Journal of Communication*, *5*, 25. <https://ijoc.org/index.php/ijoc/article/view/704>

Kaufman, S., Elliott, M., & Shmueli, D. (2003). Frames, framing and reframing. *Beyond Intractability*. <https://www.beyondintractability.org/essay/framing>

Kellner, D. (1995). Media communications vs. cultural studies: Overcoming the divide. *Communication Theory, 5*(2), 162–177. <https://doi.org/10.1111/j.1468-2885.1995.tb00104.x>

Khan, M. K., & Pratt, C. B. (2019). China's Belt and Road Initiative: Its landscape (and trajectory) in the Islamic World. In A. Visvizi, M. Lytras, X. Zhang, & J. Zhao (Eds.), *Foreign business in China and opportunities for technological innovation and sustainable economics* (pp. 117–142). IGI Global. <https://doi.org/10.4018/978-1-5225-8980-8.ch006>

Khan, M. K., Pratt, C. B., & Akhtar, N. (2023). China's public diplomacy for image making in Islamic North Africa: Frames of the Belt and Road Initiative in Daily News Egypt. In: A. A. Anani-Bossman, T. E. Mudzanani, C. B. Pratt, I. A. Blankson (Eds.), *Public relations management in Africa Volume 1.* Cham: Palgrave Macmillan. <https://doi.org/10.1007/978-3-031-26704-8_5>

Khan, M. K., Sallam, M. H., Pratt, C. B., & Farid, T. (2022). Stereotyping the Chinese in Arab Nations: The effects of media use, perceived realism and Chinese-Arab relations. *The Social Science Journal.* <https://doi.org/10.1080/03623319.2021.2025197>

Khan, M. K., Wu, F., Pratt, C. B., & Akhtar, N. (2021). Satires, narratives and journalistic divides: Discourses on free speech in Western and Islamic news media. *58*(4), 458–476. <https://doi.org/10.1016/J.SOSCIJ.2019.05.012>

Khan, Z., Changgang, G., & Afzaal, M. (2020). China-Pakistan economic corridor at the cross intersection of China, Central Asia and South Asia: Opportunities for regional economic growth. *The Chinese Economy, 53*(2), 200–215. <https://doi.org/10.1080/10971475.2019.1688005>

King, E. (2017). What framing analysis can teach us about history textbooks, peace, and conflict. In M. J. Bellino & J. H. Williams (Eds.), *(Re) constructing memory: Education, identity, and conflict* (pp. 23–48). Rotterdam: SensePublishers. <https://doi.org/10.1007/978-94-6300-860-0>

Kotler, P., & Gertner, D. (2002). Country as brand, product, and beyond: A place marketing and brand management perspective. *Journal of Brand Management, 9*(4), 249–261. <https://doi.org/10.1057/palgrave.bm.2540076>

Kunczik, M. (2016). *Images of nations and international public relations.* Routledge.

Lala, V., Allred, A. T., & Chakraborty, G. (2009). A multidimensional scale for measuring country image. *Journal of International Consumer Marketing, 21*(1), 51–66. <https://doi.org/10.1080/08961530802125407>

Lams, L. (2016). China: Economic magnet or rival? Framing of China in the Dutch- and French-language elite press in Belgium and the Netherlands. *International Communication Gazette, 78*(1–2), 137–156. <https://doi.org/10.1177/1748048515618117>

Lee, C.-C. (2002). Established pluralism: US elite media discourse about China policy. *Journalism Studies, 3*(3), 343–357. <https://doi.org/10.1080/14616700220145588>

Lehr, D. (2018, July 21). How China is winning over the Middle East. *The Diplomat.* <https://thediplomat.com/2018/07/how-china-is-winning-over-the-middle-east/>

Leung, C. C. M., & Huang, Y. (2007). The paradox of journalistic representation of the other: The case of SARS coverage on China and Vietnam by Western-led English-language media in five countries. *Journalism, 8*(6), 675–697. <https://doi.org/10.1177/1464884907083118>

Li, X., & Chitty, N. (2009). Reframing national image: A methodological framework. *Conflict & Communication, 8*(2), 1–11. <https://regener-online.de/journalcco/2009_2/pdf/li_chitty.pdf>

Liang, J. (2002). *How US correspondents discover, uncover, and cover China: China-watching transformed* (Vol. 27). Edwin Mellen Press.

Lippmann, W. (1922). The world outside and the pictures in our heads. In W. Lippmann (Ed.), *Public opinion* (pp. 3–32). MacMillan Co. <https://doi.org/10.1037/14847-001>

Liss, A. (2003). Images of China in the American print media: A survey from 2000 to 2002. *Journal of Contemporary China, 12*(35), 299–318. <https://doi.org/10.1080/1067056022000054614>

Liu, X., & Yang, Y. E. (2015). Examining China's official media perception of the United States: A content analysis of people's daily coverage. *Journal of Chinese Political Science, 20*(4), 385–408. <https://doi.org/10.1007/s11366-015-9340-8>

Luther, C. A. (2002). National identities, structure, and press images of nations: The case of Japan and the United States. *Mass Communication and Society, 5*(1), 57–85. <https://doi.org/10.1207/S15327825MCS0501_5>

Mann, J. (1999). Framing China. In R. Giles (Ed.), *Media Studies Journal Covering China* (pp. 102–107.). The Freedom Forum.

Martin, C. R., & Oshagan, H. (1997). Disciplining the workforce: The News Media frame a general motors plant closing. *Communication Research, 24*(6), 669–697.

Martin, I. M., & Eroglu, S. (1993). Measuring a multi-dimensional construct: Country image. *Journal of Business Research, 28*(3), 191–210. <https://doi.org/10.1016/0148-2963(93)90047-S>

McAndrew, F. T., Akande, A., Bridgstock, R., Mealey, L., Gordon, S. C., Scheib, J. E., Akande-Adetoun, B. E., Odewale, F., Morakinyo, A., & Nyahete, P. (2000). A multicultural study of stereotyping in English-speaking countries. *The Journal of Social Psychology, 140*(4), 487–502.

McCombs, M. (2014). *Setting the agenda: Mass media and public opinion*. John Wiley & Sons.

Mcnelly, J. T., & Izcaray, F. (1986). International news exposure and images of nations. *Journalism & Mass Communication Quarterly, 63*(3), 546–553. <https://doi.org/10.1177/107769908606300315>

Melissen, J. (2005). The new public diplomacy: Between theory and practice. In D. Lee, P. Sharp, & M. Holmes (Eds.), *Studies in diplomacy and international relations* (pp. 3–27). Springer.

Mercer, J. (2010). *Reputation and international politics*. Cornell University Press.

Miskimmon, A., O'Loughlin, B., & Roselle, L. (2014). *Strategic narratives: Communication power and the new world order* (Vol. 3). Routledge.

Mogato, M., & Petty, M. (2017, April 27). Push for South China Sea code stirs ASEAN suspicions about Beijing's endgame. *Reuters*. <https://www.reuters.com/article/us-southchinasea-asean-analysis-idUSKBN17T0A5>

Mogensen, K. (2015). International trust and public diplomacy. *International Communication Gazette, 77*(4), 315–336. <https://doi.org/10.1177/1748048514568764>

Mosher, S. W. (1992). *China misperceived: American illusions and Chinese reality* (p. 272). Basic Books.

Muhoho-Minni, P., & Lubbe, B. A. (2017). The role of the media in constructing a destination image: The Kenya experience. *Communicatio, 43*(1), 58–79. <https://doi.org/10.1080/02500167.2016.1226915>

Nassanga, G. L., & Makara, S. (2016). Perceptions of Chinese presence in Africa as reflected in the African media: Case study of Uganda. *Chinese Journal of Communication, 9*(1), 21–37. <https://doi.org/10.1080/17544750.2015.1078386>

Nisbet, E. C., & Myers, T. A. (2011). Anti-American sentiment as a media effect? Arab media, political identity, and public opinion in the Middle East. *Communication Research, 38*(5), 684–709. <https://doi.org/10.1177/0093650211405648>

Nisbet, E. C., Nisbet, M. C., Scheufele, D. A., & Shanahan, J. E. (2004). Public diplomacy, television news, and Muslim opinion. *Harvard International Journal of Press/Politics, 9*(2), 11–37. <https://doi.org/10.1177/1081180X04263459>

Nye, J. S. (2005). *Soft power: The means to success in world politics*. Public affairs. <http://www.tinyurl.com/mug36ku>

Oliver, M. B., Dillard, J. P., Bae, K., & Tamul, D. J. (2012). The effect of narrative news format on empathy for stigmatized groups. *Journalism & Mass Communication Quarterly, 89*(2), 205–224. <https://doi.org/10.1177/1077699012439020>

Ono, K. A., & Pham, V. (2009). *Asian Americans and the media* (Vol. 2). Polity.

Ono, K. A., & Yang Jiao, J. (2008). China in the US imaginary: Tibet, the Olympics, and the 2008 earthquake. *Communication and Critical/Cultural Studies, 5*(4), 406–410. <https://doi.org/10.1080/14791420802416168>

Ooi, S. M., & D'Arcangelis, G. (2018). Framing China: Discourses of othering in US news and political rhetoric. *Global Media and China, 2*(3–4), 269–283. <https://doi.org/10.1177/2059436418756096>

Peng, D. (2017). International communication strategies of Chinese Radio and TV networks: Initial observations. In *International communication strategies of Chinese Radio and TV networks: Initial observations*. <https://doi.org/10.1007/978-981-10-4460-1>

Peng, Z. (2004). Representation of China: An across time analysis of coverage in the New York Times and Los Angeles Times. *Asian Journal of Communication, 14*(1), 53–67. <https://doi.org/10.1080/0129298042000195170>

Reese, S. D. (2001). Prologue—Framing public life A bridging model for media research. In S. D. Reese, O. H. Gandy Jr, & A. E. Grant (Eds.), *Framing public life: Perspectives on media and our understanding of the social world* (pp. 7–31). Routledge. https://doi.org/10.1111/j.1460-2466.2006.00334.x

Reese, S. D. (2007). The framing project: A bridging model for media research revisited. *Journal of Communication, 57*(1), 148–154. <https://doi.org/10.1111/j.1460-2466.2006.00334.x>

Reese, S. D. (2009). Finding frames in a web of culture: The case of the war on terror. In P. D'Angelo & J. A. Kuypers (Eds.), *Doing news framing analysis: Empirical and theoretical perspectives* (1st ed., pp. 17–42). New York, NY: Routledge.

Reese, S. D., & Buckalew, B. (1995). The militarism of local television: The routine framing of the Persian Gulf War. *Critical Studies in Media Communication, 12*(1), 40–59. <https://doi.org/10.1080/15295039509366918>

Reese, S. D., Gandy Jr, O. H., & Grant, A. E. (2001). *Framing public life: Perspectives on media and our understanding of the social world.* Routledge.

Richter, C., & Gebauer, S. (2011). The Portrayal of China in German Media. *Berlin: Heinrich-Böll-Stiftung,* 1–10. <http://www.boell.de>

Riggins, S. H. E. (1997). *The language and politics of exclusion: Others in discourse.* Sage Publications, Inc.

Rivenburgh, N. K. (1992). National image richness in US-televised coverage of South Korea during the 1988 Olympics. *Asian Journal of Communication, 2*(2), 1–39. <https://doi.org/10.1080/01292989209359547>

Roth, K. P., & Diamantopoulos, A. (2009). Advancing the country image construct. *Journal of Business Research, 62*(7), 726–740. <https://doi.org/10.1016/j.jbusres.2008.05.014>

Rothbart, M., & John, O. P. (1993). Intergroup relations and stereotype change: A social-cognitive analysis and some longitudinal findings. In P. M. Sniderman, P. E. Tetlock, & E. G. Carmines (Eds.), *Prejudice, politics, and the American dilemma* (pp. 32–59). Stanford University Press. <https://psycnet.apa.org/record/1993-98327-001>

Said, E. W. (1979). *Orientalism.* Vintage.

Said, E. W. (2016). Orientalism. In W. Longhofer & D. Winchester (Eds.), *Social theory re-wired: New connections to classical and contemporary perspectives* (pp. 402–417). Routledge.

Saleem, N. (2007). US media framing of foreign countries image: An analytical perspective. *Canadian Journal of Media Studies, 2*(1), 130–162. <https://www.researchgate.net/publication/352172910_US_Media_Framing_of_Foreign_Countries_Image>

Schatz, E., & Levine, R. (2010). Framing, public diplomacy, and anti-Americanism in Central Asia. *International Studies Quarterly, 54*(3), 855–869. <https://www.jstor.org/stable/40931139>

Seiter, E. (1986). Stereotypes and the media: A re-evaluation. *Journal of Communication, 36*(2), 14–26. <https://doi.org/10.1111/j.1460-2466.1986.tb01420.x>

Semetko, H. A., Brzinski, J. B., Weaver, D., & Willnat, L. (1992). TV news and US public opinion about foreign countries: The impact of exposure and attention. *International Journal of Public Opinion Research, 4*(1), 18–36. <https://doi.org/10.1093/ijpor/4.1.18>

Seo, H. (2011). Media and foreign policy: A comparative study of journalists' perceptions of press—Government relations during the six-party talks. *Journalism, 12*(4), 467–481. <https://doi.org/10.1177/1464884910388227>

Shambaugh, D. (2013). *China goes global: The partial power.* Oxford University Press.

Shambaugh, D. (2015). China's soft-power push: The search for respect. *Foreign Affairs, 94*(4), 99–107. <https://www.jstor.org/stable/24483821>

Shaw, D. L., & Martin, S. E. (1992). The function of mass media agenda setting. *Journalism Quarterly, 69*(4), 902–920. <https://www.jstor.org/stable/2747787>

Singh, R. (2021b). Critical discourse analysis of Iran-China relations through football headlines. *English Linguistics Research, 10*(2), 1. <https://doi.org/10.5430/elr.v10n2p1>

Snow, D. A., & Benford, R. D. (2000). Clarifying the relationship between framing and ideology in the study of social movements: A comment on Oliver and Johnston. *Mobilization, 5*(1). <https://www.researchgate.net/publication/228588409_Clarifying_the_Relationship_Between_Framing_and_Ideology>

Snyder, M., & Miene, P. (2013). On the functions of stereotypes and prejudice. In M. P. Zanna & J. M. Olson (Eds.), *The psychology of prejudice: The Ontario symposium* (Vol. 7, pp. 33–54). Lawrence Erlbaum.

Soroka, S. N. (2003). Media, public opinion, and foreign policy. *Harvard International Journal of Press/Politics*, *8*(1), 27–48. <https://doi.org/10.1177/1081180X02238783>

Sparks, C. (2010). Coverage of China in the UK national press. *Chinese Journal of Communication*, *3*(3), 347–365. <https://doi.org/10.1080/17544750.2010.499637>

Sweetser, E., & Fauconnier, G. (1996). Cognitive links and domains: Basic aspects of mental space theory. In G. Fauconnier & E. Sweetser (Eds.), *Spaces, worlds, and grammar* (pp. 1–15). Chicago/London: University of Chicago Press.

Szondi, G. (2010). From image management to relationship building: A public relations approach to nation branding. *Place Branding and Public Diplomacy*, *6*(4), 333–343. <https://doi.org/10.1057/pb.2010.32>

The Pew Research Center. (2022, June 29). U.S. receives more positive ratings than China in most countries. *The Pew Research Center*, 1. <https://www.pewresearch.org/fact-tank/2022/06/29/across-19-countries-more-people-see-the-u-s-than-china-favorably-but-more-see-chinas-influence-growing/ft_2022-06-29_chinaus_01/>

Tuchman, G. (1978). Making news: A study in the construction of reality. *Social Forces*, *59*(4). <https://doi.org/10.2307/2578016>

Verlegh, P. W. J. (2001). *Country-of-origin effects on consumer product evaluations*. Wageningen University, Netherlands.

Volcic, Z. (2008). Former Yugoslavia on the World Wide Web: Commercialization and branding of nation-states. *International Communication Gazette*, *70*(5), 395–413. <https://doi.org/10.1177/1748048508094292>

Volcic, Z., & Andrejevic, M. (2011). Nation branding in the era of commercial nationalism. *International Journal of Communication*, *5*, 21. <https://ijoc.org/index.php/ijoc/article/view/849/544>

Wang, J. (2006). Managing national reputation and international relations in the global era: Public diplomacy revisited. *Public Relations Review*, *32*(2), 91–96. <https://doi.org/10.1016/j.pubrev.2005.12.001>

Wang, J. (2008a). The power and limits of branding in national image communication in global society. *Journal of International Communication*, *14*(2), 9–24. <https://doi.org/10.1080/13216597.2008.9674730>

Wang, X., & Shoemaker, P. J. (2011). What shapes Americans' opinion of China? Country characteristics, public relations and mass media. *Chinese Journal of Communication*, *4*(01), 1–20. <https://doi.org/10.1080/17544750.2011.544079>

Wang, Y. (2008b). Public diplomacy and the rise of Chinese soft power. *The Annals of the American Academy of Political and Social Science*, *616*(1), 257–273. <https://doi.org/10.1177/0002716207312757>

Wanta, W., Golan, G., & Lee, C. (2004). Agenda setting and international news: Media influence on public perceptions of foreign nations. *Journalism & Mass Communication Quarterly*, *81*(2), 364–377. <https://doi.org/10.1177/107769900408100209>

Watkins, S. C. (2001). Framing protest: News media frames of the Million Man March. *Critical Studies in Media Communication, 18*(1), 83–101. <https://doi.org/10.1080/15295030109367125>

Wekesa, B. (2013). The media framing of China's Image in East Africa: An exploratory study. *African East-Asian Affairs: The China Monitor, 1*, 15–42. <https://doi.org/10.7552/0-1-2>

Wen, J., Aston, J., Liu, X., & Ying, T. (2020). Effects of misleading media coverage on public health crisis: A case of the 2019 novel coronavirus outbreak in China. *Anatolia, 31*(2), 331–336. <https://doi.org/10.1080/13032917.2020.1730621>

White, C. L. (2012). Brands and national image: An exploration of inverse country-of-origin effect. *Place Branding and Public Diplomacy, 8*(2), 110–118. <https://doi.org/10.1057/pb.2012.6>

Wilke, J., & Achatzi, J. (2011). From Tian'anmen Square to the global world stage: Framing China in the German press, 1986–2006. *Chinese Journal of Communication, 4*(3), 348–364. <https://doi.org/10.1080/17544750.2011.594563>

Willnat, L., Aw, A., Hamdy, N. N., He, Z., Menayang, V., La Porte, M. T., Sanders, K., & Tamam, E. (2006). Media use, anti-Americanism and international support for the Iraq War. *International Communication Gazette, 68*(5–6), 533–550. <https://doi.org/10.1177/1748048506068729>

Willnat, L., & Luo, Y. (2011). Watching the Dragon: Global television news about China. *Chinese Journal of Communication, 4*(3), 255–273. <https://doi.org/10.1080/17544750.2011.594552>

Wood, S. (2017). Rebranding the nation: Germany's image politics. *International Politics, 54*(2), 161–181. <https://doi.org/10.1057/s41311-017-0027-y>

Wu, D. (2008). Glocalization and the discourses of cultural China: An introduction. In D. D. Wu (Ed.), *Discourses of cultural China in the globalizing age* (pp. 1–10). Hong Kong University Press. <https://doi.org/10.5790/hongkong/9789622099128.003.0001>

Xiang, D. (2013). China's image on international English language social media. *Journal of International Communication, 19*(2), 252–271. <https://doi.org/10.1080/13216597.2013.833535>

Xie, T., & Page, B. I. (2013). What affects China's national image? A cross-national study of public opinion. *Journal of Contemporary China, 22*(83), 850–867. <https://doi.org/10.1080/10670564.2013.782130>

Xiguang, L. (1996). *Yaomo Hua Zhongguo De Beihou [Behind Demonizing China]*. China Social Sciences Press.

Xu, S. (2014). *Chinese discourse studies*. Palgrave Macmillan.

Yang, Y. E., & Liu, X. (2012). The "China Threat" through the lens of US print media: 1992–2006. *Journal of Contemporary China, 21*(76), 695–711. <https://doi.org/10.1080/10670564.2012.666838>

Yee, H., & Storey, I. (2013). *China threat: Perceptions myths*. Routledge.

Ying, H. (2004). *U.S. media and China's national image*,. Southern Daily Press.

Yu, Y.-C., & Riffe, D. (1989). Chiang and Mao in US news magazines. *Journalism Quarterly, 66*(4), 913–919. <https://doi.org/10.1177/107769908906600042>

Yuan, Y. (2017). *Soft power of International News Media: American audiences' perceptions of China's country image mediated by trust in news*. University of Maryland.

Zambelis, C., & Gentry, B. (2008). China through Arab eyes: American influence in the Middle East. *Parameters, 38*(1), 60–73. <https://doi.org/10.55540/0031-1723.2412>

Zelizer, B., & Allan, S. (2011). *Journalism after September 11.* Taylor & Francis.

Zhang, C., & Meadows III, C. W. (2012). International coverage, foreign policy, and national image: Exploring the complexities of media coverage, public opinion, and presidential agenda. *International Journal of Communication, 6*, 20. <https://ijoc.org/index.php/ijoc/article/view/1424>

Zhang, H., Wu, Y., & Buhalis, D. (2018). A model of perceived image, memorable tourism experiences and revisit intention. *Journal of Destination Marketing and Management, 8*(February), 1–11. <https://doi.org/10.1016/j.jdmm.2017.06.004>

Zhang, J., & Cameron, G. T. (2003). China's agenda building and image polishing in the US: Assessing an international public relations campaign. *Public Relations Review, 29*(1), 13–28. <https://doi.org/10.1016/S0363-8111(02)00198-4>

Zhang, L., & Wu, D. (2017). Media representations of China: A comparison of China Daily and Financial Times in reporting on the Belt and Road Initiative. *Critical Arts, 31*(6), 29–43. <https://doi.org/10.1080/02560046.2017.1408132>

Zhang, Li. (2010). The Rise of China: Media perception and implications for international politics. *Journal of Contemporary China, 19*(64), 233–254. <https://doi.org/10.1080/10670560903444199>

Zhang, X., Wasserman, H., & Mano, W. (2016). *China's media and soft power in Africa: Promotion and perceptions.* Springer.

Zhong, L., & Zhang, J. (2016). Political myth as strategic communication: Analysis of Chinese dream's rhetoric and English news media's interpretation. *International Journal of Strategic Communication, 10*(1), 51–68. <https://doi.org/10.1080/1553118X.2015.1105229>

V

China's Global Image Perception

China's global preeminence in economic, political, and military fields and its launch of the global strategic foreign policy endeavor—the BRI have attracted the global media and public attention on an unprecedented scale and put its role, actions, and policies (past, present, and future) under critical scrutiny in international media discourse, political discussions, and international communities both at the public and country levels. Therefore, scholars, research centers, and public institutions consistently observe and measure China's global image in terms of its role, policies, and actions, and global public opinion in favor or against China in different parts of the world.

Global public opinion about China is largely bifurcated into positive or negative perceptions in the different two parts of the world: the underdeveloped world specifically the Islamic world; and the developed world, particularly the Western world where public opinion about China is negative and hostile. On the other hand, China relatively enjoys a positive and friendly image in the Islamic world.

China's image perception in the Islamic World

According to the Pew Research Center survey on the global image from 2005 through 2019, China's global image perception in the 14 Islamic countries is recorded as largely positive except for Turkey, Jordan, and Morocco. The people of the Republic of Mali recorded the highest positive opinion (92%) toward China in 2007 followed by China's all-weather strategic partner—Pakistan, where an average of 80% of people showed a positive disposition toward China between 2005 through 2019. China's positive image in Malaysia fluctuated from 78% to 83% between 2007 through 2015. The survey indicates that 77% of the people in Bangladesh held a favorable image of China in 2014. China's favorable image in Nigeria fluctuated from 70% to 76% between 2010 and 2019. China's positive image in Tunisia increased from 63% in 2018 to 70% in 2019. Similarly, the public holds a favorable image of China in Indonesia, Kuwait, Palestine, and Egypt with few exceptions. For example, China's favorable image in Indonesia declined from 53% in 2018 to 35% in 2019 though China held a favorable image in Indonesia between 2005 through 2018. However, China's image in Jordan and Turkey remained negative between 2005 through 2019. In addition, the Pew Research Center survey on China's global image also recorded negative public perception of China in Morocco in 2007. China's favorable image perception in Egypt also declined from 65% to 46% and negative perception increased from 29% to 53% between 2007 and 2014 (Table 5.1). Overall, China holds a stable and positive image in the Islamic world and the survey did not record any significant variation in the overall image perception of China in the Islamic world. The overall perception of China's unfavorable image in the Islamic world witnessed a slight decline from 30% in 2005 to 27% in 2019 (Figure 5.1), as the survey found a significant decline in public negative perception of China in Lebanon from 33% in 2017 to 22% in 2019 and from 54% to 44% in Turkey between 2017 and 2019.

Chinese leadership image in the Islamic world met with mixed responses. Although a majority Islamic countries (Malaysia, Bangladesh, Nigeria, Senegal Tunisia, Pakistan, and Indonesia) have shown confidence in Chinese leadership to "do the right thing regarding world affairs", the public opinion in four Islamic countries—Egypt, Turkey, Jordan, and Palestine did not show confidence in Chinese leadership for taking the right decision regarding the world affairs (Figure 5.2).

China also holds positive public perceptions and a favorable image in the Middle East and North Africa (MENA) region. According to the latest Arab Barometer (2021), China enjoys favorable public perception in the MENA region except for Jordan and Lebanon where negative public perceptions of China subdue the positive opinion. A majority of the population (54.7%) in the six MENA region countries—Algeria, Iraq, Lebanon, Jordan, Libya, Morocco,

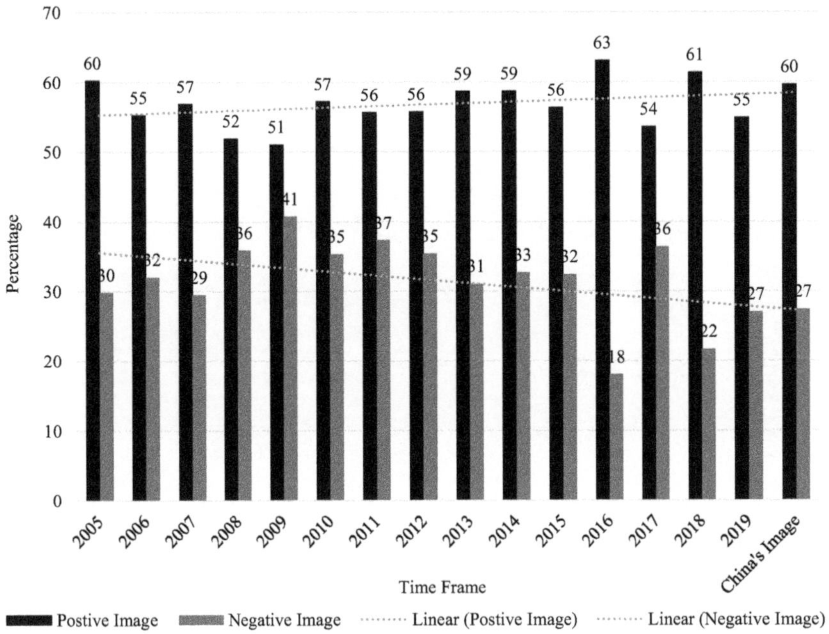

Figure 5.1: Comparative Image of China in the Islamic World during 2005 to 2019.
Source: Pew Research Center Survey 2005–2019

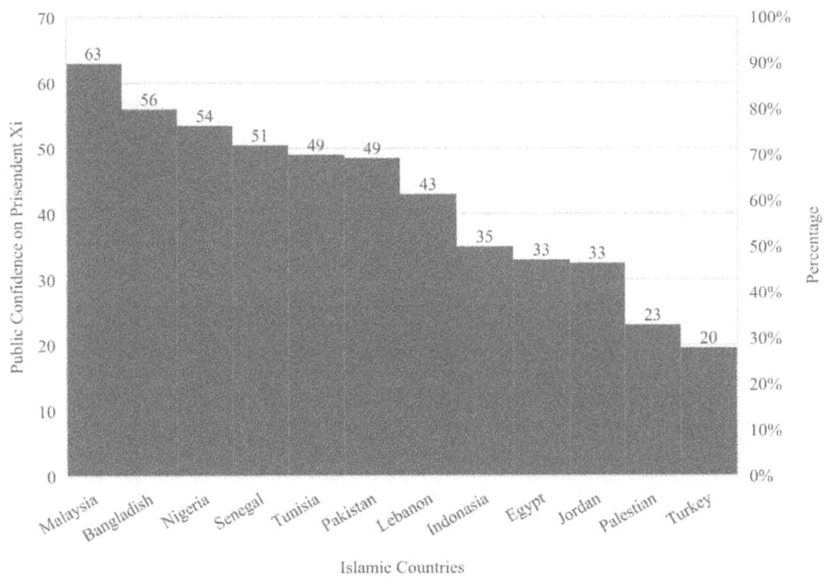

Figure 5.2: Public Confidence in Chinese Leadership to "Do the Right Thing Regarding World Affairs" in the Islamic World.
Source: Pew Research Center Survey, 2014–2019

Table 5.1: China's Favorable Image Perception in the Islamic World from 2005 through 2019.

Countries	2005	2006	2007	2008	2009	2010	2011	2012	2013	2014	2015	2016	2017	2018	2019	Avg. Score	18–19 Change
Pakistan	79	69	79	76	84	85	82	85	81	78	82	-	-	-	-	80	-
Indonesia	73	62	65	58	59	58	67	-	70	66	63	-	55	53	36	60	-7
Lebanon	66	-	46	50	53	56	59	59	56	53	52	-	63	-	68	57	-
Jordan	43	49	46	44	50	53	44	47	40	35	33	-	35	-	-	43	-
Turkey	40	33	25	24	16	20	18	22	27	21	18	-	33	-	37	26	-
Egypt	-	63	65	59	52	52	57	52	45	46	-	-	-	-	-	55	-
Malaysia	-	-	83	-	-	-	-	-	81	74	78	-	-	-	-	79	-
Mali	-	-	92	-	-	-	-	-	-	-	-	-	-	-	-	92	-
Kuwait	-	-	52	-	-	-	-	-	-	-	-	-	-	-	-	52	-
Palestine	-	-	46	-	43	-	62	-	47	61	54	-	-	-	-	52	-
Nigeria	-	-	-	-	-	76	-	-	76	70	70	63	72	61	70	70	+9
Tunisia	-	-	-	-	-	-	-	69	63	64	-	-	63	70	63	65	-7
Bangladesh	-	-	-	-	-	-	-	-	-	77	-	-	-	-	-	77	-
Morocco	-	-	26	-	-	-	-	-	-	-	-	-	-	-	-	26	-
Average Image	60	55	57	52	51	57	56	56	59	59	56	63	54	61	55	60	-6

Source: Pew Research Center, Global Indicators Database 2005–2019

and Tunisia hold a positive disposition toward China as compared to a 29.1% negative perception that prevails in the region. Algerians hold the most positive image of China and about 69.9% of people have a favorable view of China followed by Morocco where 64.7% of people like China. Public favorability of China in Libya was recorded at 60.4%, Tunisia at 59.3%, and Iraq at 56%. The survey found that the Jordanian (32.8%) and Lebanese (38.2%) people hold the least favorability of China in the MENA region (Figure 5.3). However, China's favorability as compared to the U.S. in the MENA region is significantly high. A majority of the respondents (54.7%) favor developing strategic relations with China as compared to the 40.8 % who hold favorability toward the U.S. in the MENA region. China enjoys favorability over the U.S. in Algeria, Iraq, Lebanon, Libya, and Tunisia. However, the favorability of the U.S. in Jordan and Morocco supersedes China's favorability by a thin margin as the survey recorded 34.7% favorability of the U.S. compared to 32.8% favorability toward China in Jordan. In Morocco, 65.7% of the people hold favorability toward

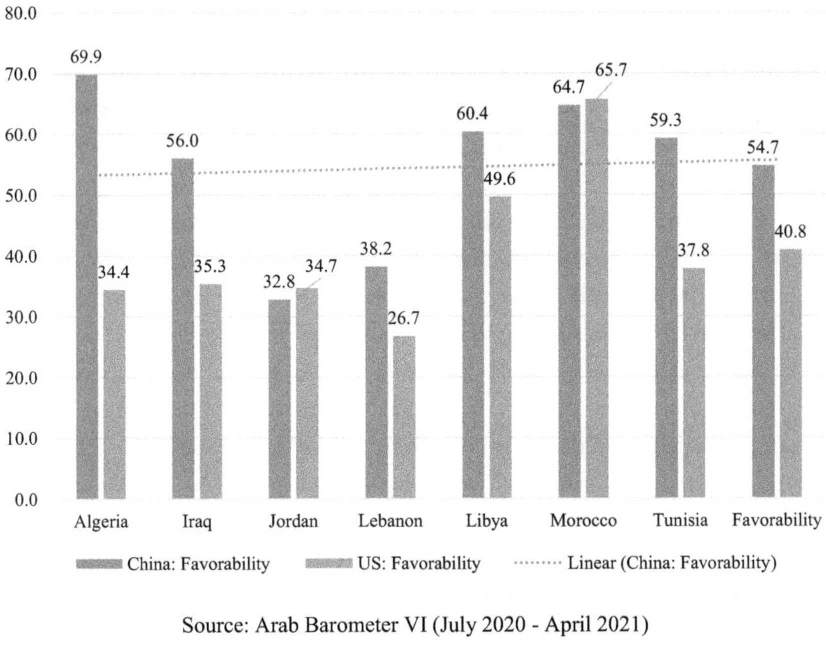

Figure 5.3: Comparative Favorability of China and the U.S. in the Middle East and North Africa (MENA) Region during 2020–2021.
Source: Arab Barometer VI (July 2020–April 2021)

the U.S. as compared to 64.7% favorability toward China during 2020–2021 (Figure 5.3). China's low favorability in Lebanon and Jordan has political and religious considerations rather than economic ones. For example, during the financial crisis in Lebanon, the Hezbollah-led government's decision to prefer China to the IMF for bail-out was strongly opposed by the other political parties that favor working with the IMF (Robbins, 2021). Lebanese society is intensively divided into sectarian lines—Muslim Sunni (36.6%), Muslim Shia (30.5%), and Christian (33.7%) and each group evaluates its relation with China in terms of its own interests. For example, Hezbollah (Shia political party) is under the strong influence of Iran, and Sunni-led political parties seek guidance from Saudi Arabia whereas Christian communities attribute more importance to stronger relations with the U.S.

China's image perception in MENA Region

BRI has driven China's strategic relations with MENA to a new height and the entire MENA region (21 countries) has signed MoUs with China to become the official partner in the BRI. China has pledged billions of U.S. dollars for investment, grants, loans, and financial aid to win the hearts and minds of the people across the MENA region. Therefore, China's popularity in the MENA has increased manifold in recent years. Arab Barometer Survey of 2019–2020 indicates that a majority of the people in the MENA region—Algeria, Iraq, Jordan, Kuwait, Lebanon, Libya, Morocco, Palestine, Sudan, Tunisia, and Yemen preferred to establish a strong economic relationship with China except for the Egyptian people who still prefer the U.S. over China for strong economic relations. The Jordanian public shows the highest preference (68.8%) to establish a strong relationship with China followed by Libya (63.1%), Tunisia (63.0%), Sudan (62%), Palestine (51.3%), Iraq (51.1%), Yemen (51%) and so on. Only Egyptian people showed the least favorability (34.4%) to establishing strong economic relations with China and instead preferred the U.S. (45.2%) for strong economic relations (Figure 5.4).

Interestingly, China's foreign policy toward the Arab world did not get popular public support in the MENA region but the support for President Xi's foreign policy is still higher than the foreign policies of U.S. President Biden toward the Arab world. The positive public perception of President Xi's foreign policy in the MENA region was recorded as high as 48.2% in Iraq, 44.7% in Libya,

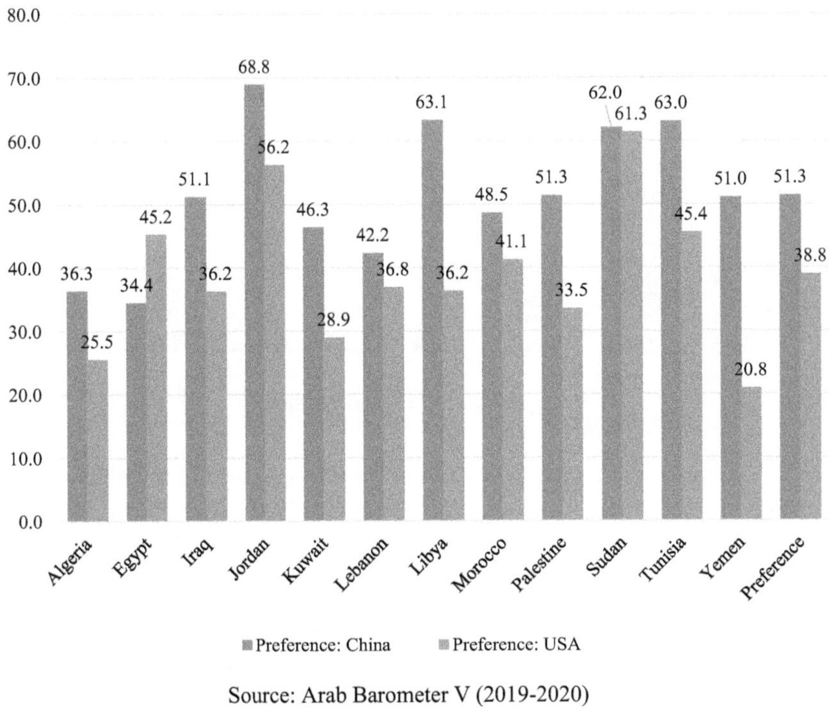

Figure 5.4: Comparative Preference for Strong Economic Relations with China and the U.S. in the MENA Region during 2019–2020.
Source: Arab Barometer V (2019–2020)

42.2% in Algeria, 41.5% in Tunisia, 40.3% in Morocco, and 25.6% in Lebanon during 2020–2021. The least favorability toward President Xi's foreign policy in the MENA region was recorded as low as 15.1% in Jordan. Public perceptions in three countries—Libya, Morocco, and Jordan indicate that people in those countries like President Biden's foreign policy more than President Xi's foreign policy toward Arab countries. For example, 46.9% of people supported President Biden's foreign policy as compared to 44.7% who supported President Xi's foreign policy toward Arab countries in Libya. Similarly, in Morocco, 44.8% supported Biden's foreign policy and only 40.3% supported President Xi's foreign policy toward Arab countries. Public support for Biden's foreign policy was recorded at 23.8% and 15.1% for President Xi's foreign policy in Jordan during 2020–2021 (Figure 5.5).

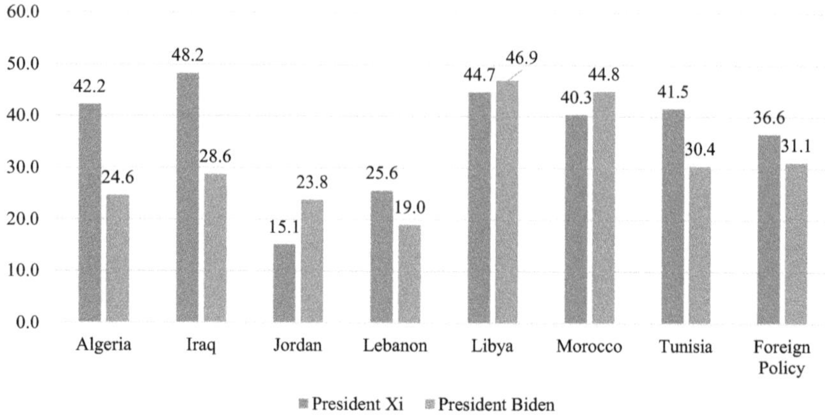

Figure 5.5: Comparative Support for Chinese President Xi and U.S. President Biden's Foreign Policy in the Middle East and North Africa (MENA) Region during 2020–2021.

The statistical data from the Arab Barometer suggests that even though China enjoys wide popularity across the MENA region and a majority of the people in the region prefer their country's economic engagement with China, China's image is still fragile and not deeply held in the region. For example, when people were asked about their preference for the origin of the company to construct quality infrastructure projects in their respective countries during the sixth wave of the Arab Barometer survey in 2020–2021. The respondents in all seven countries—Algeria, Iraq, Lebanon, Jordan, Libya, Morocco, and Tunisia opinionated that Germany will construct the best quality infrastructure project. In contrast, only one in five countries says China would build the best quality infrastructure project. Similarly, regarding the award of contracts, none of the country's citizens preferred to award a contract to a Chinese company instead German companies were preferred in four countries. Two countries preferred the U.S. companies and one opted for the French companies. Iraq was the only country where more than 15% of the citizens (22%) thought that the contract should be given to Chinese companies. In addition, only Iraqis perceived that Chinese companies pay the best salaries to the local employees. The public in four of these five countries prefers to work in U.S. companies and citizens in the other three countries pick German companies for better salaries. Therefore, public support for "China Inc" is still comparatively low in the MENA region (Robbins, 2021).

The seventh wave of the Arab Barometer survey (2021–2022) reveals that China is still more popular than the U.S. among the citizens of nine countries in the MENA region except for Morocco where people hold a more favorable perception of the U.S. than China. China holds more popularity than the U.S. in Iraq, Jordan, Lebanon, Libya, Mauritania, Palestine, Sudan, and Tunisia. However, public preference for building stronger economic ties with China has significantly decreased in 2021–2022 as compared to 2018–2019 (Table 5.2). The highest decline of 20 points in public perception of stronger economic ties with China was recorded in Jordan from 70% to 50% and in Palestine from 49% to 29% from 2018 through 2022. Public perception in Sudan decreased by 14-points from 62% to 48%; 13-points decreased in Morocco from 49% to 39%; 13-points decreased in Libya from 63% to 50%, and 5-points decreased in Lebanon from 42% to 37% in 2018 through 2022. Only a slight increase of 2-points in public perception of stronger economic ties with China was recorded in Iraq from 51% in 2018–2019 to 53% in 2020–2021 while public opinion regarding the stronger economic relationship with China in Tunisia (63%) did not change between 2018 through 2022 (Table 5.2). The fading enthusiasm in MENA for stronger economic relations with China may be the result of the weak brand name of Chinese companies and the growing perception of Chinese products as "cheap and of low quality" in the MENA region. Therefore public perception in all the nine surveyed countries indicates that the majority of the public preferred German or U.S. companies over Chinese companies for the construction of infrastructure projects in their respective country (Robbins, 2022).

Table 5.2: The Comparative Public Perception of Stronger Economic Ties with China in the MENA Region between 2018 through 2022.

Country	2018–19	2021–22	Difference
Jordan	70	50	-20
Palestine	49	29	-20
Sudan	62	48	-14
Morocco	49	36	-13
Libya	63	50	-13
Lebanon	42	37	-5
Tunisia	63	63	0
Iraq	51	53	+2

Source: Arab Barometer Survey Wave VII (October 2021–July 2022) (Robbin, 2022)

Chinese companies' poor performance and public perception of Chinese products and services as "cheap and of low quality" can affect Chinese economic activities and can damage China's national reputation in the MENA region. White (2012) argues that global companies, their brands, and products have a crucial place in people's daily lives and can potentially affect the national reputation and overall image of the country of origin. Therefore, companies through their brands and products can contribute both positively and negatively to the overall image of country-of-origin and they also can improve the country's competitive reputation on a global scale and vice versa. For example, Lee et al. (2008) noted the public consumption of South Korean companies' products resulted in their perception of South Korea in the U.S. as a "high technology" and "advanced economy". Similarly, the U.S. companies' products, policies, and adherence to corporate social responsibility enhance the U.S. influence and positive public perception in Romania and around the world (C. White et al., 2011; C. L. White, 2012).

China's popularity and favorable image in the Islamic world are largely grounded in public perception of its non-colonial outlook, its pledges of hefty economic investment under the BRI, its economic model of development, and growing anti-US sentiment in the Islamic world. The U.S. has been perceived as an economic threat in the MENA region, and China has emerged as a potential substitute both politically and economically to the U.S. in the Islamic world. The Islamic leadership and a majority of the public in the Islamic countries see the Sino-Islamic relationship as based on equal terms, mutual respect, and mutual benefits with a belief that China will never use the colonial tactics of the West to exploit the Islamic world for its own political and economic benefits. Therefore, China's interminable popularity in the Islamic world will largely depend on its ability to persuade people in the Islamic countries that its economic engagements and foreign policy will benefit the entire Muslim Ummah and the Islamic world. Failing this will likely fade China's wider public support in the Islamic world in the years to come (Khan et al., 2023; Robbins, 2021).

Africa's perception of China's image

Historically, China maintains strong political, economic, military, and sociocultural relations with the African continent. Under the auspices of the BRI, the historical relations between China and Africa have transformed into a strategic partnership and almost the entire African continent (54 countries) has officially joined BRI to enjoy Chinese investment for economic and infrastructural development (Table 1.1). Therefore, Africa has become China's largest investment destination, and Chinese foreign direct investment (FDI) in Africa reached US$5.4 billion in a single year in 2018. Chinese FDI stock in Africa has raised to US$43.4 billion in 2020, making China the single largest investor in Africa (Fu, 2021; Khan et al., 2023; Oluwole, 2022). The trade volume between China and Africa has also witnessed a rapid increase and touched US$192 billion in 2019 (Sanny & Selormey, 2021).

Under the BRI, China's economic engagement, financial support (aid, and grants), and massive investment in infrastructure, energy, and real-state sectors have increased China's popularity and influence in Africa. According to the Afro Barometer's National Survey conducted in 34 African countries—Angola, Benin, Burkina Faso, Botswana, Cabo Verde, Cameroon, Côte d'Ivoire, Eswatini, Ethiopia, Gabon, Gambia, Ghana, Guinea, Kenya, Lesotho, Liberia, Malawi, Mali, Mauritius, Morocco, Mozambique, Namibia, Niger, Nigeria, Senegal, Sierra Leone, South Africa, Sudan, Tunisia, Togo, Tanzania, Uganda, Zambia, Zimbabwe between 2019 through 2021 indicate that a majority of Africans (63%) hold a positive perception of China's economic assistance and a positive economic and political impacts on their country compared to 14% of the Africans who think otherwise. Moroccan people hold the highest positive perception of China's economic influence (80%) in their country followed by the people of Cabo Verde (77%), Mauritius (75%), Eswatini (74%), Benin (73%), Gabon (73%), Kenya (72%), Cameroon (72%), Sudan (71%), Mali (70%) . . . . and Lesotho (50%). However, positive perceptions of China's economic influence in a few African countries like Sierra Leone (21%), Malawi (38%), Zimbabwe (39%), Uganda (44%), and Ethiopia (47%) were reported by less than half of the citizens who agreed to the notion of China's positive economic influence in their respective countries (Sanny & Selormey, 2021; Table 5.3).

The comparative data of two national surveys conducted by the Afro Barometer in 2014–2015 and 2019–2021 reveal that positive public perception of China's economic influence in 24 out of 30 African countries has dwindled over the past five years, from 71% in 2014–2015 to 59% in 2019–2021 (Table 5.3). The highest decline (37-points) in the positive public perception of China's economic influence was reported in Sierra Leone followed by Zimbabwe (29-points), Botswana (24-points), Malawi (21-points), Niger (21-points), Mali (20-points) . . . .. and Cabo Verde (1-point). Only a significant increase in the positive public perception of China's economic influence was reported in Morocco (31-points) and Mauritius

Table 5.3: The Comparative Public Perception of the Positive Economic Influence of China in Africa between 2014–2015 and 2019–2021.

Country	2014–2015	2019–2021	Difference
Sierra Leone	58	21	-37
Zimbabwe	68	39	-29
Botswana	76	52	-24
Niger	80	59	-21
Malawi	59	38	-21
Mali	90	70	-20
Tongo	71	53	-18
Mozambique	68	50	-18
Burkina Faso	77	60	-17
Côte d'Ivoire	70	53	-17
Namibia	76	61	-15
Gabon	87	73	-14
Zambia	75	61	-14
South Africa	69	55	-14
Tunisia	74	61	-13
Senegal	73	60	-13
Uganda	57	44	-13
Nigeria	67	55	-12
Lesotho	61	50	-11
Guinea	72	62	-10
Cameroon	81	72	-9
Ghana	61	53	-8
Tanzania	71	64	-7
Liberia	68	61	-7
Kenya	75	72	-3
Cabo Verde	78	77	-1
Sudan	70	71	+1
Benin	70	73	+3
Mauritius	69	75	+6
Morocco	49	80	+31
Ethiopia	-	47	-
Gambia	-	51	-
Angola	-	52	-
Eswatini	-	74	-

Source: Afro Barometer National Survey—2014–2015 and 2019–2021 (Sanny & Selormey, 2021)

(6-points) followed by a slight increase in Benin (3-points), and Sudan (1-point) (Sanny & Selormey, 2021; Table 5.3).

Despite the huge economic investment under the auspices of the BRI, African countries, and its general public still prefer the U.S. model (33%) for development over China's model of development (22%) in 2019–2021. The survey indicates that 23 out of 34 surveyed countries in Africa ranked the U.S. model of development at the top whereas only five countries—Benin, Botswana, Burkina Faso, Mali, and Niger preferred China's model of development for their country. China has invested multibillion dollars in Africa and arranged substantial loans of US$153 billion to African countries between 2000 and 2019 (Pairault, 2021). In addition, the Export-Import Bank of China (EXIM) pledges a US$1 trillion investment in Africa for the next decade under the BRI (Guerraoui, 2016) but interestingly, only an average of 47% of Africans know about China's economic support and investment in Africa. And among them, a majority of 57% believe that their country has borrowed too much loan from China (Sanny & Selormey, 2021).

Another study conducted by the Ichikowitz Family Foundation—a South African non-profit organization in 15 African countries in 2022 reveals that African youth hold a positive image of China and a whopping majority of 76% of young Africans believe that China has a big positive impact on the African region. The growing popularity of China in Africa is grounded in the affordability of its cheap products, economic investments, support for infrastructure development, training and skill development of the local employees, creation of local job opportunities, and facilitation of African exports to China (Odonkor, 2022). Although China's economic engagement, hefty investments, and trade generated a positive perception of China in Africa, there is significant apprehension about the environmental, social, workplace, and labor practices of Chinese firms in Africa. The African perception of Chinese businesses in three African countries (Nigeria, Kenya, and South Africa) indicates that public perception of Chinese business is more negative than positive in 42.4% of the responses (Geerts et al., 2014). China's growing economic engagement and financial loans (debt) to African countries are also under widespread scrutiny and the West cynically criticizes it as a "debt trap diplomacy" to gain strategic benefits and political advantages in the region (Green, 2019; Scott, 2021). Afro Barometer National survey (2019–2021) also showed concerns of the African public about the growing Chinese debt in their respective country. Some scholars (Brautigam, 2020; Green, 2019) argue that China's hefty loans to African countries are unsustainable and there is a risk of losing national assets if they fail to pay back their loans to China. However, the Chinese government and various scholars (Brautigam, 2020; Jones & Hameiri, 2020; Singh, 2020) have debunked the "debt trap diplomacy" theory. There is no substantial evidence that suggests that China used predatory behavior to gain political, economic, or military advantages in Africa. Singh (2020) argues that Chinese loans are not the major drivers of debt distress in African countries and China never used debt facilities to control natural resources or strategic assets or to expand its military presence in the region. It did not deliberately entangle an African country in debt to extract unfair or strategic benefits including the "asset seizures" in Africa (Brautigam, 2020, p. 6).

Western world's perception of China

China's global image perception encounters serious challenges in Western countries and its negative image perception is recorded at or near a "historic high" in the Pew Research Center survey in 2020 (Silver et al., 2020). The unfavorable view of China in some Western countries rose to 24% between 2019 and 2020. China's global image surveys conducted by the Pew Research Center between 2005 through 2020 indicate that more than 50% of people in the 11 major Western countries (Australia, the UK, Sweden, Germany, Netherlands, the U.S., Spain, France, Canada, Italy, Belgium, and Denmark) and two East Asian nations (South Korea and Japan) hold a negative attitude toward China (Table 5.4). Although China did not hold a favorable image in a majority of those countries in the past, the recent survey indicates a drastic increase in public negative perception of China's image between 2019 and 2020. For example, the negative perception of China in Australia increased by 24% from 57% in 2019 to 81% in 2020. The unfavorable view of China in the UK increased up to 19% from 55% in 2019 to 74% in 2020. The negative public perception of China in Sweden, Germany, and the Netherlands witnessed an increase of 15% between 2019 and 2020. The U.S. public's negative perception of China increased by 13% from 60% in 2019 to 73% in 2020. South Korea witnessed an increase of 12%, Spain 10%, France 8%, Canada 6%, Italy 5%, and Japan 1% between 2019 and 2020 (Table 5.4).

In the past four years, China's global image has been damaged intensively in Asia Pacific, Europe, and North Africa and negative public perception about China is at "historic highs" in many of the 19 countries in the Asia Pacific, Europe, and North America. A majority of the people in those regions showed

Table 5.4: China's Unfavorable Image Perception in the Western World from 2005 through 2020.

Countries	2005	2006	2007	2008	2009	2010	2011	2012	2013	2014	2015	2016	2017	2018	2019	2020	Avg. Score	19–20 Change
Australia	-	-	-	40	-	-	-	-	35	-	33	39	32	47	57	81	46	+24
UK	16	14	27	36	29	35	26	35	31	38	37	44	37	35	55	74	36	+19
Sweden	-	-	40	-	-	-	-	-	-	-	-	59	49	52	70	85	59	+15
Germany	37	33	54	68	63	61	59	67	64	64	60	60	53	54	56	71	58	+15
Netherlands	34	-	-	-	-	-	-	-	-	-	-	43	42	45	58	73	49	+15
U.S.	35	29	39	42	38	36	36	40	52	55	54	55	47	47	60	73	46	+13
South Korea*	-	-	42	49	54	56	-	-	50	42	37	-	61	60	63	75	54	+12
Spain	21	38	43	56	41	38	39	46	47	55	50	56	43	48	53	63	46	+10
France	42	42	51	72	60	59	49	60	58	53	49	61	52	54	62	70	56	+8
Canada	27	-	37	-	36	-	-	-	45	-	48	40	40	45	67	73	46	+6
Italy	-	-	61	-	-	-	-	64	62	70	57	61	59	60	57	62	61	+5
Japan*	-	71	67	84	69	69	61	84	93	91	89	86	83	78	85	86	80	+1
Belgium	-	-	-	-	-	-	-	-	-	-	-	-	-	-	-	71	71	-
Denmark	-	-	-	-	-	-	-	-	-	-	-	-	-	-	-	75	75	-
Average Image	29	39	45	54	47	49	42	55	53	58	50	54	50	52	62	74	56	+11

Source: Pew Research Center, Global Indicators Database 2005–2019
*Japan and South Korea are part of East Asia.

strong resentment and negative opinions toward China's human rights policies (79%), China's growing military power (72%), economic contest with China (66%), and China's involvement in domestic country politics (59%). The U.S. favorability over China has also increased in those regions except Singapore and Malaysia (a Muslim country) where the public still views China more favorably than the U.S. (The Pew Research Center, 2022). In the last four years, public perception of China's unfavorable image increased in Japan from 78% in 2018 to 87% in 2022, negative public perception in Australia increased up to 87% in 2022, and the U.S. witnessed an increase from 79% in 2019 to 82% in 2022, in South Korea negative public perception about China raised from 60% in 2018 to 80% in 2022. Public perception in European countries that once held a positive view of China in 2018 also changed into negative perceptions in 2022. For example, China's negative perception in Poland increased from 37% in 2018 to 55% in 2022, in Hungary from 47% to 52%, in Greece from 48% to 50%, in Spain from 48% to 63%, in the UK from 35% to 69%, and negative public perception about China in Italy raised from 60% in 2018 to 64% in 2022. China's negative public perception in Israel also rose from 25% in 2018 to 46% in 2022. However, Singapore (34%) and Malaysia (39%) observed relatively low negative public perception of China in 2022 (Silver et al., 2022; The Pew Research Center, 2022).

Public opinion about China in European countries is also negative and hostile. Turcsányi et al. (2020) study of public opinion about China in 13 European countries (UK, France, Germany, Czechia (Czech Republic), Spain, Hungary, Sweden Latvia, Poland, Italy, Slovakia, Serbia, and Russia) indicates that European hold negative disposition about China and the majority views are predominantly negative. People's perception of China in 10 out of 13 European countries is negative—Western and Northern Europe hold the most negative views of China, followed by Southern and Central Europe which end up in the middle, but still anti-China sentiments are predominantly palpable. China is only viewed positively in Eastern Europe. The study recorded the highest anti-China sentiments in Sweden where 60% of respondents hold adverse views of China and only 12% feel positive about China. Public opinion of China in the UK, Germany, France, and Czechia is decisively negative. In contrast, the respondents in Russia and Serbia view China more positively, and more than 60% of them hold a very positive or positive view of China. Latvia is the only European Union (EU) country that holds a positive view of China, even though the positive ratio remained low (43%). It is higher than the negative perception (28%) in the country. Anti-China sentiments in the Visegrád Group in Central Europe—Czech

Republic, Poland, Slovakia, and Hungary are relatively low but predominant views of China in those countries are still largely negative.

China's image in the past three years has also depreciated in Europe. For example, the study reveals that two-thirds of respondents' perception of China in the UK has worsened in the past three years. Similar patterns were reported in the public perception of China in Sweden, Germany, and France. The public perception of China in three countries, i.e., Russia, Serbia, and Latvia has only improved in the past three years. The European public only views trade relations with China more positively except for the public perception in the UK, France, and Sweden that tilted toward negative sentiments. However, there is strong resentment against Chinese investment and the BRI and only a handful of countries like Russia, Serbia, Latvia, Poland, and Italy hold a positive view of Chinese investment and the BRI. Whereas the remaining countries are overwhelmed with negative perceptions. Regarding the construction of the 5G Network in Europe, cooperation with Chinese companies is least favored. Most of the respondents voted in favor of cooperation with the EU, Japan, the U.S., and South Korean companies to construct a 5G Network in their respective countries. Only Russian respondents favor cooperating with Chinese companies in this regard. In addition, China's military rise, its human rights record, and China's impacts on the global environment and democracy in other countries were also perceived negatively in Europe (Turcsányi et al., 2020). There is also fear that prevailing anti-Russia sentiments due to the Russia-Ukraine war in Europe, particularly in Central and Eastern Europe will likely create further complications for China's global image due to its congenial relations and support for Russia in the Ukraine war (Kurlantzick, 2022b).

In Europe, China is perceived as a major economic power and more powerful as compared to the U.S., Russia, and the EU. However, its soft power projection is still very limited in Europe due to a lack of public trust in China as compared to the EU and the U.S. which are far ahead of China. Though a majority of the respondents in European countries acknowledged China's support for COVID-19, they still believed in "anti-China" conspiracy theories about the origin and spread of Coronavirus reported by the mainstream Western media: "Coronavirus was artificially made in a Chinese lab and intentionally spread" and it "spread due to Chinese people eating bats and wild animals". Those allegations strengthened the cultural stereotypes about China and seriously damaged its international reputation in and across Europe (Jia & Lu, 2021; Silver et al., 2022; Turcsányi et al., 2020). For example, Gong's (2021) study of China's image-building through humanitarian public diplomacy during the global crisis of COVID-19 reveals that although China's humanitarian and medical support in the context of the COVID-19 pandemic has largely been acknowledged, it did not substantially enhance China's positive image in Southeast Asia. China's humanitarian public diplomacy faces various challenges. For example, China's initial response and pledges for a small donation to the Philippines during Typhoon Haiyan in 2013 were strongly criticized by the Western media and interpreted through the lens of the China-Philippines territorial dispute in the South China Sea (Salmons, 2019). During the Rohingya crisis, China's role was disparaged on the ground that China, instead of solving the crisis, protected self-interest and prioritized development over human rights in Bangladesh (Khan & Ahmed, 2020; McPherson et al., 2020). Similarly, China's support for Nepal was linked with the question of Taiwan and China-India rivalry for influence in the region in 2015 (Denyer, 2015).

Western scholars offered various reasons for the tumbling of China's global image in the West: (a) Western perception that China initially covered up the COVID-19 outbreak in Wuhan and later strictly implemented a zero-COVID strategy that cut it off from the rest of the world, curtailing people-to-people contacts, reduce its soft power projection due to return of foreign students, and stoppage of foreign visitors (e.g. journalists, academicians, tourists, traders, and business community), which were once-effective tools of China's public diplomacy and soft power campaign and the vital conduits of China's favorable view back in their countries, particularly in the developing world. China's strict COVID policy also steered the sharpest decline in outbound Chinese tourism that once promoted people-to-people networks between China and rest of the world and was a major source of income for many countries in Asia, Europe, Africa and other part of the world (Custer et al., 2018; Kotaky, 2022; Kurlantzick, 2022b, 2022c); (b) The rising authoritarianism at home—a shift from President Hu Jintao's consensus authoritarianism to President Xi's more authoritative one-man-rule (Kurlantzick, 2022b, 2022c); (c) alleged political repression and human rights violations in Xinjiang and Hong Kong; (d) China's enactment of assertive foreign policy to accomplish China's dream of global leadership and adoption of "belligerent public diplomacy" (e.g., "wolf warrior" diplomacy) to reciprocate the West tit for tat—a strategic foreign policy shift from Deng Xiaoping's cooperative foreign policy of "keeping a low profile" and "not seeking leadership" to Xi Jinping's more assertive and competitive foreign policy of rejuvenation of China and bidding for global influence and leadership; (e) China's alleged use of economic coercion against nation-states and multinationals (e.g., use of economic sanctions—tariff and non-tariff barrier on Australian products) (Kurlantzick,

2022b; Martin, 2021; Xie, 2021); (f) China's growing strategic partnership with Russia and support in Russia-Ukraine war; and (g) poor branding of Chinese companies and firms (e.g., allegation and ban on Huawei 5G technology) and depleting trust on Chinese model of development even within China (e.g., prolonged lockdown in China's financial hub and the largest city—Shanghai) are major contributors of China's growing negative image perception in the Western world (Kurlantzick, 2022a, 2022b, 2022c; Martin, 2021).

On the other hand, China has developed strong relations with Latin American countries under the auspices of the BRI. In recent years, China's popularity has increased in Latin America. The latest Latinobarómetro survey (2020) indicated that China holds a positive and friendly image in 18 Latin American countries, namely, Argentina, Brazil, Bolivia, Chile, Colombia, Costa Rica, EI Salvador, Ecuador, Guatemala, Honduras, Mexico, Nicaragua, Paraguay, República Dominicana, Panama, Peru, Uruguay, and Venezuela. A majority respondents (73.1%) in those countries view their country's relationship with China as "very good" or "fairly good". Only 26.9% of respondents perceived their country's relations with China as rather poor (14.7%) or very poor (12.2%). Similarly, 58.5% of the respondents in 18 Latin countries showed a positive disposition and held a favorable opinion of China in 2020. At the same time, 41.5% of the respondents hold a negative perception of China. The survey indicates that the El Salvadorian public holds the most positive perception of China and 71% of the respondents view China as a favorable country followed by Nicaragua (68.8%), Costa Rica (66.3%), the Dominican Republic (62.7%), México (61%), and so on. The least favorability (52.5%) and most negative perception (47.5%) of China were recorded in Uruguay and during 2020 (Table 5.5).

Another study by Eichenauer et al. (2021) on China's image in developing countries (Latin America) using the cross-section data from 2002 to 2013 to examine how Chinese aid, investment, and export affect public opinion about China in 18 Latin American countries overruled the widespread criticism, that China's hefty investment and economic penetration may deteriorate China's public perception in the respective country. In contrast, they found that China's economic engagement created winners and losers and boosted a more positive image of China in the economically privileged, young, and educated, populations in those countries.

Another China's global image survey (2018) conducted by the Academy of Contemporary China and World Studies in collaboration with Kantar—London based data analytics and brand consulting company in 22 countries in Asia (China, India, Indonesia, Japan, Saudi Arabia, and South Korea), Europe

Table 5.5: Descriptive Statistics of Public Perception of China in Latin America during 2020.

	Public Opinion about China			
Countries	Very Favorable	Somewhat Favorable	Somewhat Unfavorable	Very Unfavorable
Argentina (*N*=970)	113 (11.6%)	402 (41.4%)	248 (25.6%)	207 (21.3%)
Bolivia (*N*=1071)	103 (9.6%)	475 (44.4%)	297 (27.7%)	196 (18.3%)
Brazil (*N*=1051)	105 (10.0%)	443 (42.2%)	369 (35.1%)	134 (12.7%)
Chile (*N*=1069)	88 (8.2%)	549 (51.4%)	282 (26.4%)	150 (14.0%)
Colombia (*N*=1041)	145 (13.9%)	363 (34.9%)	287 (27.6%)	246 (23.6%)
Costa Rica (*N*=895)	160 (17.9%)	433 (48.4%)	158 (17.7%)	144 (16.1%)
Rep. Dominicana (*N*=875)	143 (16.3%)	406 (46.4%)	159 (18.2%)	167 (19.1%)
Ecuador (*N*=1080)	127 (11.8%)	488 (45.2%)	287 (26.6%)	178 (16.5%)
El Salvador (*N*=846)	212 (25.1%)	389 (46.0%)	139 (16.4%)	106 (12.5%)
Guatemala (*N*=703)	109 (15.5%)	318 (45.2%)	141 (20.1%)	135 (19.2%)
Honduras (*N*=738)	157 (21.3%)	291 (39.4%)	135 (18.3%)	155 (21.0%)
México (*N*=1035)	118 (11.4%)	513 (49.6%)	263 (25.4%)	141 (13.6%)
Nicaragua (*N*=756)	185 (24.5%)	335 (44.3%)	131 (17.3%)	105 (13.9%)
Panamá (*N*=893)	136 (15.2%)	386 (43.2%)	200 (22.4%)	171 (19.1%)
Paraguay (*N*=838)	65 (7.8%)	433 (51.7%)	221 (26.4%)	119 (14.2%)
Perú (*N*=1063)	149 (14.0%)	449 (42.2%)	273 (25.7%)	192 (18.1%)
Uruguay (*N*=986)	95 (9.6%)	423 (42.9%)	274 (27.8%)	194 (19.7%)
Venezuela (*N*=1095)	227 (20.7%)	414 (37.8%)	192 (17.5%)	262 (23.9%)
Total (*N*=17005)	2437 (14.3%)	7510 (44.2%)	4056 (23.9%)	3002 (17.7%)

Source: Latinobarómetro Survey, 2020

(France, Germany, Italy, Netherlands, Russia, Spain, Turkey, and the UK), North America (Canada, Mexico, and the U.S.), South America (Argentina, Brazil, and Chile), Oceania (Australia) and Africa (South Africa) clearly indicate the bifurcation of China's positive and negative image perception among the developing and developed countries. Although China is on the steady path of improving its national image on a global scale, its political image is still largely sullied and its paraphernalia of attraction is limited to the fields of science and technology, economy, and culture. China's global image is perceived more positively in the developing world where people ascribed high expectations to China for playing a leading role in all aspects of global governance. China's global influence is on the rise but still not proportionate to the U.S. and its development path and model lack predilection over the U.S. model in the majority of the countries across the world (China National Image Global Survey, 2018).

It is important to note that large-scale international surveys conducted by research centers such as the Pew Research Center and the Arab/Afro Barometer can provide statistically significant and representative findings regarding the perception of China on a global scale. However, these surveys are subject to various limitations, including sampling bias, false responses influenced by social and political desirability, exclusion or inclusion of specific groups or regions, potential bias in questioning, limited comprehension of cultural context, particularly regarding China and Chinese culture, and restricted coverage of various aspects of China's image. Most surveys tend to focus on the political and economic dimensions of China's global image, which may not capture the full range of perceptions. Therefore, it is important to consider these limitations when interpreting survey results and understanding the perception of China on a global scale.

References

Arab Barometer. (2021). *Arab Barometer VI (July 2020–April 2021)* . <https://www.arabbarometer.org/survey-data/data-downloads/>

Brautigam, D. (2020). A critical look at Chinese 'debt-trap diplomacy': The rise of a meme. *Area Development and Policy, 5*(1), 1–14. <https://doi.org/10.1080/23792949.2019.1689828>

China National Image Global Survey. (2018). <http://www.accws.cn/wp-content/uploads/2020/09/EN.pdf>

Custer, S., Russell, B., DiLorenzo, M., Cheng, M., Ghose, S., Sims, J., Turner, J., & Desai, H. (2018). *Ties that bind: Quantifying China's public diplomacy and its "good neighbor" effect.* Williamsburg, VA: AidData at William & Mary. <https://www.aiddata.org/publications/ties-that-bind>

Denyer, S. (2015, April 28). The aftermath of Nepal's earthquake exposes Asia's geopolitical fault lines. *The Washington Post.* <https://www.washingtonpost.com/news/worldviews/wp/2015/04/28/the-aftermath-of-nepals-earthquake-exposes-asias-geopolitical-fault-lines/>

Eichenauer, V. Z., Fuchs, A., & Brückner, L. (2021). The effects of trade, aid, and investment on China's image in Latin America. *Journal of Comparative Economics, 49*(2), 483–498. <https://doi.org/10.1016/j.jce.2020.08.005>

Fu, Y. (2021, November 22). The quiet China-Africa revolution: Chinese investment. *The Diplomat.* <https://thediplomat.com/2021/11/the-quiet-china-africa-revolution-chinese-investment/>

Geerts, S., Xinwa, N., & Rossouw, D. (2014). *Africans' perceptions of Chinese Business in Africa: A survey* (1st ed.). Globethics.net/Ethics Institute of South Africa.

Gong, L. (2021). Humanitarian diplomacy as an instrument for China's image-building. *Asian Journal of Comparative Politics, 6*(3), 238–252. <https://doi.org/10.1177/20578911211019257>

Green, M. (2019, April 25). China's debt diplomacy: How Belt and Road threatens countries' ability to achieve self-reliance. *Foreign Policy.* <https://foreignpolicy.com/2019/04/25/chinas-debt-diplomacy/>

Guerraoui, S. (2016, May 15). Morocco establishes 'strategic partnership' with China. *The Arab Weekly.* <https://thearabweekly.com/morocco-establishes-strategic-partnership-china>

Jia, W., & Lu, F. (2021). US media's coverage of China's handling of COVID-19: Playing the role of the fourth branch of government or the fourth estate? *Global Media and China*, *6*(1), 8–23. <https://doi.org/10.1177/2059436421994003>

Jones, L., & Hameiri, S. (2020). *Debunking the myth of "debt-trap diplomacy": How recipient countries shape China's Belt and Road Initiative.* Chatham House.

Khan, M. K., Pratt, C. B., Akhtar, N. (2023). China's public diplomacy for image making in Islamic North Africa: Frames of the Belt and Road Initiative in Daily News Egypt. In: A. A. Anani-Bossman, T. E. Mudzanani, C. B. Pratt, I. A. Blankson (Eds.), *Public relations management in Africa Volume 1.* Cham: Palgrave Macmillan. <https://doi.org/10.1007/978-3-031-26704-8_5>

Khan, M. T., & Ahmed, S. (2020). Dealing with the Rohingya crisis: The relevance of the general assembly and R2P. *Asian Journal of Comparative Politics*, *5*(2), 121–143. <https://doi.org/10.1177/2057891119868312>

Kotaky, A. (2022, March 3). China's Covid stance has created a $280 Billion Black Hole for Global Tourism. *Bloomberg News.* < https://www.bloomberg.com/news/features/2022-03-03/china-s-covid-stance-has-created-a-280-billion-black-hole-for-global-tourism>

Kurlantzick, J. (2022a). *Beijing's global media offensive: China's uneven campaign to influence Asia and the World.* New York: Oxford University Press, forthcoming.

Kurlantzick, J. (2022b). *China's collapsing global image: How Beijing's unpopularity is undermining its strategic, economic, and diplomatic goals* (Issue July, pp. 1–38). Council on Foreign Relations. <https://www.cfr.org/report/chinas-collapsing-global-image>

Kurlantzick, J. (2022c, July 22). China's poor global image is undermining its strategic goals. *The Diplomat.* <https://thediplomat.com/2022/07/chinas-poor-global-image-is-undermining-its-strategic-goals/>

Latinobarometro. (2020). *Latinobarómetro survey 2020.* <https://www.latinobarometro.org/latOnline.jsp>

Lee, S., Toth, E. L., & Shin, H. (2008). Cognitive categorisation and routes of national reputation formation: US opinion leaders' views on South Korea. *Place Branding and Public Diplomacy*, *4*(4), 272–286. <https://doi.org/10.1057/pb.2008.17>

Martin, P. (2021, October 6). Why China is alienating the world: Backlash is building—but Beijing can't seem to recalibrate. *Foreign Affairs.* <https://www.foreignaffairs.com/articles/china/2021-10-06/why-china-alienating-world>

McPherson, P., Paul, R., & Naing, S. (2020). China struggles in new diplomatic role, trying to return Rohingya to Myanmar. *Reuters.* Available at: <Https://Www.Reuters.Com/Article/Us-Myanmar-Rohingya-China-Insight-IdUSKBN1ZJ0SY> (Accessed 12 October 2020).

Odonkor, A. A. (2022, June 18). What's behind China's positive image in Africa? *GTNCGTN.* <https://news.cgtn.com/news/2022-06-18/What-s-behind-China-s-positive-image-in-Africa--1aWwlwx0EcE/index.html>

Oluwole, V. (2022, February 20). China ranks ahead of America as the largest investor in Africa since 2010. *Africa Business Insider*. <https://africa.businessinsider.com/local/markets/china-ranks-ahead-of-america-as-the-largest-investor-in-africa-since-2010/62532rh>

Pairault, T. (2021, August 11). China's presence in Africa is at heart political. *The Diplomat*. <https://thediplomat.com/2021/08/chinas-presence-in-africa-is-at-heart-political/>

Robbins, M. (2021, December 8). Fragile popularity: Arab attitudes towards China. *Manara Magazine*. <https://manaramagazine.org/2021/12/08/fragile-popularity-arab-attitudes-towards-china/#_edn1>

Robbins, M. (2022). Public views of the U.S.-China competition in MENA. *Arab Barometer, VII*, 1–17. <https://www.arabbarometer.org/wp-content/uploads/ABVII_US-China_Report-EN-1.pdf?ct=t(EMAIL_CAMPAIGN_8_11_2022_14_10_COPY_03)>

Salmons, R. (2019). Disaster relief, international status and regional order: A case study of Typhoon Haiyan. *Global Change, Peace & Security, 31*(3), 283–301. <https://doi.org/10.1080/14781158.2019.1591356>

Sanny, J. A.-N., & Selormey, E. (2021, November 15). Africans welcome China's influence but maintain democratic aspirations. *Afro Barometer, Dispatch No. 489*, 1–23. <https://www.afrobarometer.org/publication/ad489-africans-welcome-chinas-influence-maintain-democratic-aspirations/>

Scott, C. D. (2021, September 27). Does China's involvement in African elections and politics hurt democracy? *Democracy in Africa*. <http://democracyinafrica.org/does-chinas-involvement-in-african-elections-and-politics-hurt-democracy/>

Silver, L., Devlin, K., & Huang, C. (2020, October 6). Unfavorable views of China reach historic highs in many countries. *Rew Research Center*, 1–29. <https://www.pewresearch.org/global/2020/10/06/unfavorable-views-of-china-reach-historic-highs-in-many-countries/>

Silver, L., Huang, C., & Clancy, L. (2022, June 29). Negative views of China tied to critical views of its policies on Human Rights. *The Pew Research Center*. <https://www.pewresearch.org/global/2022/06/29/negative-views-of-china-tied-to-critical-views-of-its-policies-on-human-rights/>

Singh, A. (2020). The myth of "debt-trap diplomacy" and realities of Chinese development finance. *Third World Quarterly, 42*(2), 239–253. <https://doi.org/10.1080/01436597.2020.1807318>

The Pew Research Center. (2022, June 29). U.S. receives more positive ratings than China in most countries. *The Pew Research Center*, 1. <https://www.pewresearch.org/fact-tank/2022/06/29/across-19-countries-more-people-see-the-u-s-than-china-favorably-but-more-see-chinas-influence-growing/ft_2022-06-29_chinaus_01/>

Turcsányi, R. Q., Šimalčík, M., Kironská, K., Sedláková, R., Čeněk, J., Findor, A., Buchel, O., Hruška, M., Brona, A., & Bērziņa-Čerenkova, U. A. (2020). European public opinion on China in the age of COVID-19: Differences and common ground across the continent. In *Bratislava, Czech Republic: Central European Institute of Asian Studies*. <https://www.academia.edu/download/64968715/COMP_poll_final.pdf>

White, C. L. (2012). Brands and national image: An exploration of inverse country-of-origin effect. *Place Branding and Public Diplomacy, 8*(2), 110–118. <https://doi.org/10.1057/pb.2012.6>

White, C., Vanc, A., & Coman, I. (2011). Corporate social responsibility in transitional countries: Public relations as a component of public diplomacy in Romania. *International Journal of Strategic Communication*, *5*(4), 281–292. <https://doi.org/10.1080/1553118X.2010.549815>

Xie, Y. (2021, October 22). China's economic sanctions made Australia more confident. *The Interpreter*. <https://www.lowyinstitute.org/the-interpreter/china-s-economic-sanctions-made-australia-more-confident>

VI Research Methodology

The research methodology mainly depends on the proposed research questions/ hypotheses. This research study is designed to investigate China's image in the Islamic world: How Islamic English news media constructed China's image in the Islamic world and how it changed over time. Therefore, the researcher used longitudinal quantitative content analysis (Peng, 2004; Willnat & Luo, 2011; Xiang, 2013; Zhang & Cameron, 2003; Zhong & Zhang, 2016) to investigate the news coverage related to China in Islamic English news media from January 1, 2009, through December 31, 2018. The rationale behind the selection of content analysis as a method is its "objective, systematic, and quantitative description of the manifest content of communication" (Berelson, 1952, p. 18). Moreover, it is a more reliable and widely used research method for investigating the national image (Han & Wang, 2014; G. Han & Wang, 2012; He et al., 2012; Pjesivac et al., 2018; Scott, 2015; Semetko et al., 1992; Xiang, 2013; Yang & Liu, 2012).

Content analysis

Content analysis is one of the fastest-growing methods used in journalism and mass communication research (Funk, 2013; Riffe & Freitag, 1997). It is not only limited to traditional news media content (Baker & King, 2016; Bodle et al., 2011; Gicevic et al., 2016; Mastro & Sink, 2018; Riffe & Freitag, 1997) but also is widely used in social media research as well (Austin & Gaither, 2016; Bellström et al., 2016; Cheung et al., 2016; Lerman et al., 2016; Neuendorf, 2017; Rand, 2016; Wang et al., 2017). Berelson (1952) defines content analysis as an objective and systematic research method that is used for the quantitative explanation of the manifest content of communication (p. 18). Krippendorff, (1980) argues that content analysis is a more reliable and valid "research technique for making replicative and valid inferences from data to their context" (p. 21). Whereas Kolbe and Burnett (1991) argue that content analysis is an observational approach that is used by the researcher to systematically analyze the symbolic content of all forms of recorded communication. The symbolic content can be analyzed at many levels (image, word, roles, etc.) (p. 243). Therefore, content analysis is often used in all forms of communication research.

Stempel (2003) argues that content analysis is "a formal system for doing something we all do informally rather frequently—draw conclusions from observations of content" (p. 209). Whereas, Riffe et al. (2014) define it as "the systematic and replicable examination of symbols of communication, which have been assigned numeric values according to valid measurement rules and the analysis of relationships involving those values using statistical methods, to describe the communication, draw inferences about its meaning, or infer from the communication to its context, both of production and consumption" (p. 25).

Content analysis is an objective, systematic, quantitative, and referential method of scientific analysis that follows a set of procedures to reduce the text systematically and to draw valid references and conclusions. Neuendorf (2016, p. 1) termed it a "systematic, objective, quantitative analysis" that "limits itself to the produced content alone and draws conclusions based on what is there" (Poindexter & McCombs, 2000, p. 188). Journalism and communication scholars commonly use content analysis to study media texts; however, similar content analysis methods are also applied in sociology, education, political science, and other communication disciplines (Krippendorff, 2004; Neuendorf, 2017).

The study strictly follows the recommended guidelines of Wimmer & Dominick (2013) for content analysis to get better results. The study design encompasses the following steps (a) formulation of research questions, (b) definition of population, (c) selection of an appropriate sample from the population, (d) selection of unit of analysis, (e) construction of distinct categories of content, and (g) establishing the quantifications system.

Population

The study investigates China's overall image in the Islamic world, therefore, the researcher analyzes the news coverage related to China in the six most influential English newspapers from the most powerful Islamic countries in the Islamic world: Saudi Arabia (*Arab News*), Pakistan (*The Nation*), Turkey (*Daily Sabah*), Iran (*Tehran Times*), Egypt (*Daily News Egypt*) and Qatar for its vibrant global media outlet (*Al-Jazeera English*) for the period from January 1, 2009, through December 31, 2018. Saudi Arabia, Pakistan, Turkey, Iran, Egypt, and Qatar are the major political, economic, and military powers in the Islamic world. The specific reasons for the selection of the above-mentioned Islamic countries and their news media were as follows:

Saudi Arabia (Arab News)

The selection of Saudi Arabia and its newspaper *Arab News* has strong merits. *First*, Saudi Arabia is one of the strongest and most capable political and economic forces in the Islamic world, particularly in the Sunni Islamic bloc. It is the birthplace of Islam, the largest Arabic country that enjoys great significance and respect in the Islamic world as a custodian of two Holy Mosques ("Al-Masjid-al-Haram" in Mecca and "Al-Masjid an-Nabawi" in Medina), consecrated to the Muslim Ummah (Hussain, 2016). *Second*, Saudi Arabia has a stronger and more traditional influence in the Middle East and Gulf regions. The Kingdom has often been termed a heavyweight in the region (Elmagherbi, 2010; Hussain, 2016). It has established the world's twelfth-largest economy, the largest economy in West Asia, the largest oil producer in the world, and a capable and strong force in global politics, specifically in the Sunni-Islamic world (Hussain, 2016).

Third, China and Saudi Arabia have maintained strong political and economic relations since the establishment of official diplomatic relations in the 1990s (Elmagherbi, 2010). Initially, the bilateral relations between the two countries focused more on energy and trade and, therefore, were often labeled as marginal relations. But now the relationship has fully grown into a new level of "comprehensive strategic partnership" in recent years (Al-Tamimi, 2022). The burgeoning relationships between China and Saudi Arabia indicate that both nations intend to move the relations beyond energy security and development into new inviolable strategic and political realms (Macgillivray, 2019).

China and Saudi Arabia have both synchronized their ambitious future-oriented mega initiatives, China's BRI and Saudi Vision 2030 to further expand the bilateral relations into the fields of nuclear energy, space technology, renewable energy, engineering, trade, and economic development (Foley, 2017; Fulton, 2020; Shay, 2018). *Fourth*, China is the largest importer of Saudi crude oil and conversely, the Kingdom has emerged as the single largest importer of Chinese goods in the Middle East and North Africa and the fifth-largest importer of Chinese products at the global level (Elmagherbi, 2010; Elmagherbi & Wang, 2011; Foley, 2017; Hussain, 2016). The trade volume (both import and export) between the two countries has significantly increased in the last ten years from US$26.7 billion in 2007 to US$44.9 billion in 2016 (UN Comtrade, 2018). The bilateral trade between the two nations has now reached US$ 65.2 billion in 2022 (Al-Tamimi, 2022).

Fifth, the economic, political, and strategic relationship between the two countries has increased manifold in recent years. Saudi Crown Prince Mohammad bin Salman Al-Saud named China as the Kingdom's biggest economic partner during his visit to Beijing in August 2016 (Salman, 2016). But still, a sizable Saudi population harbors a negative perception of China. Al-Sudairi (2013) noted that Saudi people consider China a "godless" Communist country and the Kingdom's relationship with China is un-Islamic. Though the Kingdom has started to support China's point of view on Xinjiang, it strongly criticized China's policies toward Uyghur Muslims in Xinjiang in the past (Al-Sudairi, 2013; Al-Tamimi, 2022; Hussain, 2016). The Saudi leadership also feels discomfort with China's growing strategic relations with Iran, particularly the military relations and its support for Iran's nuclear deal with the world's powers (P5+1: UNSC permanent members plus Germany) that may shatter the confidence in future China-Saudi Arabia relations. Saudis considers Iran a major threat to its national security and strategic interests in the Middle East (Al-Tamimi, 2022; Macgillivray, 2019). The recently signed "strategic accord—a 25 years comprehensive strategic cooperation agreement" that includes the comprehensive strategic, economic, military, and security cooperation between China and Iran also exacerbated the negative sentiments in Saudi security circles which believes it could further inspire professed Iranian belligerence in the Middle East region (Houghton, 2022).

Sixth, the Kingdom of Saudi Arabia is an "absolute authoritarian monarchy" where the King is the head of state and government. Saudi Arabia's basic laws do not permit to election of a King outside the royal family—the "Al-Saud". The constitution is guided by the Quran and Sunnah (Islamic Sharia) and is subjected to the interpretation of Saudi religious clerics (Al-Rasheed, 2010; Niblock, 2004). In addition, political, religious, and social freedom are strictly regulated by the Kingdom. Saudi public has no significant role in the Kingdom's decision-making and policy formulation, therefore, public opinion may not be an important factor in China's image construction in Saudi state control media (Al-Sudairi, 2013; Hussain, 2016).

Finally, Arab News is a leading, dynamic, and influential English daily newspaper launched in 1975 in Saudi Arabia. It is the first and oldest English-language newspaper in Saudi Arabia that is widely circulated in and outside Saudi Arabia (Mishra, 2007; Rampal, 1994).

Arab News has a diverse readership comprising various segments of Saudi society, including government officials, company executives and workers, intellectuals, students, and the public. It is also popular among foreign expatriates, NGOs, financial institutions, and policy think tanks. The newspaper is widely read in the Gulf region and has a daily readership in the United Arab Emirates (UAE), Bahrain, Kuwait, Oman, Qatar, Pakistan, North and East Africa, Europe, Japan, and the United States. Additionally, its website edition (*www.arabnews.com*) receives hundreds of thousands of views every day (*Arab News*, 2015, 2023).

Arab News is also considered a mouthpiece of the Kingdom's foreign policy and the first choice of the executives and policymakers in Saudi Arabia. *Arab News* fairly presents Saudi's perspective on the Arabic Islamic world, particularly in Middle East countries (Arab News, 2023; Mishra, 2007; Rampal, 1994).

Pakistan (The Nation)

Historically, the geostrategic, geopolitical, and geoeconomic concerns of both China and Pakistan converge with one another around multiple areas of mutual strategic interests, particularly, mutual economic cooperation, shared internal security challenges, uninterrupted access to affordable energy resources, and safeguarding of joint geostrategic interests in Asia and beyond. Therefore, China's image evaluation in Pakistan has various merits. *First*, Pakistan and China have enjoyed deep economic, political, and strategic relationships since 1951. The relationship between the two countries is often coined as "Iron Brothers" (巴铁) "All weather friends" and "time-tested and reliable strategic partners" etc. (Lim, 2015; Vandewalle, 2015). Beijing and Islamabad need each other for their bright future. Beijing is interested in transforming global politics and ensuring the continuity of its economic growth while Islamabad is looking to boost its deteriorated economy and overcome the energy crisis through the China-Pakistan Economic Corridor (CPEC)—a multi-billion dollars flagship project of China's ambitious Belt and Road Initiative (Fels, 2017; Khan & Pratt, 2019; Rizvi, 2016; Small, 2015). CPEC is one of the leading projects of China's BRI, with more than

US$62 billion in investment. It links the New Silk Route with the 21st Century New Maritime Silk Route to reduce the 9,000-kilometer distance and connect China with the Middle East and Africa through Gwadar Port, constructed in Balochistan, Pakistan. Pakistan considers CPEC a game-changer and a ray of hope to bring economic prosperity through infrastructure development, energy projects, and regional connectivity. It will also provide China with a gateway to the energy-rich Middle East region. Pakistan believes that this corridor will open new opportunities for attracting foreign investment in the region and is equally beneficial for all the neighboring countries. Likewise, China considered CPEC as a strategic project that will provide China with an alternative route to the oil-rich Middle East and Africa and improve its image in its neighboring countries (Akhtar et al., 2021; Kamel, 2018; Shah, 2018). Chaziza (2016a) argues that a strong Pak-China relationship will provide China's geo-economic and geostrategic leverage not only in South Asia and the Middle East but will also foster its influence in the broader Asia region where both China and the US are competing with each other to strengthen their sphere of influence.

Second, Pakistan is the only nuclear power among the Islamic states, and therefore, enjoys a special status and strong political influence in the Islamic world. In the past, Pakistan played an important role in getting the support of Islamic courtiers for China to earn a permanent seat in the United Nations and also facilitate China's relationship with the outer world, particularly with the United States during the Cold War era when the two countries became bitter enemies (Cohen, 2010; Khan & Pratt, 2019).

Third, Pakistan's strategic position in the region makes it a cornerstone for China's strategy for South Asia, West Asia, and Central Asia. In recent years, the U.S. and India exacerbated the geopolitical competition and zero-sum game thinking in the region. Particularly, the U.S. Indo-Pacific strategy, its promotion of military competition through QUAD (a security quadrilateral security alliance between the U.S., India, Australia, and Japan), and the newly established AUKUS (trilateral security pact between Australia, the U.K., and the U.S.) pose serious security and strategic challenges to China's core interests in the Indo-Pacific region. The growing strategic alliance between the U.S. and India and the U.S. demand for a greater role of India in Afghanistan may also spoil and undermine the emerging stability in Afghanistan due to its 20 years of support for anti-Taliban forces. Resulting in spill-over effects on Afghanistan's close neighbouring countries China and Pakistan. Therefore, both China and Pakistan need to work hand in hand to maintain and promote regional stability and global security (Zongyi, 2021).

Fourth, Pakistan is a parliamentary democratic country where press freedom and democratic rights are widely recognized. Even though there are few restrictions on freedom of expression, comparatively Pakistani media is freer than other Islamic countries. Therefore, coverage of China-related news is more impartial and represents the true image of China in Pakistan.

Finally, *The Nation* is an old, influential, and respected English daily newspaper in Pakistan. The newspaper enjoys a special position in the Pakistani media landscape and is also the most cited Pakistani newspaper at the international level. *The Nation* presents a constructive, bold, impartial, and critical point of view on national and international issues. Its motto is to provide "credible, insightful, and balanced" news to the audience. It is one of the most popular English newspapers in Pakistan and is widely followed by educated people, bureaucrats, decision-makers, policy formulators, and opinion-makers in Pakistan. *The Nation* has a wide range of circulation within and outside the country. Its online edition is also available (*www.nation.com.pk*) for the audience and has more than 1.6 million active followers on Facebook. The newspaper has been published by the oldest and most reputable Pakistani media group "Nawaiwaqt" since 1940 (*The Nation*, 2023).

Turkey (renamed as Türkiye) (Daily Sabah)

First, Turkey is an important and major Islamic country located between Eastern Europe and the Western Asia region. The country is often coined as the genuine leader of the Muslim world for its strong and active leadership role in raising Muslim grievances and concerns on the world stage (Colakoglu, 2015; Fuller, 2008; Zhu, 2010). Particularly, its incessant support for the independent Palestine cause (a major issue in the Middle East region) and Kashmiri's right to self-determination (an internationally recognized territory under dispute between Pakistan and India since 1947) (Ahmad, 1993; Kalin, 2011; Komath, 2022; Pope & Pope, 2000).

Second, China-Turkey relations have been experiencing unsteadiness since 1949. Turkey preferred to establish diplomatic relations with the Republic of China (ROC) in Taiwan over the People's Republic of China (PRC) in mainland China in 1949. But later it officially recognized and established diplomatic relations with PRC in 1971. During the 1970s and 1980s, both governments maintained relatively good economic and security relations but in the 1990s the relations between the two nations stagnated again due to the Xinjiang issue (alleged mistreatment of Uyghur Muslims in Xinjiang) and the re-establishment of Ankara's political relations with Taipei (Taiwan). However, relations regained momentum when Turkish Deputy Prime Minister Bülent Ecevit met Chinese President Jiang Zemin during his official visit to China in 1998 to improve the bilateral relationships between the two countries (Colakoglu, 2015). Though the relations between Turkey and China improved significantly since 2000, they remained erratic due to the Muslim Uyghur issue in Xinjiang (Colakoglu, 2015; Temiz, 2018). Uyghur is of Turkish origin. Therefore, the "East Turkistan" issue and China's punitive crackdown on Uyghur Muslims in Xinjiang in 2009, which was labeled as "a kind of genocide" by Turkey's Prime Minister Tayyip Erdogan seriously hunted the relationship between the two countries (Chen, 2011; Hille, 2009). Turkish public perception of China remained most unfavorable in the Islamic World (Ergenc, 2015; Pew Research Center, 2017; Xie & Page, 2013). Ergenc (2015) argues that although the foreign policies of the two nations are compatible, the dynamics of domestic politics and public opinion in Turkey hinder the veritable engagements between the two countries. The negative public perception of China is manifested mainly in the negative media coverage, anti-China protests, and the Uyghur diaspora's lobbying for Turkey-Xinjiang relations.

Third, Turkey enjoys an important strategic position in global politics—both historically and geographically. Its strategic location between Asia and Europe can work as a window for China to extend its influence in Europe and the Islamic world (Kalin, 2011). Turkey is one of the most westward partners in the BRI—China's key partner in the West Asian corridor and a gateway to Europe. It is pivotal to China's BRI—New Eurasian Land Bridge corridor which connects China to Europe through Turkey.

Fourth, China and Turkey established strong economic ties in recent years. Since 1990, the trade volume between the two countries has increased significantly. From 2007 through 2017, the trade volume between China and Turkey extended from US$13.2 billion in 2007 to US$22.0 billion in 2016 (UN Comtrade, 2018). Consequently, the trade deficit between the two countries also increased significantly. For example, Turkey imported US$62.8 billion of products from China between 2018 and 2020, whereas Turkey's exports to China remained at US$8.5 billion, contributing to a huge trade deficit of US$54.3 billion (2.8% of Turkey's GDP) to the Turkish economy during the same period. The trade deficit between Turkey and China was recorded at US$20.2 billion—41% of Turkey's total trade deficit in 2020 (Yilmaz, 2022). Researchers (e.g., Ergenc, 2015; Temiz, 2018) noted that China's cheapest products easily penetrated Turkish markets but Turkish businessmen failed to take advantage of the economic relationship between the two countries due to a lack of understanding of the Chinese market demand. Therefore, China's exports to Turkey steadily increased but China's imports from Turkey drastically decreased. The growing trade deficit may spill over negative effects on future relations between the two countries.

Finally, Daily Sabah is the most circulated English-language regional daily newspaper in Turkey. It is considered a pro-government newspaper that is available in English, Arabic, German, and Russian languages. The *Daily* claims to represent the facts and adhere to the commitments to safeguard democracy, human rights, the rule of law, and liberty.

Daily Sabah is popular among young educated adults (aged between 18 and 40 years) and its online edition (*www.dailysabah.com*) monthly attracts more than 1.9 million readers mainly from Turkey (17.36%), United States (16.55%), Ireland (6.67%), United Kingdom (6.24%), Bangladesh (5.59%) and from other regional and international countries (40.67%) (Similarweb, 2023).

Iran (Tehran Times)

First, Iran is the largest Shiite Islamic country in the world and enjoys strategic importance in the Persian Gulf region. After the Islamic revolution in Iran in 1979, the country has emerged as a strong regional power that possesses a strong influence on the Shia communities (the second largest sect of Islam) around the world, particularly in the Middle East region (Louër, 2008). Iran is the de-facto leader of the Shia Islamic world and holds a strong influence on Islamic countries like Yemen, Iraq, Syria, Bahrain, and Lebanon.

Second, Iran has ranked fourth in holding the largest proven oil reservoirs in the world. After the successful nuclear deal with major world powers and the removal of UN sanctions in 2016, Iran is looking to upgrade its petroleum infrastructure, build new oil refineries, and enhance oil and gas exports to the world (Morello & DeYoung, 2016). China has emerged as the largest foreign investor in Iran's petroleum sector and is also a major importer of its oil and liquefied natural gas. In 2004, both countries signed an oil and natural gas agreement worth US$70 billion through which China will acquire 250 million tons of liquefied natural gas over 30 years from Iran (Dorraj, 2013). In January 2016, Chinese President Xi was the first world leader who pay a state visit to Iran when international sanctions were removed and signed 17 economic agreements with the Iranian government to boost the bilateral trade up to US$600 billion by 2026 (Conduit & Akbarzadeh, 2019). In March 2021, China and Iran signed another "strategic accord—a 25-year comprehensive strategic cooperation agreement" to fortify bilateral cooperation in the fields of politics, economy, infrastructure, technology, and national security (Houghton, 2022; Vaisi, 2022). Under the agreement, China pledges to invest US$400 billion in Iranian infrastructure development under the auspice of BRI to further enhance bilateral trade and economic cooperation (Shira & Assoiciates, 2021). Although Sino-Iran relations have strengthened in recent years, Iran's heavy reliance on China has led to a flood of cheap Chinese goods in the Iranian market and harmed local artisans, businesses, and industrialists. Therefore, some Iranians think that the Iranian government has "sold Iran to China" and the Persian heritage of 2500 years is at risk of wiping out in the next 25 years due to the abundance of Chinese cheap products in the market (Vaisi, 2022).

Third, China and Iran have developed a strong economic relationship under the BRI framework, and trade volume (both import and export) between the two countries has increased from US$21.0 billion in 2007 to US$31.8 billion in 2016 (UN Comtrade, 2018). However, the trade volume between the two countries witnessed a sharp decline to US$23.02 billion after the reimposition of the U.S. sanction on Iran in 2019 (Shira & Assoicates, 2021).

Fourth, In the past, Iranian news media and the public expressed popular resentment toward China's support of the UN Security Council's Resolution 1929, a "yes vote" that enacted economic and military sanctions on Iran in 2010 (Chen, 2011). *Fifth,* during the period of Iranian revolutionary activism (1979), Iranian religious scholars' unauthorized visits to Xinjiang for the promotion of Islam outside of China's officially sanctioned channels significantly strained the China-Iran relationship. China officially conveyed to Tehran to respect its sovereignty and to assure Iran's "noninterference in Xinjiang" (Temiz, 2018, p. 63). In the recent past, Iranian clerics have openly criticized China's military crackdown on Uyghur Muslims in Xinjiang in 2009 (Chen, 2011). The recent analysis of Farsi-language news sources about China-Iran relations also indicates a bifurcated attitude of reformists and conservatives in Iran toward China. The reformists held an unfavorable image of China due to ethnic tension in Xinjiang and insisted on approaching Europe to break Tehran's economic and diplomatic isolation instead of deepening economic cooperation with China, which they termed "Chinese exploitation" and China cannot be trusted as a reliable ally—contradicting the conservatives and Iran's official stance on Sino-Iran relationship (Ehteshami et al., 2018).

Sixth, China, and Iran are natural allies and have a common interest to contain U.S. influence both regionally and globally (Currier & Dorraj, 2010; Osiewicz, 2018). Iran possesses a significant geostrategic location in the Persian Gulf region. It is an aspirant regional power and a major player in the global energy market. Iran is also a significant and major partner in China's BRI—a New Silk Road project. Erdbrink (2017) argues that Iran will be the center of everything in terms of Chinese investment and outbound trade. Therefore, China wants positive and stronger ties with Iran to access Iran's untapped oil and gas resources and to use its political influence to secure its energy interests in the Middle East (Macgillivray, 2019; Mackenzie & Misc, 2010). In addition, China is the largest foreign investor in Iran (Chen, 2011). On the other hand, Tehran also wants China's political and economic support to avoid U.S. aggression and to refurbish its national economy (Ehteshami et al., 2018; Mackenzie & Misc, 2010; Morello & DeYoung, 2016).

Finally, the *Tehran Times* is the first and oldest most popular English daily newspaper in Iran that provides reliable news to local and international readers in more than 80 different countries. The newspaper claims to represent the "voice of Islamic revolution" and "loudspeaker for the oppressed people of the world". Most intellectuals and foreign media outlets follow the *Tehran Times* for its authentic journalism and reliable news sources (*Tehran Times*, 2018). The readership of the newspaper is mainly based on young educated Iranians, foreign envoys, foreign media outlets, government officials, and policymakers as well as regional and international audiences. It is one of the most authentic and reliable sources that are freely available to the foreign public to know about the government's official position on important national, regional, and international affairs. Therefore, the *Tehran Times* is a landmark media outlet to gauge China's image in Iran.

Egypt (Daily News Egypt)

First, Egypt is an influential and powerful Islamic country that holds the strongest and largest military in the Arab Islamic world, therefore, it enjoys strong political and military influence in the Islamic North Africa, and West Asia region, particularly Egyptian role in the Middle East as a "diplomatic mediator" and a "peace contributor" is widely recognized (Alterman, 2016; Chaziza, 2016b; Zhu, 2010). Egypt is also one of the most politically active and founding members of the various powerful regional and international organizations such as the United Nations (UN), the Organization of Islamic Cooperation (OIC), the Arab League (AL), the African Union (AU), and the Non-Aligned Movement (NAM), etc.

Second, Egypt is among the first Islamic countries that developed diplomatic relations with China in 1956 and also facilitated China's diplomatic relations with other Islamic countries (Elmagherbi, 2010). However, Sino-Egypt relations remained stressful over trade deficit issues and on the issues of Taiwan in the past.

Zhu (2011) argues that the past governments in Egypt often used Taiwan as a trading chip to leverage economic benefits from China.

Third, Egypt is the largest Muslim country in the Arab Islamic world and maintains the second-largest economy in the African region (Chaziza, 2016b; Shapshak, 2016). Under the BRI, China has developed strong economic relations with Egypt and pledges to invest more than US$50 billion in infrastructural development in Egypt, particularly multi-billion dollar investments in Egypt's new capital and the Suez Canal cooperation zone (Kliman & Grace, 2018). China and Egypt are also bonded on a "comprehensive strategic partnership" agreement that enhanced the geo-economic, geopolitical, and geostrategic cooperation between the two countries. Thereafter, the trade volume (both import and export) between the two countries increased significantly and reached US$14.56 billion in 2020. However, it has created a new economic problem for Egypt in the form of huge trade deficit, as China export to Egypt reached US$13.64 billion and imports from Egypt stalled at US$0.92 billion in 2020, making China the single largest contributor to the trade deficit in the Egyptian economy (Mena, 2021; Sun & Xu, 2022).

Fourth, the public perception of China in Egypt is negative. In recent years, Egyptian public perception of China's positive image has declined from 57% in 2011 to 39% in 2013, and conversely, China's negative image perception in Egypt increased from 39% in 2011 to 54% in 2014 (Khan et al., 2023; Pew Research Center, 2017; Xie & Page, 2013).

Finally, Daily News Egypt is the "only independent" English daily newspaper that provides "unbiased and forthright" news analysis to the audiences. The newspaper holds an emblem of freedom of expression and was banned twice for its independent editorial policies in 2012 and 2017. Therefore, it is often regarded as free from state control (Khan et al., 2023; Khazbak, 2012). The *Daily* holds a strong appeal to young Egyptian elites, the business community, corporate entities, and government officials and is widely circulated in Egypt as part of the world's leading English daily "*International Herald Tribune*" (*Daily News Egypt*, 2018). Its web edition (*www.dailynewsegypt.com*) is freely available and accessed around the world.

Qatar (Al-Jazeera English)

First, Qatar is a modern Arabic Islamic state with a high-income economy. The country possessed the world's third-largest natural gas reservoirs after Iran and Russia and ranked first in the world's richest per-capita state (Fromherz, 2017;

Reader, 2013; Zahlan, 2016). *Second,* Qatar enjoys significant power in the world, particularly in Arabic Islamic countries due to its vibrant media outlet "*Al-Jazeera Media Network*".

Finally, Al-Jazeera is considered one of the most popular, influential, and free media outlets in the Islamic world (Worth & Kirkpatrick, 2011). It has emerged as a strong competitor to traditional Western media outlets like *BBC, CNN,* and *Voice of America* in the global media sphere by providing a "voice to the voiceless" around the world (*Al-Jazeera*, 2018; Powers, 2009). It effectively challenged the Western narratives and presented an alternative storyline of the issues by providing voices to the unnoticed, isolated, and ignored audiences in the world, particularly the Muslim Ummah (El-Nawawy & Powers, 2010; Miles, 2006). *Al-Jazeera English* has promoted a new mode of reconciliatory news journalism and rebukes the traditional approach of "stereotypical and counter-productive attitudes towards cultural 'Others'" (El-Nawawy & Powers, 2010, p. 62).

Al-Jazeera English is considered the true voice of the Islamic world and is evenly popular among young and old people. The monthly readership of its online edition (www.aljazeera.com) has reached up to 38.6 million. Additionally, it is equally popular in Arab countries as well as in other parts of the world, particularly in the U.S., UK, EU, Australia, Canada, and India (Similarweb, 2023). Therefore, it is a vital media source to assess China's global image-making in the Islamic world.

To summarize, this research analyzes how China's global image is portrayed in the English-language news media of the six most influential Islamic countries. Together, these countries have a significant political, religious, and economic influence over the Islamic world, and their news media has a greater impact at local, regional, and international levels.

Data collection

This study selected the six most influential English language newspapers from six prominent Islamic countries (that is, Saudi Arabia [*Arab News*], Pakistan [*The Nation*], Turkey [*Daily Sabah*], Iran [*Tehran Times*], Egypt [*Daily News Egypt*] and Qatar [*Al-Jazeera English*]) to measure and analyze China's global image in the Islamic world. The researcher used the keywords i.e., "China" or "Chinese" in "LexisNexis Database Search Engine" to extract the complete data set with full texts related to the China-related news coverage from Islamic English news media (i.e., *Arab News, The Nation, Tehran Times, Daily News Egypt* and *Al-Jazeera*

Table 6.1: The Descriptive Statistics of the News Articles Related to China in Islamic English News Media from January 1, 2009, through December 31, 2018.

			Attention Intensity			
Years	*Arab News*	*Daily News Egypt*	*The Nation*	*Tehran Time*	*Daily Sabah*	*Al-Jazeera English*
2009	186	468	379	0	0	0
2010	90	649	1161	0	20	0
2011	188	554	1033	0	199	0
2012	595	353	1317	0	134	0
2013	181	291	2469	261	60	0
2014	444	229	1814	534	844	794
2015	418	450	2235	556	1515	1023
2016	352	648	2641	455	1617	901
2017	526	555	2834	698	2174	1054
2018	627	656	2269	1162	1506	1167
Total	**3607**	**4853**	**18152**	**3666**	**8069**	**4939**

English) for the period from January 1, 2009, through December 31, 2018 (Armony, 2012; He, Xianhong, & Xing, 2012). Data for *Daily Sabah* was directly extracted from the newspaper website (*www.dailysabah.com*) due to unavailability at the LexisNexis database. The keywords approached retrieved a total of 43, 286 news articles related to China published in Islamic English news media. The contribution of *Arab News* was 3,607 news articles (8.4 %); *The Nation,* 18,152 articles (41.9 %); *Daily Sabah,* 8,069 articles (18.6 %); *Tehran Times,* 3,666 articles (8.5 %); *Daily News Egypt,* 4,853 articles (11.2 %) and *Al-Jazeera English,* 4,939 news articles (11.4 %) related to China for the period from January 1, 2009, through December 31, 2018 (Table 6.1). The data set includes all types of China-related newspaper articles (e.g., news, columns, editorials, features, interviews, and letters to the editor) published in Islamic English news media from January 1, 2009, through December 31, 2018 (Ferguson, 2000).

Sampling technique

The twofold sampling technique was used to analyze China's image in Islamic English news media. *First*, the researcher used keywords to search ("China" or

"Chinese") in the LexisNexis database and retrieved a total of 43, 286 news articles related to China published in Islamic English news media to measure the intensity of the attention paid to China by the Islamic English news media. *Second*, the researcher used a stratified random sampling technique (that is, one hundred articles randomly selected for each year) to measure China's image and its precise dimensions e.g., political image, cultural image, economic image, technological image, and social image in the Islamic world. A total of 4,870 newspaper articles were selected for content analysis through stratified random sampling for the period from January 1, 2009, through December 31, 2018. (Teddlie & Yu, 2007). The share of contributions from each newspaper was: *Arab News* (990 articles), *The Nation* (1000 articles), *Daily Sabah* (780 articles), *Tehran Times* (600 articles), *Daily News Egypt* (1000 articles), and 500 articles from *Al-Jazeera English*. The disparity in the stratified random sample size is due to the unavailability of complete data sets of the following newspapers, i.e., *Tehran Times* and *Al-Jazeera English* in the LexisNexis database. In addition, *Arab News* produced 24 articles in 2008 and 90 articles in 2010 related to China. Similarly, the study found zero articles related to China in *Daily Sabah* for 2009, only 20 articles in 2010, and 60 articles in 2013 respectively. All these articles were selected as a sample (Table 6.2).

Table 6.2: The Descriptive Statistic of the Stratified Random Sample Chosen from Islamic English News Media from January 1, 2009, through December 31, 2018.

Years	*Arab News*	*Daily News Egypt*	*The Nation*	*Tehran Time*	*Daily Sabah*	*Al-Jazeera English*
2009	100	100	100	0	0	0
2010	90	100	100	0	20	0
2011	100	100	100	0	100	0
2012	100	100	100	0	100	0
2013	100	100	100	100	60	0
2014	100	100	100	100	100	100
2015	100	100	100	100	100	100
2016	100	100	100	100	100	100
2017	100	100	100	100	100	100
2018	100	100	100	100	100	100
Total	990	1000	1000	600	780	500

A well-exhausted and mutually inclusive coding sheet was prepared after a rigorous literature review and mutual consultation between coders. A single article was used as a unit of analysis in this study and each article was coded based on its domain theme (i.e., political, economic, culture, social, science and technology, and miscellaneous). The prescribed code sheet is attached as Appendix A.

Conceptualizing and measurement

Media attention intensity

Media attention is the first component of a country's image perception. Scholars argue that the level of media attention to a particular foreign country indicates its significance and importance in international relations as the salience of the countries in international news flow remained unequal (Chang, 1998; Golan & Wanta, 2003; Jones et al., 2013). Studies found a positive correlation between the level of media attention and the level of importance attached to that particular country. A high level of attention intensity prioritizes the targeted place, actor, or issue in the policy-making agenda (Liu & Yang, 2015; C. Zhang & Meadows III, 2012). Therefore, to gauge China's importance and significance in the Islamic world, this study measured the media attention intensity through the number of articles related to China published in Islamic English news media for the period from January 1, 2009, through December 31, 2018.

China's image

China's image refers to the evaluation, interpretation, construction, and dissemination of China-related news in Islamic English news media. Scholars argue that image is the first perception that comes from news media about a country or a nation. Therefore, media play a pivotal role in constructing, shaping, and disseminating a country or nation's image through affective judgments, interpretation, and "national branding" or "national stereotypes" (Archetti, 2012; Huang & Leung, 2005; Seo, 2011; Soroka, 2003; C. Zhang & Meadows III, 2012). The media's image of the country as a "friend" or "enemy" determines how a state should interpret and analyze that country's behavior and take effective policy measures to deal with it accordingly. For example, the U.S. media's image of the Soviet Union as an "enemy" greatly affected the relationship between the U.S. and the Soviet Union during the Cold War (Cottam, 1994; Herrmann, 1985; Herrmann & Fischerkeller, 1995).

Manheim and Albritton (1983) noted that media portrays two primary dimensions of a nation or country's image: visibility and valence. Visibility refers to the amount of media coverage a country receives, and valance refers to the degree of favorability and unfavourability of media content related to that country. Valance can also be labeled as value i.e., favorable vs. unfavorable or positive vs. negative evaluation of a nation or a country's image. "Positive references included such points of discussion as a country's progress, advances, resources, assets, strengths, continuity, stability, reliability, or dependability", while "negative references included any mention of decline, weakness, poverty, liabilities, lack of progress, instability, or unreliability on the part of a given country" (Manheim, 2015; Manheim & Albritton, 1983, p. 647; L. Zhang & Wu, 2017). Therefore, the researchers often used the tracing approach to measure the country's image through the implicit or explicit connotation, tone, and expression used in news media, government documents, official announcements, and reports of the particular county (Armony, 2012; Fong & Chia, 2017; Liu & Yang, 2015). As the study focuses on China's image in the Islamic world, the researcher classifies the overall tone of each selected newspaper's article based on three categories, i.e., positive, negative, and neutral to determine China's overall image in the Islamic world (Liu & Yang, 2015).

China's image dimensions

Each country has a multifaceted image that comprises various dimensions: social, political, cultural, economic, technological, etc. (Buhmann, 2016; Liu & Yang, 2015; Pjesivac et al., 2018). Countries enjoy a polygonal relationship with other states and the media tried to cover every aspect of the bilateral relationship between the countries. Therefore, public perception of a foreign country's image is formed at two levels, i.e., the holistic image and the issue-specific or dimensional image. The holistic image is the overall country's image without any distinctive dimension while issue-specific or dimensional image is the second level of public perception and comprehensively refers to a precise country's image dimension as social, political, cultural, economic, technological, etc. This study analyzed the holistic image as well as the issue-specific or dimensional image (i.e., political, cultural, economic, technological, and social) of China in Islamic English news media. China's holistic image as well as those of specific dimensional images in the Islamic English news media was classified into three categories, that is, positive, negative, and neutral (Khan et al., 2023; Liu & Yang, 2015).

China's political image

China's political image was coded into three categories: Political and diplomatic relations; Defense and security; and Global values:

(a) Political and diplomatic relations frame refers to the all-news reports related to China's foreign policy, its role in international politics and diplomatic relations such as public diplomacy, regional and global political affairs, China's role in transnational political institutions [e.g., Shanghai Cooperation Organization (SCO), United Nations (UN), United Nation Security Council (UNSC), Paris Club (PC)], China's role in international political negotiations, dispute settlements and conflict management and mediations (e.g., North Korea and Iran Nuclear Issues, War in Afghanistan, Syria, Iraq, Libya, Yemen), and China's political and diplomatic relations with other countries, etc.

(b) Defense and security frame refers to the all-news reports about China's military engagements and activities such as military training, equipment, and international joint exercises, its role in global security and counter-terrorism activities (e.g., United Nations Peace Forces, China's anti-piracy patrols in the Gulf of Aden), modernization of China's Arm Forces, its new military installations (e.g., a military installation in the South China Sea) and China's military relations with other countries, etc.

(c) Global values frame refers to human rights, civil rights, democratic rights, freedom of expression, religious freedom, environment protection, copyrights, etc. All the news stories related to these themes were included in the global values category.

China's economic image

China's economic image was coded into six categories: Business, trade, and investment; Economic growth; Infrastructure development; Natural resources; Economic policies and reforms; and Economic aid and loans:

(a) Business, trade, and investment frame refer to China's business, trade, and investment-related news articles e.g., China's US trade relation, China's investment in Islamic countries, China's business activities in Asia, Europe, Africa, South and North America, Australia and beyond.

(b) Economic growth frame, refers to the articles that reported China's economic growth and its impact on national and international economies.
(c) Infrastructure development frame, refers to the news reports related to China's infrastructural development activities within or outside the country. The category also included China's BRI-related infrastructure development work around the world.
(d) Natural resources frame, refers to China's oil, gas, and mineral-related work and activities around the world.
(e) Economic policies and reforms frame, refers to China's economic policies, its economic reform agenda, and new economic institutions [e.g., Asian Infrastructure Investment Bank (AIIB), National Silk Road Fund (NSRF), New Development Bank (NDB)] and its role in international economic institutions, e.g., International Monetary Fund (IMF), Asian Development Bank (ADB), World Bank (WB), Paris Club (PC) and World Trade Organization (WTO).
(f) Economic aid and loans frame, refers to China's economic aid and loans to the international community, charity organizations, and sovereign states.

China's cultural image

China's cultural image was coded into nine categories: Sport; Tourism; History and artifacts; Media and entertainment; Fine art; Ethnicity; Education; Chinese language; and Chinese cuisines:

(a) Sports frame, refers to the articles related to sports activities.
(b) Tourism frame, refers to the articles related to the tourism industry, Chinese tourists, natural sights, scenic areas, tourist spots, etc.
(c) History and artifacts frame, refers to the articles related to China's rich history, ancient cultures, and artifacts.
(d) Media and entertainment frame, refer to the articles related to Chinese media, films, dramas, theatre, folk music, entertainment industries, etc.
(e) Fine art frame, refers to articles related to Chinese art, painting, calligraphy, etc.
(f) Ethnicity frame, refers to the articles related to the Chinese ethnic community.
(g) Education frame, refers to the articles related to China's education system, scholarships, education reforms, education institutions, education development, education standards, etc.

(h) Chinese language frame, refers to the articles related to the Chinese language, its growth, evolution, and importance.
(i) Chinese cuisines, refers to the articles related to Chinese cuisines.

China's social image

China's social image was coded into seven categories: Health; Welfare; Corruption; Natural disasters; Crime; and the Gender gap:

(a) Health frame, refers to the articles related to health, diseases, medicines, disease prevention, etc.
(b) Welfare frame, refers to the articles related to China's welfare activity toward the domestic and international community.
(c) Corruption frame, refers to the articles related to the spreading of and prevention of corruption and corrupt practices in China and Chinese.
(d) Poverty frame, refers to the articles related to poverty growth and alleviation in China.
(e) Natural disasters frame, refers to the articles related to flood, coal, and mineral mining incidents and earthquakes, etc.
(f) Crime frame, refers to the articles related to social crimes in China.
(g) Gender gap frame, refers to the articles related to gender imbalance in China.

China's technological image

China's technological image was coded in a single category: Science and technology which included China's scientific achievements, technological development, and innovation, such as a breakthrough in, nuclear technology, space technology, information and communication technology, artificial intelligence, virtual and augmented reality, advanced military equipment both innovation in hardware and software, engineering breakthroughs, such as space rockets, aircraft, high-speed rails, tunnels, bridges, and other scientific contributions.

Journalistic attitude

Journalistic attitudes toward China were measured in five categories: (a) Neutral; (b) Positive descriptive; (c) Positive analytical; (d) Negative descriptive; and

(e) Negative analytical (Reason & García, 2007). All those articles that showed no clear discernible attitude toward China were coded as neutral. Articles that cover China with a positive attitude were coded as Positive descriptive. Whereas positive analytical articles were those which reached on positive conclusion after following analytical reflection on events related to China.

Similarly, articles that showed negative attitudes toward China were coded as negative descriptive and those that reached on negative conclusion after following analytical reflection on the events related to China were coded as negative analytical (Reason & García, 2007).

Article size

An article size was determined by the number of words. Based on the number of words, articles were divided into three categories: (a) short article (*N* = <500 words); (b) standard article (*N* = 501—1000 words); and (c) long article (*N* = >1001 words).

Effects of economic relations on China's image

The effects of economic relations on China's image were measured by the volume of trade (import and export) between China and that Islamic country. United Nations statistics division and trade statistics of imports and exports between China and that particular country were used as an independent variable to measure its impact on China's image construction in that particular Islamic country. China's imports and exports to each particular country from 2009 through 2018 were used as an independent variable to measure their impact on China's image construction in that country.

Effects of the political/government system on China's image

The effects of political and government systems were measured through the country's political system i.e., Absolute Authoritarian Monarchy in Saudi Arabia, the Federal Parliamentary system in Pakistan, the Presidential system in Turkey, Theocracy in Iran, the Semi Presidential system in Egypt, and the Constitutional Monarchy in Qatar. The country's political system was used as an independent variable to measure its influence on China's image construction in that Islamic country. All these government systems have unique values and practices that may implicate China's image construction in that country.

Effects of the Belt and Road Initiative

To measure the BRI effects on China's image construction in the Islamic world, data were divided into two categories: (a) China's image before the launch of the BRI (2009–2013); and (b) China's image after the inauguration of the BRI (2014–2018). Articles that were published before the launch of the BRI (2009–2013) were coded as zero (0) and those articles that were published after the launch of the BRI (2014–2018) were coded as one (1). BRI was used as an independent variable to measure its effects on China's image construction in the Islamic world.

Intercoder reliability

The researchers always aim to achieve the highest reliability. However, perfect reliability in the content analysis may not be reached due to complex coding processes which require elaborative cognitive processes. Even though content analysis is an "objective" and "systematic" process (Neuendorf, 2017, p. 1; Berelson, 1952, p. 18), the research questions always drive it toward subjectivity (Krippendorff, 2004). Moreover, the coder's cognitive abilities and personal characteristics (cultural, social, political, and professional background) may also influence the reliability of the results. Therefore, to ensure higher reliability and to reduce the subjective impact of the coders on the results, the researcher should strictly adhere to the standard coding scheme and undergo vigorous training exercises before starting the coding processes (Krippendorff, 2004; Neuendorf, 2017; Poindexter & McCombs, 2000; Weber, 1990).

Peter and Lauf (2002) argue that to ensure a high level of reliability in coding processes, the coders should have essential knowledge about the social, political, and cultural background of the country in which the study has been conducted. Moreover, the coders should be recruited from the same educational and professional background. Krippendorff (2012) reinforced these arguments that the coders "must have the necessary cognitive abilities, but what is perhaps more important is that they have appropriate backgrounds" (p. 127).

The researcher gave due consideration to the advice and suggestions of the scholars mentioned above and recruited six independent coders based on their strong educational backgrounds (graduate and postgraduates) for content analysis. Most importantly, all coders had vast experience in the social, political, and cultural understanding of Islamic countries. The coders' unique ability to understand Islamic culture and the historical relationship between China and the Islamic world increased the intercoder agreement level and helped in refining the categories and subcategories of the proposed dimensions of China's image. It reduced subjectivity by achieving the highest reliability standard in the coding process (Krippendorff, 2004; Neuendorf, 2017; Peter & Lauf, 2002).

The researcher used the following steps for the coding process: (a) A well-defined code sheet was prepared well before starting the formal coding process; (b) All the categories and subcategories were well-defined, exhaustive, and mutually exclusive; (c) The coders were provided appropriate training through vigorous exercises on the texts randomly chosen from the relevant population to ensure the maximum understanding and consensuses of related terms, categories, and subcategories used in this research study (Neuendorf, 2017); (c) After achieving the maximum agreement level, 500 articles were randomly selected from the complete set of data and the same study sample was coded by all six coders independently to check the intercoder reliability between them; (d) The intercoder reliability among the six coders was measured by using Krippendorff's Alpha (α) which is a standardized reliability statistic for content analysis and is often used for three or more coders in communication research (Krippendorff, 2004, 2007). Krippendorff's Alpha is suitable to measure the agreements for the nominal, ordinal, interval, and ratio data and allows researchers to measure the "reliability data with missing categories or scale points, a frequent reality that none of the [other] measures has been able to cope with" (Krippendorff & Hayes, 2007, p. 82).

The researcher used the KALPHA macro program written by Krippendorff and Hayes (2007) for SPSS and SAS to facilitate the measurement of Krippendorff's α for the intercoder reliability. First coding data of all six coders were entered in SSPS and then run the following command after activating the KALPHA macro in SSPS:

KALPHA judges = obsl obs2 obs3 obs4 obs5 obs6/level = 1/detail = 0/
boot = 10000

Note: "obsl, obs2, obs3. . ..... obs6" represents the observations of coderl, coder2, coder3. ... .. coder6 respectively. Whereas "/level" represents the measurement of the judgments (1 = nominal, 2 = ordinal, 3 = interval, 4 = ratio). The "/detail= 0" command suppresses the additional information (Krippendorff & Hayes, 2007, p. 82). The results indicated the relatively higher intercoder reliability between six coders on the specific dimension of China's image in Islamic media (α = .89). Whereas the intercoder reliability for subdimensions of China's image was also relatively high (α = .83). The intercoder reliability for other categories, that is, tone of the article (α = .92), journalistic attitude (α = .87), name of newspaper, type of new article, and date were recorded as (α = 1.0).

Krippendorff and Hayes (2007) argue that Kapha = .80 or more indicates the higher intercoder reliability between coders. The minimum intercoder reliability of .67 or even .60 can be adopted for certain variables if specific information is provided in support of low intercoder reliability between coders. Therefore, the intercoder reliability of this study which ranged from .83 to 1.0 for all variables is relatively high.

Research questions

China's image is extensively explored in Western news media. However, there is little known about China's image construction, interpretation, and dissemination in Islamic English news media. Therefore, this study convened to explore China's image construction, interpretation, and dissemination in the Islamic world. The following research questions were addressed:

RQ1: What is the intensity of the overall attention paid to China-related news by the Islamic English news media and how does the media attention change over time?

RQ 2: How does the Islamic English news media construct China's image in the Islamic world and how did it change over time?

RQ 3: How does Islamic English news media construct different dimensions of China's image in the Islamic world and how do these dimensions change over time?

RQ 4: How do different dimensions of China's image in the Islamic world interrelate and affect each other?

RQ 5: What impact, if any, does China's economic relationship (imports and exports) with particular Islamic countries (i.e., Saudi Arabia, Pakistan, Turkey, Iran, Egypt, and Qatar) exert on China's image in that particular country's news media?

RQ 6: What impact, if any, does the degree of compatibility in the political system (government system) between China and particular Islamic countries (i.e., Saudi Arabia, Pakistan, Turkey, Iran, Egypt, and Qatar) have on China's image in that particular country's media?

RQ 7: What impact, if any, does the Belt and Road Initiative exert on China's image construction in the Islamic world (i.e., Saudi Arabia,

Pakistan, Turkey, Iran, Egypt, and Qatar) and how does BRI relate to the different dimensions of China's image in the Islamic world?

References

Ahmad, F. (1993). *The making of modern Turkey*. London: Routledge.

Akhtar, N., Khan, H. U., Jan, M. A., Pratt, C. B., & Jianfu, M. (2021). Exploring the determinants of the China-Pakistan economic corridor and its impact on local communities. *SAGE Open, 11*(4). <https://doi.org/10.1177/21582440211057127>

Al-Jazeera. (2018, January 22). Who we are. *Al-Jazeera*. <http://www.aljazeera.com/aboutus/>

Al-Rasheed, M. (2010). *A history of Saudi Arabia*. Cambridge University Press.

Al-Sudairi, M. T. (2013). China in the eyes of the Saudi Media. *Gulf Research Center, February*(February), 1–38. <https://www.ictsd.org/sites/default/files/downloads/2013/04/china-in-the-eyes-of-the-saudi-media.pdf>

Al-Tamimi, N. (2022). Saudi Arabia's once marginal relationship with China has grown into a comprehensive strategic partnership. In J. Gunter & H. Legarda (Eds.), *Beyond blocs: Global views on China and US-China relations* (pp. 73–79). Mercator Institute for China Studies. <https://merics.org/sites/default/files/2022-08/MERICS-Papers-On-China-Beyond-blocs-Global-views-on-China-and-US-China-relations-3.pdf>

Alterman, J. B. (2016). *Making choices: The future of the U.S.-Egyptian Relationship*. <https://www.csis.org/analysis/making-choices-future-us-egyptian-relationship>

Arab News. (2015, July 21). Arab News is most widely read English daily in the Arab world: Survey. *Arab News*. <https://www.arabnews.com/node/779336/amp>

Arab News. (2023, July 19). About us. *Arab News*. <http://www.arabnews.com/node/51199>

Archetti, C. (2012). The impact of new media on diplomatic practice: An evolutionary model of change. *The Hague Journal of Diplomacy*, *7*(2), 181–206. <https://doi.org/10.1163/187119112X625538>

Armony, A. C. (2012). A view from Afar: How Colombia sees China. *The China Quarterly*, *209*, 178–197. <https://doi.org/10.1017/S0305741011001536>

Austin, L. L., & Gaither, B. M. (2016). Examining public response to corporate social initiative types: A quantitative content analysis of Coca-Cola's social media. *Social Marketing Quarterly*, *22*(4), 290–306. <https://doi.org/10.1177/1524500416642441>

Baker, L. M., & King, A. E. H. (2016). Let's get theoretical: A quantitative content analysis of theories and models used in the journal of applied communications. *Journal of Applied Communications*, *100*(1), 67–80. <https://doi.org/10.4148/1051-0834.1021>

Bellström, P., Bellström, P., Magnusson, M., Magnusson, M., Pettersson, J. S., Pettersson, J. S., Thorén, C., & Thorén, C. (2016). Facebook usage in a local government: A content analysis of page owner posts and user posts. *Transforming Government: People, Process and Policy*, *10*(4), 548–567. <https://doi.org/10.1108/TG-12-2015-0061>

Berelson, B. (1952). *Content analysis in communication research*. New York: Free Press.

Bodle, J. T., Burriss, L., Farwell, T., Hammaker, S., & Joshi, J. (2011). Gender and journal scholarship in mass communication: How well are women doing? A twenty-year content analysis. *Journalism & Mass Communication Educator, 66*(2), 117–133. <https://doi.org/10.1177/107769581106600202>

Buhmann, A. (2016). The constitution and effects of country images: Theory and measurement of a central target construct in international public relations and public diplomacy. *Studies in Communication Sciences, 16*(2), 182–198. <https://doi.org/10.1016/j.scoms.2016.10.002>

Chang, T.-K. (1998). All countries not created equal to be news: World system and international communication. *Communication Research, 25*(5), 528–563. <https://doi.org/10.1177/009365098025005004>

Chaziza, M. (2016a). China–Pakistan relationship: A game-changer for the Middle East? *Contemporary Review of the Middle East, 3*(2), 147–161. <https://doi.org/10.1177/2347798916638209>

Chaziza, M. (2016b). Comprehensive strategic partnership: A new stage in China-Egypt relations. *Middle East Review of International Affairs, 20*(3), 41–51. <https://www.proquest.com/openview/1457e4966613369ec6fe3a6476acbaca/1?pq-origsite=gscholar&cbl=54955>

Chen, J. (2011). *The emergence of China in Middle East* (Issue 271, pp. 1–8). National Defense University, Washington, DC. <https://doi.org/10.1111/j.1539-6975.2009.01318.x>

Cheung, Y. T. D., Chan, C. H. H., Wang, M. P., Li, H. C. W., & Lam, T. (2016). Online social support for the prevention of smoking relapse: A content analysis of the WhatsApp and Facebook Social Groups. *Telemedicine and E-Health*. <https://doi.org/10.1089/tmj.2016.0176>

Cohen, W. I. (2010). *America's response to China: A history of Sino-American relations*. Columbia University Press.

Colakoglu, S. (2015). Dynamics of Sino–Turkish relations: A Turkish perspective. *East Asia, 32*(1), 7–23. <https://doi.org/10.1007/s12140-015-9225-7>

Conduit, D., & Akbarzadeh, S. (2019). Great power-middle power dynamics: The case of China and Iran. *Journal of Contemporary China, 28*(117), 468–481. <https://doi.org/10.1080/10670564.2018.1542225>

Cottam, M. L. (1994). *Images and intervention: US policies in Latin America*. University of Pittsburgh Pre.

Currier, C. L., & Dorraj, M. (2010). In arms we trust: The economic and strategic factors motivating China-Iran relations. *Journal of Chinese Political Science, 15*(1), 49–69. <https://doi.org/10.1007/s11366-009-9082-6>

Daily News Egypt. (2018, January 22). About us. *Business News for press, publishing and distribution company*. <https://www.linkedin.com/company/the-daily-news-egypt>

Dorraj, M. (2013). *Iran's expanding relations with China and their strategic dimensions* (12th ed.). Emirates Center for Strategic Studies and Research.

Ehteshami, A., Horesh, N., & Xu, R. (2018). Chinese-iranian mutual strategic perceptions. *The China Journal, 79*(79), 1–20. <https://doi.org/10.1086/693315>

El-Nawawy, M., & Powers, S. (2010). Al-Jazeera English: A conciliatory medium in a conflict-driven environment? *Global Media and Communication, 6*(1), 61–84. <https://doi.org/10.1177/1742766510362019>

Elmagherbi, F. I. (2010). A case study of China's relations with the Arab World. *2010 2nd IEEE International Conference on Information and Financial Engineering*, 646–650. <https://doi.org/10.1109/ICIFE.2010.5609442>

Elmagherbi, F. I., & Wang, R. (2011). Optimum plan to improve the economic relation between China and Arab world. *Modern Applied Science*, *5*(6), 181–187. <https://doi.org/10.5539/mas.v5n6p181>

Erdbrink, T. (2017, July 25). For China's global ambitions, "Iran is at the center of everything." *The New York Times*. <https://www.nytimes.com/2017/07/25/world/middleeast/iran->china-business-ties.html

Ergenc, C. (2015). Can two ends of Asia Meet? An overview of contemporary Turkey-China relations. *East Asia*, *32*(3), 289–308. <https://doi.org/10.1007/s12140-015-9242-6>

Fels, E. (2017). Pakistan: "Iron Brother" to Beijing, reluctant partner for Washington. In *Shifting power in Asia-Pacific?* (pp. 437–505). Springer.

Ferguson, S. D. (2000). *Researching the public opinion environment: Theories and methods* (Vol. 3). Sage.

Foley, S. (2017). When oil is not enough: Sino-Saudi relations and vision 2030. *Asian Journal of Middle Eastern and Islamic Studies*, *11*(1), 107–120. <https://doi.org/10.1080/25765949.2017.12023296>

Fong, Y. L., & Chia, T. Y. (2017). Framing diplomatic relations. *China Report*, *53*(4), 467–489. <https://doi.org/10.1177/0009445517727925>

Fromherz, A. J. (2017). *Qatar: A modern history*. Georgetown University Press.

Fuller, G. E. (2008). *The new Turkish Republic: Turkey as a pivotal state in the Muslim world*. United States Institute of Peace.

Fulton, J. (2020). China-Saudi Arabia Relations Through the "1+ 2+ 3" Cooperation Pattern. *Asian Journal of Middle Eastern and Islamic Studies*, *14*(4), 516–527. <https://doi.org/10.1080/25765949.2020.1841991>

Funk, M. J. (2013). *Analyzing content deviance in American Community Journalism Websites and Social Media* [The University of Texas, Austin]. <https://repositories.lib.utexas.edu/handle/2152/22983>

Gicevic, S., Aftosmes-Tobio, A., Manganello, J. A., Ganter, C., Simon, C. L., Newlan, S., & Davison, K. K. (2016). Parenting and childhood obesity research: A quantitative content analysis of published research 2009–2015. *Obesity Reviews*, *17*(8), 724–734. <https://doi.org/10.1111/obr.12416>

Golan, G., & Wanta, W. (2003). International elections on US network news: An examination of factors affecting newsworthiness. *International Communication Gazette*, *65*(1), 25–39. <https://doi.org/10.1177/0016549203065001135>

Han, G. K., & Wang, X. C. (2014). Analysis finds U. S. Newspapers use six frames for "Made in China". *Newspaper Research Journal*, *35*(2), 6–24. <https://doi.org/10.1177/073953291403500202>

Han, G., & Wang, X. (2012). Understanding "made in China": Valence framing and product-country image. *Journalism and Mass Communication Quarterly*, *89*(2), 225–243. <https://doi.org/10.1177/1077699012439034>

He, Z., Xianhong, C., & Xing, W. (2012). The image of the United States in the Chinese media: An examination of the evaluative component of framing. *Public Relations Review*, *38*(5), 676–683. <https://doi.org/10.1016/j.pubrev.2012.09.001>

Herrmann, R. K. (1985). *Perceptions and behavior in Soviet foreign policy.* University of Pittsburgh Pre.

Herrmann, R. K., & Fischerkeller, M. P. (1995). Beyond the enemy image and spiral model: Cognitive–strategic research after the cold war. *International Organization*, *49*(3), 415–450. <https://doi.org/10.1017/S0020818300033336>

Hille, K. (2009). Xinjiang Widens crackdown on Uighurs. *Financial Times.* <https://www.ft.com/content/5aa932ee-747c-11de-8ad5-00144feabdc0>

Houghton, B. (2022). China's balancing strategy between Saudi Arabia and Iran: The view from Riyadh. *Asian Affairs*, *53*(1), 124–144. <https://doi.org/10.1080/03068374.2022.2029065>

Huang, Y., & Leung, C. C. M. (2005). Western-Led press coverage of Mainland China and Vietnam during the SARS crisis: Reassessing the concept of "Media representation of the other." *Asian Journal of Communication*, *15*(3), 302–318. <https://doi.org/10.1080/01292980500261621>

Hussain, Z. (2016). *Saudi Arabia in a multipolar world.* Routledge.

Jones, T. M., Van Aelst, P., & Vliegenthart, R. (2013). Foreign nation visibility in US news coverage: A longitudinal analysis (1950–2006). *Communication Research*, *40*(3), 417–436. <https://doi.org/10.1177/0093650211415845>

Kalin, İ. (2011). Soft power and public diplomacy in Turkey. *Perceptions*, *XVI*(3), 5–23.

Kamel, M. S. (2018). China's Belt and Road Initiative: Implications for the Middle East. *Cambridge Review of International Affairs*, *31*(1), 76–95. <https://doi.org/10.1080/09557571.2018.1480592>

Khan, M. K., & Pratt, C. B. (2019). China's Belt and Road Initiative: Its landscape (and trajectory) in the Islamic World. In A. Visvizi, M. Lytras, X. Zhang, & J. Zhao (Eds.), *Foreign business in China and opportunities for technological innovation and sustainable economics* (pp. 117–142). IGI Global. <https://doi.org/10.4018/978-1-5225->8980-8.ch006

Khan, M. K., Pratt, C. B., & Akhtar, N. (2023). China's public diplomacy for image making in Islamic North Africa: Frames of the Belt and Road Initiative in Daily News Egypt. In: A. A. Anani-Bossman, T. E. Mudzanani, C. B. Pratt, I. A. Blankson (Eds.), *Public relations management in Africa Volume 1.* Cham: Palgrave Macmillan. <https://doi.org/10.1007/978-3-031-26704-8_5>

Khazbak, R. (2012, April 23). Daily News Egypt leaves a legacy of independent journalism. *Egypt Independent.* <https://egyptindependent.com/daily-news-egypt-leaves-behind-legacy-independent-journalism/>

Kliman, D., & Grace, A. (2018, June 18). China smells opportunity in the Middle East's Crisis. *Foreign Policy.* <https://foreignpolicy.com/2018/06/14/china-smells-opportunity-in-the-middle-easts-crisis/>

Kolbe, R. H., & Burnett, M. S. (1991). Content-analysis research: An examination of applications with directives for improving research reliability and objectivity. *Journal of Consumer Research*, *18*(2), 243–250. <https://doi.org/10.1086/209256>

Komath, A. (2022). The Kashmir Litmus test: An examination of international Islamic solidarity and co-operation. *India Review, 21*(1), 53–76. https://doi.org/10.1080/14736489.2021.2018202

Krippendorff, K. (1980). Content analysis an introduction to its Methodology. London: Sage.

Krippendorff, K. (2004). *Content analysis: An introduction to its methodology* (2nd ed.). Sage Publications.

Krippendorff, K. (2007). *Testing the reliability of content analysis data: What is involved and why.* https://studylib.net/doc/7447747/testing-the-reliability-of-content-analysis-data

Krippendorff, K. (2012). Content Analysis: An Introduction to Its Methodology (3rd ed.). Thousand Oaks, CA: Sage Publications.

Krippendorff, K., & Hayes, A. F. (2007). Answering the call for a standard reliability measure for coding data. *Communication Methods and Measures, 1*(1), 77–89. <https://doi.org/10.1080/19312450709336664>

Lerman, B. I., Lewis, S. P., Lumley, M., Grogan, G. J., Hudson, C. C., & Johnson, E. (2016). Teen depression groups on Facebook A content analysis. *Journal of Adolescent Research, 32*(6). <https://doi.org/10.1177/0743558416673717>

Lim, A. C.-H. (2015). Iron Brothers': Sino-Pakistani relations and the China-Pakistan economic corridor. *Eurasia Review.* <https://www.academia.edu/12286990/_Iron_Brothers_Sino_Pakistani_Relations_and_the_China_Pakistan_Economic_Corridor>

Liu, X., & Yang, Y. E. (2015). Examining China's official media perception of the United States: A content analysis of people's daily coverage. *Journal of Chinese Political Science, 20*(4), 385–408. <https://doi.org/10.1007/s11366-015-9340-8>

Louër, L. (2008). *Transnational Shia politics: Religious and political networks in the Gulf.* Columbia University Press.

Macgillivray, I. (2019). Maturing Sino-Saudi strategic relations and changing dynamics in the Gulf. *Global Change, Peace and Security, 31*(1), 61–80. <https://doi.org/10.1080/14781158.2018.1475350>

Mackenzie, P., & Misc, D. A. (2010). *A closer look at China-Iran relations: Roundtable report* (Issue September). <https://www.cna.org/reports/2010/D0023622.A3.pdf>

Manheim, J. B. (2015). Images in the news. *Discourse studies reader: Essential excerpts.* <https://doi.org/10.5040/9781472541925.ch-010>

Manheim, J. B., & Albritton, R. B. (1983). Changing national images: International public relations and media agenda setting. *American Political Science Review, 78*(3), 641–657. <https://doi.org/10.2307/1961834>

Mastro, D., & Sink, A. (2018). Measuring extremes: A quantitative content analysis of prime time TV depictions of body type. *Journal of Broadcasting & Electronic Media, 62*(2), 320–336. <https://doi.org/10.1080/08838151.2018.1451853>

Mena. (2021, March 29). Trade exchange between Egypt, China reaches $14.56B in 2020. *Egypt Today.* <https://www.egypttoday.com/Article/3/100267/Trade-exchange-between-Egypt-China-reaches-14-56B-in-2020>

Miles, H. (2006). *Al-Jazeera: The inside story of the Arab news channel that is challenging the West.* Grove Press.

Mishra, S. (2007). "Liberation" vs. "purity": Representations of Saudi women in the American press and American women in the Saudi press. *Howard Journal of Communications, 18*(3), 259–276. <https://doi.org/10.1080/10646170701490849>

Morello, C., & DeYoung, K. (2016, January 16). International sanctions against Iran lifted. *The Washington Post.* https://www.washingtonpost.com/world/national-security/world-leaders-gathered-in-anticipation-of-iran-sanctions-being-lifted/2016/01/16/72b8295e-babf-11e5-99f3-184bc379b12d_story.html?utm_term=.a8972fe24f1c

Neuendorf, K. A. (2016). *The content analysis guidebook.* London: Sage.

Neuendorf, K. A. (2017). *The content analysis guidebook* (2nd ed.). Sage publications.

Niblock, T. (2004). *Saudi Arabia: Power, legitimacy and survival.* Routledge.

Osiewicz, P. (2018). The Belt and Road Initiative (BRI): Implications for Iran-China relations. *Przeglad Strategiczny, 11*(September), 221–232. <https://doi.org/10.14746/ps.2018.1.16>

Peng, Z. (2004). Representation of China: An across time analysis of coverage in the New York Times and Los Angeles Times. *Asian Journal of Communication, 14*(1), 53–67. <https://doi.org/10.1080/0129298042000195170>

Peter, J., & Lauf, E. (2002). Reliability in cross-national content analysis. *Journalism & Mass Communication Quarterly, 79*(4), 815–832. <https://doi.org/10.1177/107769900207900404>

Pew Research Center. (2017). *China Image: Do you have a favorable or unfavorable view of China?* <http://www.pewglobal.org/database/indicator/24/survey/17/response/Unfavorable/>

Pjesivac, I., Luther, C. A., & Imre, I. (2018). Constructing an image of the United States in the British and French editorials about WikiLeaks. *Journal of International Communication, 24*(2), 216–237. <https://doi.org/10.1080/13216597.2018.1492432>

Poindexter, P. M., & McCombs, M. E. (2000). *Research in mass communication: A practical guide.* Macmillan.

Pope, N., & Pope, H. (2000). *Turkey unveiled: A history of modern Turkey.* Overlook Books.

Powers, S. (2009). *The geopolitics of the news: The case of the Al Jazeera network.* University of Southern California.

Rampal, K. R. (1994). Saudi Arabia. In Y. Kamalipour & H. Mowlana (Eds.), *Mass media in the Middle East: A comprehensive handbook* (pp. 244–1260). London: Greenwood Press.

Rand, A. (2016). # Feminism: The influence of feminist social media on the Millennial College Student. *Revaluing Feminist Communities.* <https://digitalcommons.winthrop.edu/sewsa/2016/fullschedule/53/>

Reader, S. L. (2013, November 12). Qatar shows how money can solve most problems. *BusinessDay.* <https://www.businesslive.co.za/archive/2013-11-12-qatar-shows-how-money-can-solve-most-problems/>

Reason, M., & García, B. (2007). Approaches to the newspaper archive: Content analysis and press coverage of Glasgow's year of culture. *Media, Culture & Society, 29*(2), 304–331. <https://doi.org/10.1177/0163443707074261>

Riffe, D., & Freitag, A. (1997). A content analysis of content analyses: Twenty-five years of Journalism Quarterly. *Journalism & Mass Communication Quarterly, 74*(3), 515–524. <https://doi.org/10.1177/107769909707400414>

Riffe, D., Lacy, S., & Fico, F. (2014). *Analyzing media messages: Using quantitative content analysis in research.* Routledge.

Rizvi, H.-A. (2016). The military and politics in Pakistan. *South Asia Journal of South Asian Studies, 31*(2), 65–76. <https://www.jstor.org/stable/41394233>

Salman, M. bin. (2016, September 3). Fusing vision 2030 with Belt Road Initiative. *Arab News.* <http://www.arabnews.com/node/979346/saudi-arabia>

Scott, D. (2015). China's public diplomacy rhetoric, 1990–2012: Pragmatic image-crafting. *Diplomacy and Statecraft, 26*(2), 249–265. <https://doi.org/10.1080/09592296.2015.1034563>

Semetko, H. A., Brzinski, J. B., Weaver, D., & Willnat, L. (1992). TV news and US public opinion about foreign countries: The impact of exposure and attention. *International Journal of Public Opinion Research, 4*(1), 18–36. <https://doi.org/10.1093/ijpor/4.1.18>

Seo, H. (2011). Media and foreign policy: A comparative study of journalists' perceptions of press—Government relations during the six-party talks. *Journalism, 12*(4), 467–481. <https://doi.org/10.1177/1464884910388227>

Shah, A. R. (2018). How does China–Pakistan economic corridor show the limitations of China's "One Belt One Road" Model? *Asia & The Pacific Policy Studies, December 2017.* <https://doi.org/10.1002/app5.224>

Shapshak, T. (2016, May 12). South Africa's economy falls to third behind Nigeria, Egypt. *Forbes Media LLC.* <https://www.forbes.com/sites/tobyshapshak/2016/05/12/south-africas-economy-falls-to-third-behind-nigeria-egypt/#4ac582244b78>

Shay, S. (2018). Saudi Arabia and the "nuclearization" of the Middle East. *Institute for Policy and Strategy, March.* <https://www.runi.ac.il/media/bnbddxrh/shaul_shay18_03_18.pdf>

Shira, D., & Assoicates. (2021, August 20). China and Iran: Bilateral trade relationship and future outlook. *China Briefing.* <https://www.middleeastbriefing.com/news/china-and-iran-bilateral-trade-relationship-and-future-outlook/>

Small, A. (2015). *The China-Pakistan axis: Asia's new geopolitics.* Oxford University Press.

Similarweb. (2023). <https://www.similarweb.com/website/dailysabah.com/#overview>

Similarweb. (2023). <https://www.similarweb.com/website/aljazeera.com/#overview>

Soroka, S. N. (2003). Media, public opinion, and foreign policy. *Harvard International Journal of Press/Politics, 8*(1), 27–48. <https://doi.org/10.1177/1081180X02238783>

Stempel, G. H. (2003). Content analysis. In G. H. Stempel, D. H. Weaver, & G. C. Wilhoit (Eds.), *Mass communication research and theory* (pp. 209–2119). Allyn & Bacon Boston, Massachusetts.

Sun, D., & Xu, R. (2022). China and Egypt's comprehensive strategic partnership in the Xi-sisi era: A "role theory" prism. *Mediterranean Politics, 00*(00), 1–21. <https://doi.org/10.1080/13629395.2022.2035139>

Teddlie, C., & Yu, F. (2007). Mixed methods sampling: A typology with examples. *Journal of Mixed Methods Research, 1*(1), 77–100. <https://doi.org/10.1177/1558689806292430>

Tehran Times. (2018, January 21). About us. *Tehran Times Daily Newspaper.* <http://www.tehrantimes.com/news/300000/about-us>

Temiz, K. (2018). An illustration of Sino-Turkish relations: The Cyprus question. *Insight Turkey, 20*(1). <https://www.insightturkey.com/articles/an-illustration-of-sino-turkish-relations-the-cyprus-question>

The Nation. (2023, July 20). About us. *Nawaiwaqt Group of Newspapers.* <https://nation.com.pk/about-us>

UN Comtrade. (2018, January 19). Trade statistics. *United Nations Statistics Division.* <https://comtrade.un.org/data/>

Vaisi, G. (2022, March 1). The 25-year Iran-China agreement, endangering 2,500 years of heritage. *Middle East Institute.* <https://www.mei.edu/publications/25-year-iran-china-agreement-endangering-2500-years-heritage>

Vandewalle, L. (2015, June 18). Pakistan and China: "Iron brothers" forever. *Think Tank European Parliament.* <https://www.europarl.europa.eu/thinktank/en/document/EXPO_IDA(2015)549052>

Wang, R., Kim, J., Xiao, A., & Jung, Y. J. (2017). Networked narratives on humans of New York: A content analysis of social media engagement on Facebook. *Computers in Human Behavior, 66*, 149–153. <https://doi.org/10.1016/j.chb.2016.09.042>

Weber, R. P. (1990). *Basic content analysis* (Issue 49). Sage.

Willnat, L., & Luo, Y. (2011). Watching the Dragon: Global television news about China. *Chinese Journal of Communication, 4*(3), 255–273. <https://doi.org/10.1080/17544750.2011.594552>

Wimmer, R. D., & Dominick, J. R. (2013). *Mass communication research: An introduction* (10th ed.). Cengage Learning.

Worth, R. F., & Kirkpatrick, D. D. (2011). Seizing a moment, Al Jazeera Galvanizes Arab frustration. *New York Times, 27.* <https://www.nytimes.com/2011/01/28/world/middleeast/28jazeera.html>

Xiang, D. (2013). China's image on international English language social media. *Journal of International Communication, 19*(2), 252–271. <https://doi.org/10.1080/13216597.2013.833535>

Xie, T., & Page, B. I. (2013). What affects China's national image? A cross-national study of public opinion. *Journal of Contemporary China, 22*(83), 850–867. <https://doi.org/10.1080/10670564.2013.782130>

Yang, Y. E., & Liu, X. (2012). The "China threat" through the lens of us print media: 1992–2006. *Journal of Contemporary China, 21*(76), 695–711. <https://doi.org/10.1080/10670564.2012.666838>

Yilmaz, B. (2022). Trade relations between China and Turkey: A comparison with the European Union. In *Stiftung Wissenschaft und Politik German Institute for International and Security Affairs.* <https://www.swp-berlin.org/publications/products/arbeitspapiere/WP01_22_FG7_Yilmaz_China_Turkey.pdf>

Zahlan, R. S. (2016). *The making of the modern Gulf States: Kuwait, Bahrain, Qatar, the United Arab Emirates and Oman* (Vol. 10). Routledge.

Zhang, C., & Meadows III, C. W. (2012). International coverage, foreign policy, and national image: Exploring the complexities of media coverage, public opinion, and presidential agenda. *International Journal of Communication, 6*, 20. <https://ijoc.org/index.php/ijoc/article/view/1424>

Zhang, J., & Cameron, G. T. (2003). China's agenda building and image polishing in the US: Assessing an international public relations campaign. *Public Relations Review, 29*(1), 13–28. <https://doi.org/10.1016/S0363-8111(02)00198-4>

Zhang, L., & Wu, D. (2017). Media representations of China: A comparison of China Daily and Financial Times in reporting on the Belt and Road Initiative. *Critical Arts, 31*(6), 29–43. <https://doi.org/10.1080/02560046.2017.1408132>

Zhong, L., & Zhang, J. (2016). Political myth as strategic communication: Analysis of Chinese dream's rhetoric and English news media's interpretation. *International Journal of Strategic Communication, 10*(1), 51–68. <https://doi.org/10.1080/1553118X.2015.1105229>

Zhu, W. (2010). On the strategic relationship between China and Islamic countries in the Middle East. *Journal of Middle Eastern and Islamic Studies (in Asia), 4*(3), 1–27. https://doi.org/10.1080/19370679.2010.12023159

Zhu, W. (2011). On the Strategic Relationship between China and Islamic Countries in the Middle East. *Journal of Sino-Islamic Communications, 3*(1), 1–27.

Zongyi, L. (2021, October 2). Why is it essential for China, Pakistan to enhance coordination against terrorists, safeguard regional stability? *Global Times*. <https://www.globaltimes.cn/page/202110/1235584.shtml>

VII Research Findings

This study used univariate and multivariate analysis to examine China's image in Islamic English news media. The univariate analysis was used as a descriptive statistic, that is, frequency tables and graphs (bar charts, pie charts, and line charts) to examine the trends and patterns regarding China's importance to the Islamic world, its overall image, and specific image dimensions in the Islamic world while multivariate analysis (e.g., correlations, chi-square, and regression) was used to measure the relationship between different dimensions of China's image in Islamic English news media and the possible effects of China's economic relations, its political system, and the Belt and Road Initiative on China's image construction, interpretation, and dissemination in the Islamic world from January 1, 2009, through December 31, 2018.

Descriptive statistics

Media attention intensity

Media attention is a fundamental component of a country's image perception. Scholars (Chang, 1998; Golan & Wanta, 2003; Jones et al., 2013) argue that the level of media attention to a particular foreign country indicates its significance in international relations as the salience of the countries in international news flow remains unequal. Scholarship indicates a positive correlation between the level of media attention and the level of importance attached to that particular country. A high level of attention intensity prioritizes the target place, actor, or issue in the policy-making agenda (Liu & Yang, 2015; Zhang & Meadows III, 2012).

This study found a total of 43,286 articles related to China in the six prominent Islamic English news media (that is, *Arab News* [Saudi Arabia], *The Nation* [Pakistan], *Daily Sabah* [Turkey], *Tehran Times* [Iran], *Daily News Egypt* [Egypt] and *Al-Jazeera English* [Qatar]) from January 1, 2009, through December 31, 2018. The study found 18,152 articles (42%) related to China in the Pakistani newspaper *The Nation,* followed by *the* Turkish newspaper *Daily Sabah* (8,069 articles, 19%). *Al-Jazeera English* published 4,939 articles (11%), *Daily News Egypt* published 4,853 articles (11%), and the Iranian newspaper *Tehran Times* published 3,666 articles (9%) related to China during the study. Whereas only 3,607 articles (8%) were found in the Saudi newspaper, *Arab News.* The results indicate that the Pakistani daily "*The Nation*" published the highest number of articles (N = 8,069) related to China. Whereas, Saudi daily *Arab News* published the lowest number of articles (N = 3,607) related to China from January 1, 2009, through December 31, 2018 (Figure 7.1). The higher media attention intensity paid to China-related articles by Pakistan daily *The Nation* indicates the strong economic and political relationship between the two countries. Historically, both countries enjoyed strong strategic relationships; and currently, China has pledged an amount of US$62 billion in investment through the China-Pakistan Economic Corridor (CPEC)—a flagship project of the Belt and Road Initiative in Pakistan (Bhola, 1986; Chaziza, 2016; Khan & Pratt, 2019; Lim, 2015). Scholars argue (Chang, 1998; Golan & Wanta, 2003; Jones et al., 2013; Liu & Yang, 2015; Zhang & Meadows III, 2012) that media attention to a particular foreign country indicates its importance and significance in foreign policy of that country. For example, scholars (Besova & Cooley, 2009; Wanta et al., 2004; Zhang & Meadows III, 2012) noted that the intensity of U.S. media attention to a particular country prioritizes its importance and perception of worth to the U.S. interests. Therefore, Pakistani media paid high attention to China-related news as both nations bonded in strong relationships as "Iron Brothers" (巴铁) "All weather friends" and "time tested and reliable strategic partners" (Lim, 2015; Vandewalle, 2015).

The study also found an upward trend and continuous increase in the media attention to China-related articles in the Islamic world, X^2 (df = 9, N = 4870) = 299.8, p < .001. The Islamic English news media published 1,033 articles (2.4%) related to China in 2009 and that number increased to 7387

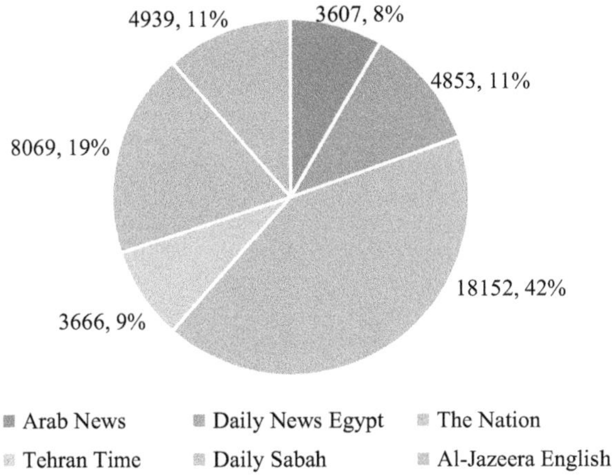

Figure 7.1: Number of Articles Related to China in Islamic English News Media.

articles (17.1%) in 2018. Thus, the study reported a total of 14.7% fluctuation in the number of China-related articles in Islamic media between 2009 and 2018 (Figure 7.2). However, results indicate a significant difference, X^2 ($df = 5$, $N = 4870$) = 302.6, $p < .001$ in the level of media attention paid to China-related news by the different Islamic English news media from January 1, 2009, through December 31, 2018 (Figure 7.1 and Table 6.1).

Pakistani daily *The Nation* published the highest number of articles (18,152, 42%) related to China in the Islamic world whereas *Arab News* published the lowest number of articles related to China (3,607, 8.3%). The results indicate the lowest number of articles related to China in 2009 (1033, 2.3%) and the highest number of articles in 2017 (7,841, 18.1%). The contribution of newspapers to the peak in 2017 was: *The Nation* (2,834 articles, 36.1%), *Daily Sabah* (2,174 articles, 27.3%), *Al-Jazeera English* (1,054 articles, 13.4%), *Tehran Times* (698 articles, 8.9%), *Daily News Egypt* (555 articles, 7.0%) and *Arab News* (526 articles, 6.7%), respectively (Figure 7.3). The higher media attention to China-related news by Islamic English news media in 2017 may be a result of China's hosting of the first successful Belt and Road Initiative Forum for International Cooperation since the commencement of BRI in 2013 which was attended by heads of state and governments from 29 countries, along with more than 1500 representatives from 130 countries and 70 international organizations—most of whom belong to the Islamic world in Beijing in May 2017. That event got global media attention, particularly Islamic English news media paid more attention to BRI-related news coverage than other international events coverage by Islamic news media in

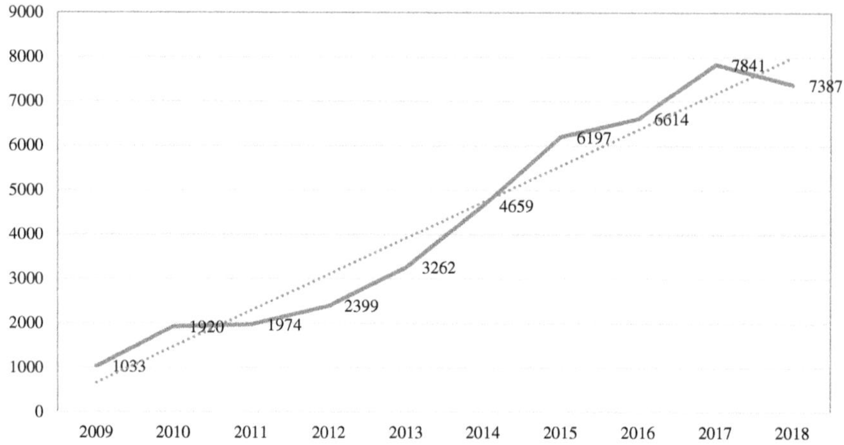

Figure 7.2: Trends and Changes in Attention Intensity Paid to China's Image in Islamic English News Media from January 1, 2009, through December 31, 2018.

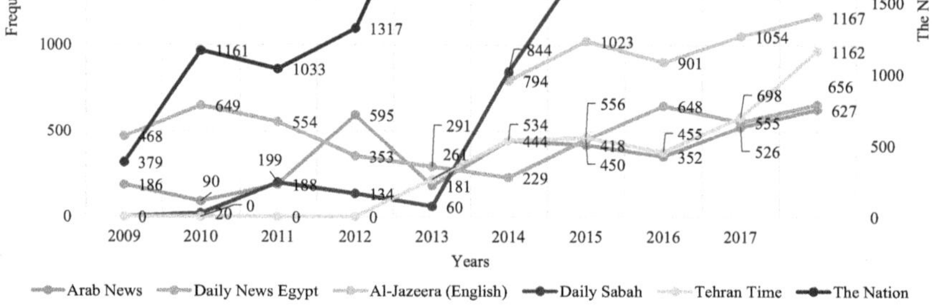

Figure 7.3: Trends and Changes in the Number of Articles Related to China in Specified Islamic English News Media.

the past. Interestingly, the study found a slight decline in the number of China-related articles (7387, 17.1%) in Islamic English news media in 2018 (Figure 7.2). The highest decline (668 articles) in media coverage of China was reported in the *Daily Sabah* from 2174 articles in 2017 to 1506 articles in 2018. Similarly, the Pakistani daily *The Nation* also reported a decline of 565 articles from 2834 articles related to China in 2017 to 2269 articles in 2018. The decline of China-related news coverage might be the result of a change in government in Pakistan and newly elected Prime Prime Minister Imran Khan's decision to review and reevaluate some major CPEC projects and put them on hold in the quest for compelling evidence to proceed carefully while keeping in mind the tottering national economy (Anderlini et al., 2018; Kiani, 2019).

China's BRI kicks off a larger media debate about China's new role in global economic and infrastructural development. Results indicate that the media attention intensity toward China significantly increased after the commencement of the Belt and Road Initiative projects in September 2013. This study found that Islamic English news media's attention intensity toward China-related news coverage increased from 24% of China's media coverage before the commencement of BRI (10,588 articles between 2009 and 2013) to 76% (32,698 articles between 2014 and 2018) after the commencement of the BRI projects in the Islamic world. However, the increase in China's related news coverage was not equally distributed. After the announcement of BRI, China-related coverage in *The Nation* increased from 6,358 articles (35%) to 11,793 articles (65%), in *Daily Sabah* from 413 articles (5%) to 7,656 articles (95%), in *Al-Jazeera English* from zero articles (0%) to 4,939 articles (100%). However, it is important to note that news coverage of China before the commencement of the BRI in *Al-Jazeera English* was not found in the LexisNexis database. China-related news coverage after the commencement of the BRI in *Tehran Times* increased from 261 articles (7%) to 3,405 (93%), in *Daily News Egypt* from 2,315 articles (48%) to 2,538 articles (52%), and in *Arab News* from 1,240 articles (34%) to 2,367 articles (66%), respectively (Figure 7.4). Results indicate that China-related coverage in *Daily Sabah* showed the highest increase (90%) after the commencement of the BRI while the least increase in media attention intensity was reported in *Daily News Egypt* (4%) (Figure 7.4). Under the ambit of BRI, China, and Turkey have strengthened their strategic partnership and started to work on common interests to further enhance their political and economic cooperation. Therefore, *Daily Sabah*'s coverage of China-related news has intensified in recent years.

Type of articles

The study found six types of articles related to China news coverage in the Islamic English news media, i.e., news, opinion, feature, editorial, interview, and letters to the editor. News is the most dominating type of article that frequently appeared (*N*=3,217, 66.1%) in the Islamic English news media. The second major type of

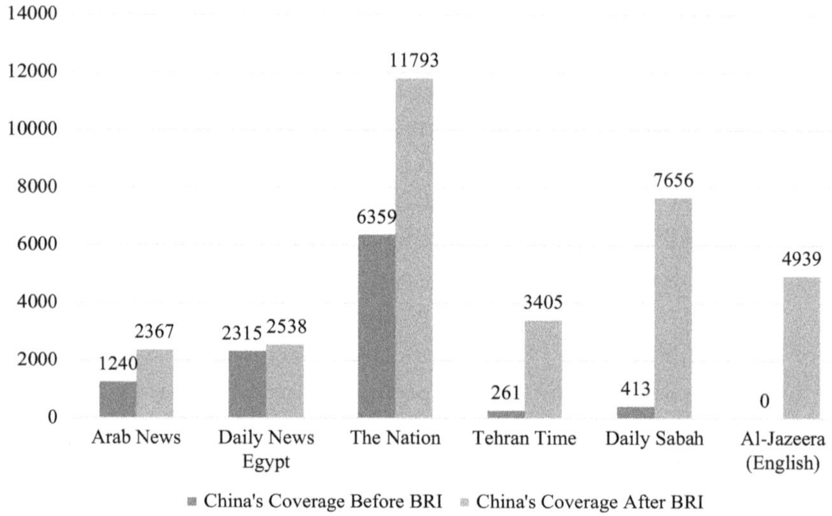

Figure 7.4: Media Attention Intensity Before and After China's Belt and Road Initiative.

article was opinion (*N*=1,469, 30.2%). News and opinion contributed 96.3% to the total type of articles related to China published by the Islamic English news media from January 1, 2009, through December 31, 2018. The other types of articles were features (*N*=104, 2.1%), interviews (*N*=56, 1.1%), editorials (*N*=17, 0.3%), and letters to the editor (*N*=7, 0.1%) respectively (Table 7.1).

Tone of the articles

Most of the articles related to China published by the Islamic English news media were positive (2,741, 56.3%). However, the study also found 1,252 (25.7%) negative articles and 877 (1.8%) neutral articles related to China in the Islamic English news media from January 1, 2009, through December 31, 2018 (Table 7.2).

Results found a significant increase in positive coverage of China, X^2 (df = 2, N = 4870) = 1195.8, p < 001) in the Islamic English news media from January 1, 2009, through December 31, 2018. Positive coverage related to China increased from 185 articles in 2009 to 323 articles in 2018. However, the study also found a slight increase in negative articles (N = 71) and neutral articles (N = 44) related to China to 143 negative articles and 134 neutral articles from 2009 to 2018 (Figure 7.5).

Table 7.1: Type of Articles Related to China in Islamic English News Media.

	Frequency	Percent
Opinion	1469	30.2
News	3217	66.1
Feature	104	2.1
Interview	56	1.1
Editorial	17	.3
Letters to the Editor	7	.1
Total	4870	100.0

Table 7.2: Tone of the Articles Related to China in Islamic English News Media.

	Frequency	Percent
Positive	2740	56.3
Neutral	877	18.0
Negative	1253	25.7
Total	4870	100.0

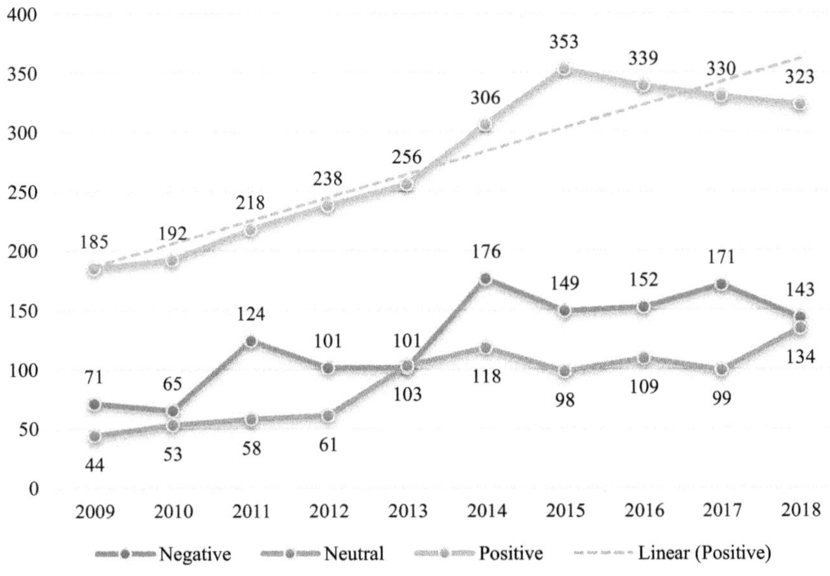

Figure 7.5: Trends and Changes in Negative, Positive, and Neutral Tone of the Articles.

Table 7.3: Journalistic Attitudes toward China-related Articles in Islamic English News Media.

	Journalistic Attitude		
Tone of the Articles	Analytical (*N*=1363, 28%)	Descriptive (*N*=2630, 54%)	Neutral (*N*=87, 18%)
Positive	894 (65.6%)	1847 (70.2%)	0 (0.0%)
Negative	469 (34.4%)	783 (29.8%)	0 (0.0%)
Neutral	0 (0.0%)	0 (0.0%)	87 (100.0%)

Journalistic attitude

Journalistic attitudes towards China-related articles in the Islamic English news media were mainly based on descriptive narratives (2,630 articles, 54%). Whereas, 1,363 articles (28%) used an analytical approach, and 18% (877 articles) were reported as neutral. Results indicate that journalists predominantly used positive descriptive approaches (1,847 articles, 70.2%) to write news about China. However, there were also negatively descriptive (783 articles, 29.8%) articles about China in the Islamic English news media. Positive analytical (894 articles, 65.6%) approaches were also used in discourse about China in the Islamic English news media. A few negative analytical articles (469, 34.4%) related to China also appeared in the Islamic English news media from January 1, 2009, through December 31, 2018 (Table 7.3).

Themes related to China

The study found five prominent themes in the articles related to China published in the Islamic English news media from January 1, 2009, through December 31, 2018. Interestingly, Politics was identified as the main dominant theme (1,989 articles, 40.8%) of the articles related to China in the Islamic English news media from January 1, 2009, through December 31, 2018. The economy was the second most domain theme (1,259 articles, 25.9%) that appeared in the Islamic English news media. Both politics and economy together contributed 66.7% to the overall themes related to China's image appearing in the Islamic English news media while culture (530 articles, 10.9%), science and technology (269 articles, 5.5%), social issues (243 articles, 5.0%), and Misc. (580 articles, 11.9%) were also reported by the Islamic English news media from January 1, 2009, through December 31, 2018 (Table 7.4).

Table 7.4: Themes related to China Reported by Islamic English News Media.

Themes	Frequency	Percent
Politics	1989	40.8
Economy	1259	25.9
Culture	530	10.9
Science and Technology	269	5.5
Social Issues	243	5.0
Misc.	580	11.9
Total	4870	100.0

Sub-Themes related to China

The study found a total of 26 sub-themes in the articles related to China. Political themes were represented by three major sub-themes: (a) Political and diplomatic relations (1,254 articles, 63%); (b) Defense and security (397 articles, 20%); and (c) Global values (338 articles, 17%). The economy was represented by six sub-themes: (a) Business, trade, and investment were reported as a dominant subtheme (878 articles, 70%); (b) Economic growth (156 articles, 13%); (c) Infrastructure development (99 articles, 8%); (d) Natural resources (89 articles, 7%); (e) Economic policies and reforms (21 articles, 2%) (e.g., China's economic policies, its economic reform agenda, and new economic institutions); and (f) Economic aids and loans (16 articles, 1%) respectively (Table 7.5).

The culture was represented by nine subthemes: (a) Sport (210 articles, 40%) emerged as the most prominent subtheme of culture in cultural articles related to China in Islamic English news media; followed by the sub-themes (b) Tourism (86 articles, 16%); (c) Education (70 articles, 13%); (d) History and artifacts (40 articles, 8%); (e) Media and entertainment (35 articles, 7%); (f) Fine arts (34 articles, 6%); (g) Ethnicity (27 articles, 5%); (h) Chinese language (18 articles, 3%); and (i) Chinese cuisines (10 articles, 2%) were also reported as a subtheme of culture in this study (Table 7.5).

Social issues were represented by seven subthemes: Health (135 articles, 56%) emerged as the most prominent subtheme in the social articles related to China in the Islamic English news media. Other prominent subthemes were welfare (35 articles, 14%), corruption (23 articles, 10%), poverty (18 articles, 7%), natural disasters (16 articles, 7%), crime (10 articles, 4%), and gender gap (6 articles, 2%)

Table 7.5: Sub-Themes related to China in Islamic English News Media.

	Frequency	Percent
Politics (*N*=1989)		
Political and Diplomatic Relations	1254	63.0
Defense and Security	397	20.0
Global Values	338	17.0
Economy (*N*=1259)		
Business, Trade, and Investment	878	69.7
Economic Growth	156	12.4
Infrastructure Development	99	7.9
Natural Resources	89	7.1
Economic Policies and Reforms	21	1.7
Economic Aid and Loans	16	1.3
Culture (*N*=530)		
Sport	210	39.6
Tourism	86	16.2
Education	70	13.2
History and Artifacts	40	7.5
Media and Entertainment	35	6.6
Fine-Art	34	6.4
Ethnicity	27	5.0
Chinese Language	18	3.4
Cuisines	10	1.9
Social Issues (*N*=243)		
Health	135	55.6
Welfare	35	14.4
Corruption	23	9.5
Poverty	18	7.4
Natural Disasters	16	6.5
Crime	10	4.1
Gender Gap	6	2.5
Science and Technology (*N*=269)		
Science and Technology	269	100
Misc. (*N*=580)		
Misc.	580	100

respectively. Articles related to science and technology were coded under single subthemes: science and technology (269 articles, 100%). The study reported 580 articles as miscellaneous (Table 7.5).

China's image construction, interpretation, and dissemination

The Islamic English news media constructed a positive image of China in the Islamic world. Positive discourses related to China dominated the Islamic English news media as the study found 2,741 positive articles (56.3%) related to China from January 1, 2009, through December 31, 2018. However, China's negative image was also reported in the Islamic English news media. The study found 1,252 negative articles (25.7%) related to China during the same study period while 877 articles (18.0%) represented China's image as neutral (Figure 7.6).

The Nation's framing of China's image in the Islamic world was reported as the most positive/favorable and least negative/unfavorable image of China in the Islamic world. The study indicates that *The Nation* published 73.7% of the positive articles (N = 737) related to China during the study period. 207 articles (20.7%) were neutral and only 5.6% of articles (N=56) were negative.

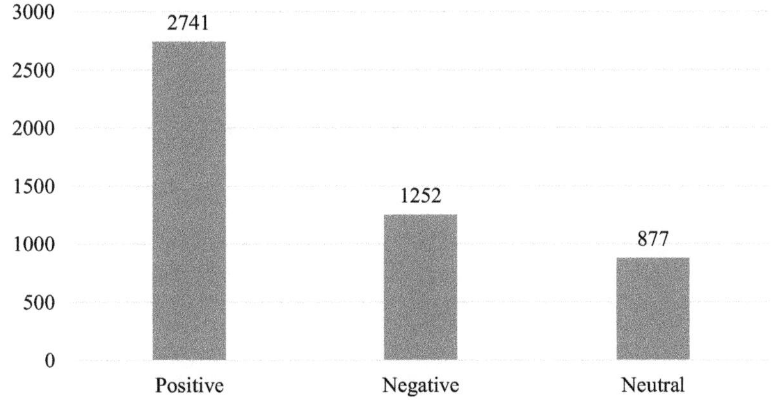

Figure 7.6: China's Image Construction in Islamic English News Media from January 1, 2009, through December 31, 2018.

These findings are very much consistent with the prevailing positive perception of China in Pakistan. According to the public opinion poll conducted by Pew Research Center from 2005 through 2017, an average of 80% of people hold a favorable image of China, and relatively less than 4.4% of people have an unfavorable image of China in Pakistan (Pew Research Center, 2017). In addition, China is a close ally, all-weather strategic partner of Pakistan, and the largest investor in the Pakistani economy in recent years.

Tehran Times was ranked second in positive China's image construction in the Islamic world. More than 61% of the articles (N = 371) published by the *Tehran Times* were positive, 157 articles (26.2%) were neutral and only 12% (71 articles) were negative. Positive coverage of China by the *Tehran Times* reflects the strong diplomatic and economic relationship between China and Tehran in the recent decade. *Arab News* was ranked third in positive coverage of China's image in the Islamic world. More than 60% of the total articles published by *Arab News* related to China were positive but a substantial number of articles (N=296, 30%) reported China's image as negative.

Results indicate that China's overall image construction by *Daily News Egypt* was positive (N=502, 50.2%) but there is a substantial number of articles (N= 333, 33.3%) that reported China's image as negative. Similarly, overall, China's image construction by *Daily Sabah* was positive (N= 351, 45.0%) but the number of negative articles related to China was pretty high (N= 277, 35.5%). According to the Pew Research Center (2017), general populations in Turkey and Egypt hold relatively negative opinions about China. More than 68% of people in Turkey and 53% in Egypt held an unfavorable image of China in 2013 (Pew Research Center, 2017). Therefore, the study found a significant number of negative articles related to China published in *Daily News Egypt* and *Daily Sabah* from January 1, 2009, through December 31, 2018.

The findings suggest that *Al Jazeera English* has presented China's image in a more negative light (N=218, 43.6%) than positive light (N=184, 36.8%). Reasons behind the negative image of China may be the relatively free (without any government control) and critical news approach by *Al Jazeera English*. It is considered one of the freest and most critical news media in the Islamic world that claims to provide voices to the unnoticed, isolated, and ignored audiences in the world, particularly the Muslim Ummah (El-Nawawy & Powers, 2010; Miles, 2006). It mainly focuses on political issues such as fundamental human rights, i.e., freedom of expression, freedom of religion, democratic rights, etc. which is the fragile and vulnerable part of China's image (Corkin, 2014; Li, 2008). The study noticed that 60% (n = 299) of articles related to China published by *Al Jazeera English*

Table 7.6: China's Image Construction by Islamic English News Media.

	China's Image		
	Positive (2,741, 56.3%)	Neutral (877, 18.0%)	Negative (1,252, 25.7%)
The Nation	737 (73.7%)	207 (20.7%)	56 (5.6%)
Tehran Times	371 (61.8%)	157 (26.2%)	72 (12.0%)
Arab News	596 (60.2%)	98 (9.9%)	296 (29.9%)
Daily News Egypt	502 (50.2%)	165 (16.5%)	333 (33.3%)
Daily Sabah	351 (45.0%)	152 (19.5%)	277 (35.5%)
Al Jazeera English	184 (36.8%)	98 (19.6%)	218 (43.6%)

are of a political theme. Therefore, China's image is constructed as more negative than positive in *Al Jazeera English* (Table 7.6).

China's image dimensions

The study found five different dimensions of China's image in the Islamic English news media: political, economic, cultural, social, and technological. China's political image received higher attention intensity as compared to other frames found in Islamic English news media. A total of 1,989 articles (41%) discuss China's political stature, its political issues, and its emerging role in global politics. China's economic image also received substantial coverage in Islamic English news media. A total of 1,259 articles (26%) discuss China's economic relations and its role in global economic governance. Results indicate that political and economic image dominated China's overall image in Islamic English news media and contributed an aggregate total of 67% to China's overall image in the Islamic world. Islamic English news media also paid attention to China's cultural image (11%), miscellaneous image (12%), social image (5%), and technological image (5%) respectively (Figure 7.7).

This study found a significant shift, X^2 $(df = 5, N = 4870) = 2841.9$, in China's image dimensions over time. China's political image and economic image have received a significant increase in news media attention in the Islamic world over time. For example, the political image received 117 articles in 2009 and it reached 244 articles in 2018. Similarly, economic coverage increased from 61 articles to 218 articles from 2009 to 2018. However, the study did not find any significant change in cultural, social, and technological coverage of China's image from January 1, 2009, through December 31, 2018 (Figure 7.8).

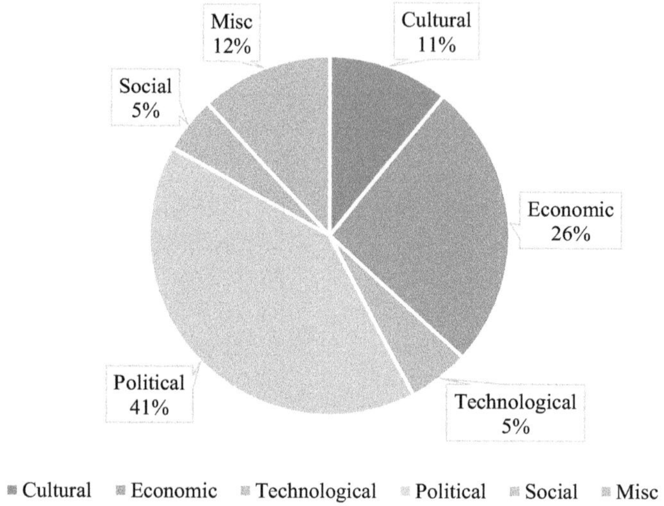

Figure 7.7: China's Image Dimensions in the Islamic World.

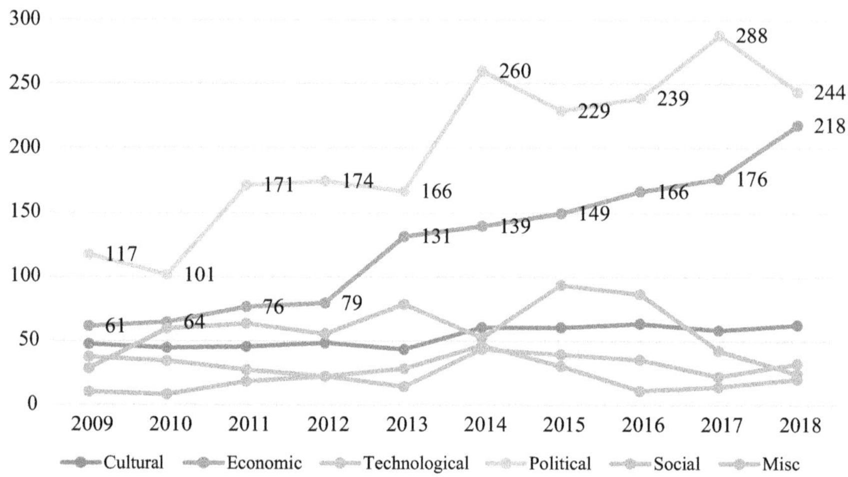

Figure 7.8: Trends and Changes Across Different Dimensions of China's Image from January 1, 2009, through December 31, 2018.

Interestingly, China's technological image received the most positive coverage in Islamic English news media than all other dimensions of China's image in the Islamic world. This study found that 73.6% of articles related to science and technology were positive, 16% were neutral and only 10.4% were negatively presented by Islamic English news media (Table 7.7). China's economic image also received positive reporting from Islamic English news media as 59.6% of the articles related to China's economic engagement and cooperation received a positive evaluation from the Islamic English news media. However, 22.2% of articles reported China's economic engagement with other countries in a negative tone. 18.2% of articles produced neutral discourses about China's economic role in the global economy. The cultural image received 55.4% positive coverage, 24.7% neutral, and 19.8% negative coverage in Islamic English news media. The social image received a 52.6% positive evaluation from Islamic English news media. However, a significant number of articles (33.8%) related to China's social image received a negative representation in Islamic English news media. This may be the result of stories related to corruption and corrupt practices in China while 13.6% of articles related to social image were reported as neutral. China's political image received the lowest number of positive evaluations (52.4%) among all the dimensions of China's image and a substantially higher number of negative presentations 30.1% in Islamic English news media while 17.5% of articles related to the political image received neutral coverage. The miscellaneous image received 56.7% positive, 27.2% negative, and 17.5% neutral coverage in Islamic English news media from January 1, 2009, through December 31, 2018 (Table 7.7).

China's technological image

The technological image was the most promising image dimension of China's national image in the Islamic world. It was dominated by science and technology-related discourses (269 articles) in the Islamic English news media. The study found a higher number of positive discourses (198 articles, 74%) related to

Table 7.7: Construction of China's Image Dimension in Islamic English News Media.

	China's Image Dimension		
	Positive	Neutral	Negative
Technological	198 (73.6%)	43 (16.0%)	28 (10.4%)
Economic	750 (59.6%)	229 (18.2%)	280 (22.2%)
Cultural	294 (55.4%)	131 (24.7%)	105 (19.8%)
Social	128 (52.6%)	33 (13.6%)	82 (33.8%)
Political	1042 (52.4%)	348 (17.5%)	599 (30.1%)
Misc.	329 (56.7%)	93 (16.0%)	158 (27.2%)

Table 7.8: China's Technological Image in Islamic English News Media.

	China's Technological Image		
	Positive	Neutral	Negative
Science and Technology	198 (73.6%)	43 (15.9%)	28 (10.4%)

China's technological image in Islamic English news media. Whereas 16% of articles related to the technological image were neutral and only 10% of articles projected China's negative technological image in the Islamic world from January 1, 2009, through December 31, 2018 (Table 7.8).

China's economic image

The second most promising dimension of China's national image is its economic image in the Islamic world. China's economic image was dominated by business, trade, and investment. A total of 70% of news coverage of China's economic image focuses on business, trade, and investment, 12.4% is related to economic growth, 7.9% is related to infrastructural development, 7.1% is related to natural resources, 1.7% is related to economic policies and reforms, and only 1.3% coverage is related to the economic aid and loans.

However, economic aid and loans received more positive coverage than other dimensions of China's economic image. A total of 93.8% of news coverage of economic aid and loans were positive whereas only 6.3% were reported as negative. Islamic English news media highly appreciated China's economic policies and reforms (85.7%) and only 9.5% of news reports cited it as negative. Infrastructure development also received positive coverage (72.7%). However, 21.2% of news reports cited China's infrastructure development projects as negative. Islamic English news media also give positive coverage (65.4%) of China's economic growth. However, 20.5% reported a decline in China's economic growth.

China's business, trade, and investment were also reported positively (57.9%). However, 20.1% of reports related to China's business, trade, and investment were negative. Interestingly, China's economic engagement in natural resources (e.g., oil and gas) received the lowest positive (46.1%) and highest negative (37.1%) coverage in Islamic new media from January 1, 2009, through December 31, 2018 (Table 7.9).

Table 7.9: China's Economic Image in Islamic English News Media.

		China's Economic Image		
		Positive	Neutral	Negative
Business, Trade, and Investment	(*N*=878, 69.7%)	501 (57.1%)	185 (21.1%)	192 (21.8%)
Economic Growth	(*N*=156, 12.4%)	102 (65.4%)	22 (14.1%)	32 (20.5%)
Infrastructure Development	(*N*=99, 7.9%)	72 (72.7%)	6 (6.1%)	21 (21.2%)
Natural Resources	(*N*=89, 7.1%)	41 (46.1%)	15 (16.9%)	33 (37.1%)
Economic Policies and Reforms	(*N*=21, 1.7%)	18 (85.7%)	1(4.8%)	2 (9.5%)
Economic Aid and Loans	(*N*=16, 1.3%)	15 (93.8%)	0 (0.0%)	1 (6.3%)

China's social image

Discourses related to China's social image were dominated by health-related news. A total of 56% of articles focus on health-related news, 14% on welfare, 10% on corruption, 7% on poverty, 7% on natural disasters, 4% on crime, and 3% on the gender gap. China's poverty alleviation efforts were predominantly reported positively (72.2%) in Islamic English news media. However, the study also found some negative news related to poverty (11.1%) in China during the study period. China's welfare initiative also got positive coverage (65.7%). However, there was also criticism of the welfare issues (20%). Health-related coverage remains positive (56.3%). However, 29.6% of articles related to health facilities in China were reported as negative. Corruption and corrupt practices of Chinese officials and state enterprises received equal reporting of positive (47.8%) coverage in battling corruption and negative (47.8%) coverage in case of prevailing corrupt practices in China in the Islamic English news media. Articles related to crime (90%), gender gap (83.3%), and natural disaster management (50%) were reported as the most negative aspects of China's social image in the Islamic world (Table 7.10).

China's cultural image

China's cultural image was dominated by sports (40%), followed by education (16%), tourism (13%), history and artifacts (8%), media and entertainment (7%),

Table 7.10: China's Social Image in Islamic English News Media.

		China's Social Image		
		Positive	Neutral	Negative
Health	(*N*=135, 55.6%)	76 (56.3%)	19 (14.1%)	40 (29.6%)
Welfare	(*N*=35, 14.4%)	23 (65.7%)	5 (14.3%)	7 (20.0%)
Corruption	(*N*=23, 9.5%)	11 (47.8%)	1 (4.4%)	11 (47.8%)
Poverty	(*N*=18, 7.4%)	13 (72.2%)	3 (16.7%)	2 (11.1%)
Natural Disasters	(*N*=16, 6.5%)	4 (25.0%)	4 (25.0%)	8 (50.0%)
Crime	(*N*=10, 4.1%)	1 (10.0%)	0 (0.0%)	9 (90.0%)
Gender Gap	(*N*=6, 2.5%)	0 (0.0%)	1 (16.7%)	5 (83.3%)

fine art (6%), ethnicity (5%), Chinese language (3%) and Chinese cuisine (2%) respectively. Chinese language-related news received the most positive coverage (94.4%) in the Islamic English news media. Education was the second most positive (74.3%) and less negative (11.4%) aspect of China's cultural image. Chinese cuisine received 60% positive and 20% negative coverage in the Islamic English news media. History and artifacts received 57.5% positive coverage. However, it also received 20% negative coverage. Media and entertainment received 57.5% positive coverage and 25.7% negative coverage. Tourism received 50% positive coverage but 29.1% negative coverage which made it the worst part of China's cultural image. The sports received 50% positive coverage and 19.5% negative coverage while ethnicity received 44.4% positive coverage and 22.2% negative coverage in Islamic English news media from January 1, 2009, through December 31, 2018 (Table 7.11).

China's political image

China's political and diplomatic engagement with the rest of the world dominated its political image (63%), followed by defense and security-related matters (20%). Global values received 17% coverage in the Islamic English news media. China's political and diplomatic role in international relations was the most positive aspect of China's political image (58.9%). However, it also received 23.8% negative and 17.2% neutral coverage. Defense and security-related engagement received 51.9% positive coverage and 25.9% negative coverage in Islamic English news media. 22.2% of coverage related to China's defense and security-related issues was neutral. Global values were the most negative aspect (58.3%) of China's political image. However, there was also positive (28.7%) and neutral (28.7%)

Table 7.11: China's Cultural Image in Islamic English News Media.

		China's Cultural Image		
		Positive	Neutral	Negative
Sports	(*N*=210, 39.6%)	105 (50.0%)	64 (30.5%)	41 (19.5%)
Tourism	(*N*=86, 16.2%)	43 (50.0%)	18 (20.9%)	25 (29.1%)
Education	(*N*=70, 13.2%)	52 (74.3%)	10 (14.3%)	8 (11.4%)
History and Artifacts	(*N*=40, 7.5%)	23 (57.5%)	9 (22.5%)	8 (20.0%)
Media and Entertainment	(*N*=35, 6.6%)	20 (57.1%)	6 (17.1%)	9 (25.7%)
Fine-Art	(*N*=34, 6.4%)	16 (47.1%)	12 (35.3%)	6 (17.6%)
Ethnicity	(*N*=27, 5.0%)	12 (44.4%)	9 (33.3%)	6 (22.2%)
Chinese Language	(*N*=18, 3.4%)	17 (94.4%)	1 (5.6%)	0 (0.0%)
Cuisines	(*N*=10, 1.9%)	6 (60.0%)	2 (20.0%)	2 (20.0%)

Table 7.12: China's Political Image in Islamic English News Media.

		China's Political Image		
		Positive	Neutral	Negative
Political and Diplomatic Relations	(*N*=1254, 63.0%)	739 (58.9%)	216 (17.2%)	299 (23.8%)
Defense and Security	(*N*=397, 20.0%)	206 (51.9%)	88 (22.2%)	103 (25.9%)
Global Values	(*N*=338, 17.0%)	97 (28.7%)	44 (13.0%)	197 (58.3%)

coverage related to China's adherence to the global values in Islamic English news media from January 1, 2009, through December 31, 2018 (Table 7.12).

China's comparative image in the Islamic World

China did not possess a unified image in the Islamic world. Results indicate a significant difference in China's image, X^2 [(df = 5, N = 1000) = 1248.7, p < 001] in the Islamic English news media. However, there is some similarity in China's image projection among these Islamic media. For example, China's image projection in *Al Jazeera English* (Qatar) is correlated (r = .346, p < 01) with *Daily*

Table 7.13: Correlation Between China's Global Image in the Islamic World.

	1	2	3	4	5	6
1. China's Image in Qatar	1					
2. China's Image in Saudi Arabia	.000	1				
3. China's Image in Egypt	.034	.001	1			
4. China's Image in Turkey	.346**	-.027	-.025	1		
5. China's Image in Iran	.672**	-.001	.028	.394**	1	
6. China's Image in Pakistan	-.078*	-.018	-.070*	.042	-.026	1

**p < .01, *p < .05

Sabah (Turkey); and with *Tehran Times* (Iran) (r = .672, p < 01). The study also found a significant relationship (r = .394, p < 01) between *Tehran Times* (Iran) and *Daily Sabah* (Turkey). Those three news media have paid more attention to China's political image than other aspects of China's image. Results indicate that there was a negative correlation between China's Image in Pakistan and Qatar (r = -.078, p < 01); and between Pakistan and Egypt (r = -.070, p < 01) (Table 7.13).

China's image in a specific Islamic Country

China holds a mixed image (both positive and negative) in the Islamic world. The results indicate that China's image in Pakistan (r = .178, p < 01), Saudi Arabia (r = .040, p < 01), and Iran (r = .042, p < 01) were significantly positive while the study found China's negative image projection in Turkey (r = .098, p < 01), Egypt (r = .088, p < 01), and Qatar (r = .138, p < 01) (Table 7.14). These results are consistent with China's historical image perception in Turkey and Egypt as negative (Al-Sudairi, 2013; Pew Research Center, 2017; Xie & Page, 2013).

Interestingly, the study found China's positive image projection in Saudi Arabia and Iran which contradicts the findings of prior studies on China's image perception in Saudi Arabia and Iran (Al-Sudairi, 2013; J. Chen, 2011; Ehteshami et al., 2018). The projection of China's positive image in Saudi Arabia and Iran may be the result of China's improving economic and political relationship with Saudi Arabia and Iran in recent years.

China's image dimensions, in particular, Islamic English News Media

This study found a significant difference, X^2 [(df = 5, N = 4870) = 2879.4, p < 001] in China's image dimensions in Islamic English news media from January

Table 7.14: China's Positive and Negative Image in the Islamic World.

	Positive Image	Negative Image
China's Image in Qatar	-.133**	.138**
China's Image in Saudi Arabia	.040**	.048**
China's Image in Egypt	-.062**	.088**
China's Image in Turkey	-.099**	.098**
China's Image in Iran	.042**	-.118**
China's Image in Pakistan	.178**	-.234**

**$p < .01$

1, 2009, through December 31, 2018. *Al-Jazeera English* mainly focused on the political aspect of China's image. The study found that 60% of coverage about China on *Al-Jazeera English* was related to politics. The economic aspect of China's image received less attention in *Al-Jazeera English* (14.2%). *Arab News* focuses more on the political (32.5%) and economic (28.4%). However, 20.5% of miscellaneous themes were also reported related to China's image in *Arab News*. *Daily Egypt News* focuses more on political (41.5%) and economic (28.9%) issues while political discourses (45.3%) related to China dominated in *Daily Sabah*. Economic themes received only 12.9% coverage whereas 22.8% of themes were miscellaneous. *Tehran Time* also paid more attention to political themes (51.5%). However, considerable attention was paid to economic themes (28.2%) as well. *The Nation* paid more attention to the economic (34.8%) aspect of China's image, followed by political (29.1%) and technological image (19.4%) (Table 7.15).

Results indicate that China's economic ($r = .039$, $p < 01$) and technological image ($r = .084$, $p < 01$) received more positive coverage in Islamic English news media. Whereas China's political image ($r = .084$, $p < 01$) was reported negatively in Islamic English news media. Historically, China's political image remained unstable and was often portrayed negatively in news media coverage (Corkin, 2014; Li, 2008). Social and cultural images were not found significant in this study (Table 7.16).

Effects of China's political system on China's image

The study found a positive relationship between the political system and China's image ($r = .229$, $p < 01$) construction in Islamic English news media. Constitutional monarchy in Qatar has shown a negative association with a

Table 7.15: Coverage of China's Image Dimensions in Islamic English News Media.

	Cultural	Economic	Technological	Political	Social	Misc.
Al-Jazeera English	43 (8.6%)	71 (14.2%)	9 (1.8%)	299 (59.8%)	31 (6.2%)	47 (9.4%)
Arab News	88 (8.9%)	281 (28.4%)	19 (1.9%)	322 (32.5%)	77 (7.8%)	203 (20.5%)
Daily Egypt News	114 (11.4%)	289 (28.9%)	12 (1.2%)	415 (41.5%)	35 (3.5%)	135 (13.5%)
Daily Sabah	64 (8.2%)	101 (12.9%)	23 (2.9%)	353 (45.3%)	61 (7.8%)	178 (22.8%)
Tehran Time	85 (14.2%)	169 (28.2%)	12 (2.0%)	309 (51.5%)	8 (1.3%)	17 (2.8%)
The Nation	136 (13.6%)	348 (34.8%)	194 (19.4%)	291 (29.1%)	31 (3.1%)	0 (0.0%)

Table 7.16: Positive and Negative Aspects of China's Image Dimensions in the Islamic World.

	Positive Image	Negative Image
Cultural Image	-.021	-.037
Economic Image	.039**	-.047**
Technological Image	.084**	-.085**
Political Image	-.065**	.084**
Social Image	.004	.022

$^{**}p < .01$

positive image (r = -.133, p < 01) and a positive (r = .138, p < 01) association with a negative image. Absolute authoritarian monarchy in Saudi Arabia was positively correlated with both positive (r = .040, p < 01) and negative image (r = .048, p < 01) construction. Presidential (r = .098, p < 01) system in Turkey and the semi-presidential system (r = .088, p < 01) in Egypt were positively associated with a negative image and negatively (r = -.099, p < 01; r = -.062, p < 01) associated with positive image respectively. Whereas theocracy (r = .042, p < 01) in Iran and the federal parliamentary system (r = .178, p < 01) in Pakistan have shown a positive relationship with a positive image and a negative relationship (r = -.118, p < 01; r = -.234, p < 01) with negative image respectively (Table 7.17).

Table 7.17: Effects of the Country's Political System on China's Image Construction in the Islamic World.

	Positive Image	Negative Image
Constitutional Monarchy (Qatar)	-.133**	.138**
Absolute Authoritarian Monarchy (Saudi Arabia)	.040**	.048**
Semi Presidential System (Egypt)	-.062**	.088**
Presidential System (Turkey)	-.099**	.098**
Theocracy (Iran)	.042**	-.118**
Federal Parliamentary System (Pakistan)	.178**	-.234**

$^{**}p < .01$

Effects of economic relationship on China's image

China's economic relationship with the Islamic world partially affected its image in Islamic English news media. The study found a negative association between China's economic relations and its positive image ($r = -.057, p < 01$) in the Islamic world. China's exports were positively associated with China's negative image construction in the Islamic news world ($r = .045, p < 01$) while China's imports from the Islamic world did not show any significance to its positive or negative image in the Islamic world. China's image in Qatar has shown a positive correlation with imports and exports. The positive correlation may be the result of China's balanced economic relationship with Qatar. Interestingly, China's image in Pakistan has also shown a positive correlation with China's imports from Pakistan ($r = .045, p < 05$). China's image in Saudi Arabia, Egypt, Turkey, and Iran does not show any significant relationship with imports or exports in China (Table 7.18). China is a major exporter to the Islamic world, but China's import from the Islamic world is relatively low. Therefore, there is a significant trade imbalance between China and the Islamic world (UN Comtrade, 2018). Turkey and Egypt have shown their concerns regarding the trade deficit with China (Ergenc, 2015; Temiz, 2018; Zhu, 2010). Therefore, it may contribute to China's negative image projection in the Islamic world (Table 7.18).

Table 7.18: Effects of China's Economic Relationship on China's Image Construction in the Islamic World.

	Imports	Exports
Positive Image	-.024	-.057**
Negative Image	-.024	.045**
China's Image in Qatar	.486**	.635**
China's Image in Saudi Arabia	-.032	-.041
China's Image in Egypt	-.042	-.043
China's Image in Turkey	.053	.059
China's Image in Iran	-.067	.079
China's Image in Pakistan	.077*	-.008

**$p < .01$, *$p < .05$

Effects of the Belt and Road Initiative on China's image

Belt and Road Initiative (BRI) significantly contributed to China's positive image (r = .031, p < 05) construction in the Islamic world. Results indicate that BRI contributed positively to China's technological image (r = .083, p < 01) and to China's economic image (r = -.087, p < 01). But showed a negative association with a political image (r = -.030, p < 05). However, the study did not find any significant impact of the BRI on China's social and cultural image (Table 7.19).

Results indicate that China's Belt and Road Initiative also contributed positively to China's positive image construction in Saudi Arabia (r = .115, p < 01), Egypt (r = .121, p < 01), and Pakistan (r = .121, p < 01). The study also found a negative correlation between BRI and China's image in Qatar (r = -.267, p < 01) and Iran (r = -.167, p < 01). However, the BRI did not affect China's image in Turkey (Table 7.19).

Table 7.19: Effects of the Belt and Road Initiative on China's Image Construction in the Islamic World.

	Effects of Belt and Road Initiative
China's Image	
Positive Image	.031*
Negative Image	-.018
China's Image Dimensions	
Cultural image	.021
Economic Image	.070**
Technological Image	.083**
Political Image	-.030*
Social Image	-.022
China's Image in Particular Country	
China's Image in Qatar	-.267**
China's Image in Saudi Arabia	.115**
China's Image in Egypt	.121**
China's Image in Turkey	-.022
China's Image in Iran	-.167**
China's Image in Pakistan	.121**

**$p < .01$, *$p < .05$.

Belt and Road Initiative is used as an independent variable to measure its effects on China's overall image, image dimension, and China's image in a particular Islamic country.

References

Al-Sudairi, M. T. (2013). China in the eyes of the Saudi Media. *Gulf Research Center, February*(February), 1–38. <https://www.ictsd.org/sites/default/files/downloads/2013/04/china-in-the-eyes-of-the-saudi-media.pdf>

Anderlini, J., Sender, H., & Bokhari, F. (2018, September). Pakistan rethinks its role in Xi's Belt and Road plan. *Financial Times*. <https://www.ft.com/content/d4a3e7f8-b282-11e8-99ca-68cf89602132>

Besova, A. A., & Cooley, S. C. (2009). Foreign news and public opinion: Attribute agenda-setting theory revisited. *Ecquid Novi African Journalism Studies, 30*(2), 219–242. <https://doi.org/10.3368/ajs.30.2.219>

Bhola, P. L. (1986). *Pakistan-China relations: Search for Politico-Strategic Relationship*. RBSA Publishers.

Chang, T.-K. (1998). All countries not created equal to be news: World system and international communication. *Communication Research*, *25*(5), 528–563. <https://doi.org/10.1177/009365098025005004>

Chaziza, M. (2016). China–Pakistan relationship: A game-changer for the Middle East? *Contemporary Review of the Middle East*, *3*(2), 147–161. <https://doi.org/10.1177/2347798916638209>

Chen, J. (2011). *The emergence of China in Middle East* (Issue 271, pp. 1–8). National Defense University, Washington, DC. <https://doi.org/10.1111/j.1539-6975.2009.01318.x>

Corkin, L. J. (2014). China's rising soft power: The role of rhetoric in constructing China-Africa relations. *Revista Brasileira de Politica Internacional*, *57*, 49–72. <https://doi.org/10.1590/0034-7329201400204>

Ehteshami, A., Horesh, N., & Xu, R. (2018). Chinese-Iranian mutual strategic perceptions. *The China Journal*, *79*(79), 1–20. <https://doi.org/10.1086/693315>

El-Nawawy, M., & Powers, S. (2010). Al-Jazeera English: A conciliatory medium in a conflict-driven environment? *Global Media and Communication*, *6*(1), 61–84. <https://doi.org/10.1177/1742766510362019>

Ergenc, C. (2015). Can two ends of Asia meet? An overview of contemporary Turkey-China Relations. *East Asia*, *32*(3), 289–308. <https://doi.org/10.1007/s12140-015-9242-6>

Golan, G., & Wanta, W. (2003). International elections on US network news: An examination of factors affecting newsworthiness. *International Communication Gazette*, *65*(1), 25–39. <https://doi.org/10.1177/0016549203065001135>

Jones, T. M., Van Aelst, P., & Vliegenthart, R. (2013). Foreign nation visibility in US news coverage: A longitudinal analysis (1950–2006). *Communication Research*, *40*(3), 417–436. <https://doi.org/10.1177/0093650211415845>

Khan, M. K., & Pratt, C. B. (2019). China's Belt and Road Initiative: Its landscape (and trajectory) in the Islamic World. In A. Visvizi, M. Lytras, X. Zhang, & J. Zhao (Eds.), *Foreign business in China and opportunities for technological innovation and sustainable economics* (pp. 117–142). IGI Global. <https://doi.org/10.4018/978-1-5225-8980-8.ch006>

Kiani, K. (2019, January 14). Govt puts major CPEC power project on hold. *Dawn*. <https://www.dawn.com/news/1457449>

Li, M. (2008). *Soft power in Chinese discourse : Popularity and prospect*. <http://hdl.handle.net/10220/4552>

Lim, A. C.-H. (2015). Iron Brothers': Sino-Pakistani relations and the China-Pakistan economic corridor. *Eurasia Review*. <https://www.academia.edu/12286990/_Iron_Brothers_Sino_Pakistani_Relations_and_the_China_Pakistan_Economic_Corridor>

Liu, X., & Yang, Y. E. (2015). Examining China's official media perception of the United States: A content analysis of people's daily coverage. *Journal of Chinese Political Science*, *20*(4), 385–408. <https://doi.org/10.1007/s11366-015-9340-8>

Miles, H. (2006). *Al-Jazeera: The inside story of the Arab news channel that is challenging the West*. Grove Press.

Pew Research Center. (2017). *China Image: Do you have a favorable or unfavorable view of China?* <http://www.pewglobal.org/database/indicator/24/survey/17/response/Unfavorable/>

Temiz, K. (2018). An illustration of Sino-Turkish relations: The Cyprus question. *Insight Turkey, 20*(1). <https://www.insightturkey.com/articles/an-illustration-of-sino-turkish-relations-the-cyprus-question>

UN Comtrade. (2018, January 19). Trade statistics. *United Nations Statistics Division.* <https://comtrade.un.org/data/>

Vandewalle, L. (2015, June 18). Pakistan and China: "Iron brothers" forever. *Think Tank European Parliament.* <https://www.europarl.europa.eu/thinktank/en/document/EXPO_IDA(2015)549052>

Wanta, W., Golan, G., & Lee, C. (2004). Agenda setting and international news: Media influence on public perceptions of foreign nations. *Journalism & Mass Communication Quarterly, 81*(2), 364–377. <https://doi.org/10.1177/107769900408100209>

Xie, T., & Page, B. I. (2013). What affects China's national image? A cross-national study of public opinion. *Journal of Contemporary China, 22*(83), 850–867. <https://doi.org/10.1080/10670564.2013.782130>

Zhang, C., & Meadows III, C. W. (2012). International coverage, foreign policy, and national image: Exploring the complexities of media coverage, public opinion, and presidential agenda. *International Journal of Communication, 6*, 20. <https://ijoc.org/index.php/ijoc/article/view/1424>

Zhu, W. (2010). On the strategic relationship between China and Islamic countries in the Middle East. *Journal of Middle Eastern and Islamic Studies (in Asia), 4*(3), 1–27. <https://doi.org/10.1080/19370679.2010.12023159>

VIII

Discussion and Conclusion

The study investigates China's stature and image in the Islamic English news media and helps guide its policy in—and engagement with—the Islamic world. It provides an understanding of how the economic relationship, BRI and political system of the different Islamic countries have influenced China's image construction, interpretation, and dissemination in Islamic English news media.

Discussion

China's westward policy "Westward March" to engage Islamic countries for strategic, political, and economic purposes and the Islamic world's eastward push (toward China) to realign its strategic calculus to form a new strategic alliance with China for strategic, political, and economic leverages has fortified the geopolitical, geo-economic, and geostrategic relationship between the two great civilization (Galal, 2014; Guzansky & Orion, 2017; Khan et al., 2018; Khan & Pratt, 2019). As a result, China-related news coverage has become more prominent in Islamic English news media. The news media's attention intensity toward China has increased manifold in the Islamic world during the last decade. The study found that China's coverage in the Islamic English news media (i.e., *The*

Nations, Arab News, Daily Sabah, Al-Jazeera English, Daily News Egypt, and *Tehran Times*) has expanded to a total of 43, 286 news articles from January 1, 2009, through December 31, 2018. The study finds a significant increase in the number of articles related to China in the Islamic English news media from 1,033 articles in 2009 to 7,387 articles in 2018. This indicates the increasing influence and importance of China in the Islamic world. Particularly, after the commencement of China's Belt and Road Initiative, China's coverage in the Islamic English news media increased from 24% of the total coverage of China between 2009 and 2013 to 76% of the news coverage of China between 2014 and 2019. The increase in media attention to China-related news in the Islamic English news media manifests the importance and relevance of China's new role in the Islamic world. Scholars (Chang, 1998; Jones et al., 2013; Liu & Yang, 2015; Zhang & Meadows III, 2012) argue that media attention significantly mediates the importance and significance of the reported country (i.e., China) in the foreign policy of that particular reporting country. Therefore, media attention to China-related news is not equally persistent in the Islamic English news media (Chang, 1998). Being the "all-weather friends" and "Iron Brothers", the Pakistani newspaper, *The Nation* had paid more attention to China-related news coverage than other Islamic English news media outlets in the Islamic world, as the study found 18,152 news articles (42%) related to China in Pakistani daily (*The Nation*) during the study period. The higher media attention to China-related news by Pakistani news media signifies the importance of China in Pakistani foreign policy and strong strategic relations between the two countries. Historically, China and Pakistan are considered strategic partners in Asia and beyond. The relationship between the two countries is often labeled as "Iron Brothers" (巴铁) "all-weather friends" and "time-tested and reliable strategic partners" etc (Fels, 2017; Lim, 2015; Vandewalle, 2015).

China is a major foreign investor in Pakistan and its latest venture, China-Pakistan Economic Corridor (CPEC) is one of the leading projects of China's Belt and Road Initiative, with more than US$62 billion investment. The project is considered a "game-changer" and a "ray of hope" to bring economic prosperity through infrastructure development, energy projects, and regional connectivity to Pakistan and China (Kamel, 2018; Rizvi, 2016; Shah, 2018; Small, 2015). Therefore, Pakistani news media paid significantly higher attention to China-related news in Pakistan. The Turkish newspaper, *Daily Sabah* emerged as the second-highest news media in the Islamic world which paid significant attention to China-related news (8,069 articles, 19%), followed by *Al-Jazeera English* (4,939 articles, 11%), *Daily News Egypt* (4,853 articles, 11%), *Tehran Times* (3,666 articles, 9%) respectively. Increasing media attention of China in a Turkish newspaper, *Daily Sabah* is due to the emergence of a new strategic partnership between the two countries. Both countries have recently integrated their ambitious flagship projects (i.e., China's BRI and Turkey's Middle Corridor) for better economic engagement and cooperation in the region.

Saudi newspaper, *Arab News* paid the least coverage to China-related news (3,607 articles, 8%) in the Islamic English news media. The reason behind the low media attention toward China in Saudi Arabia may be the result of the wobbly relationship between the two countries. Saudi Arabia is the last Arab country that established a diplomatic relationship with China in 1990. But the post-haste changes in geo-economics, geo-politics, and geostrategic dynamics, particularly after 9/11 brought the two nations closer and the incumbent Saudi King Abdullah bin Abdulaziz Al Saud chose China as his first foreign destination for an official visit despite being a close ally of the U.S. in the Middle East while ascending to the throne in January 2006. Recently, Saudi Crown Prince Mohammed bin Salman visited Beijing to integrate Saudi Vision 2030 with China's BRI to strengthen Sino-Saudi Arabia relations in August 2016, but the Kingdom still relies more on the U.S. than China for geo-political and geostrategic support in world affairs (Al-Sudairi, 2013; Grey, 2017; Khan & Pratt, 2019). Therefore, Saudi mainstream news media did not pay much attention to China in Saudi Arabia.

China-related news received predominantly positive coverage in the Islamic English news media and the majority of the articles related to China published by the Islamic English news media were positive (2,741 articles, 56.3%). However, the study also found a significant number of negative (N = 1,252, 25.7%) and neutral articles (N = 877, 18.0%) related to China in Islamic English news media. China's positive news coverage in Islamic English news media is the result of journalists' descriptive attitude toward China-related news reporting that chiefly dominated the media discourses. The study found more descriptive discourses (2,630 articles, 54%) about China as compared to analytical or interpretative discourses (1,362 articles, 28%) in the Islamic English news media. Journalists working for the Islamic English news media often follow the descriptive style of news writing to report the news about China that merely communicates the descriptive account of the events, persons, things, places, and time by focusing on what, who, when, where, and how—while ignoring the answer of the most important tenet of news writing—why and with what effect—in other words, explaining the impacts, consequences, and interpretation of the given situation. In contrast, Western journalists employ a more independent approach to interpretive news reporting that not only explains what happens but also why it happens—explaining the background, evaluating and interpreting the situations while underlying the impacts and consequences of the events (Albæk, 2011; Salgado & Strömbäck, 2012). The journalist employs different approaches to news coverage that facilitate the beneficiaries of the news messages. Therefore, descriptive reporting is often adopted for or against any state without a careful analysis of the emerging socio-economic and political realities, but simply carrying forward the messages of the government, political elites, interest groups, or audiences.

In recent years, China and the Islamic countries have improved their relationships and signed new comprehensive strategic partnership agreements under the BRI framework. The perception of China in the Islamic world has also enhanced and people in the Islamic world started to view China as an alternative responsible global power that can help resolve the Islamic world's lingering regional disputes, haunting economic challenges, and much-needed infrastructure development to foster economic growth and to improve people living standards in the Islamic countries (Khan et al., 2018; Khan & Pratt, 2019). The recent China-facilitated peace deal between Saudi Arabia and Iran further cemented this argument and strengthened China's political stature in the Islamic world. Whereas the Islamic world's concerns over the Western powers' meddling in the internal affairs of the Islamic countries, perceived perennial distrust over Western political directives, and hegemonic stance on regional issues have been aggravated (see the contentious issues between the Islamic world and the West—the lingering dispute between Israel and Palestine, the wars in Iraq, Syria, Libya and Afghanistan, and Iran's nuclear program, etc.) and brought the two great civilization closer to each other (Al-Ghwell, 2018; Almedia, 2018; Khan & Pratt, 2019). Therefore, the Islamic English news media started to pay more attention to China and projected its positive image in more descriptive and less critical ways in the Islamic world.

The Islamic English news media constructed a diverse image of China in the Islamic world. The study found five prominent themes (politics, economy, culture, science and technology, and social issues) and 26 sub-themes (Tables 7.4 & 7.5) in China-related news coverage in Islamic English news media from January 1, 2009, through December 31, 2018. Politics was a major theme (1,989 articles, 40.8%) related to China that appeared in the Islamic English news media. Whereas economy (1,259 articles, 25.9%) was the second major theme that frequently appeared in the Islamic English news media. Both politics and economy together contributed 66.7% to the overall themes related to China that appeared in Islamic English news media. The cultural and technological dimensions (theme) of China's image also received palpable coverage in the Islamic English news media. Whereas social issues-related themes received the lowest attention (243 articles, 5%) in Islamic English news media (Table 7.4).

The Western news media coverage ofttimes represents China in one dimension—extensively focuses on the political dimension (theme) of China's image, playing up the human rights issues, freedom of expression, political suppression, anti-communist framing, etc. It pays less or little heed to China's social transformation (education, social issues, science, and technology), cultural prestige, technological and economic achievements, etc. (Lams, 2016; Richter & Gebauer, 2011; Willnat & Luo, 2011). In contrast, the Islamic English news media accentuated both the political and economic themes and hearkened to the social, cultural, and technological themes as well during the study period.

The Islamic English news media constructed China's positive image in the Islamic world (Figure 7.6). However, the construction of China's positive image varied significantly in different Islamic English news media. Pakistani news media, *The Nation* has constructed the most positive image of China in the Islamic world, followed by *Tehran Times* (Iran) and *Arab News* (Saudi Arabia). China's image projection and construction in Turkey, Egypt, and Qatar was partially negative. Those results are somehow consistent with historical facts that China holds the most favorable image perception in Pakistan. Historically, Pakistan and China enjoy friendly relations and Pakistani people hold a positive perception of China. More than 80% of the people view China-Pakistan relations positively as indicated by the Pew Research Center survey on China's global image conducted between 2005 through 2015 (Pew Research Center, 2017). China-Pakistan Economic Corridor (CPEC)—China's flagship investment of US$62 billion in Pakistan further magnifies the positive sentiments about China and, therefore, Pakistani news media jampacked with positive and friendly framing of China as an "iron brother" and "all-weather friend" (Ittefaq et al., 2021). However, some intricacies and sensitivities related to the CPEC and BRI also appeared in the Pakistani news media (Afzaal et al., 2019; Khan et al., 2020).

The study indicates that China's image projection in Iran and Saudi Arabia's news media is positive which contradicts the previous research findings of China's negative public perception in these countries (Al-Sudairi, 2013; Chen, 2011; Ehteshami et al., 2018). China's positive image projection in Saudi Arabia and Iran might be the result of China's growing bilateral relationship with these countries. China has become a major foreign investor in Iran and the relationship between the two countries has evolved from a security partnership to an economic and strategic partnership in recent years. China carefully supported Iran in the United Nations Security Council and also emerged as a major importer and investor in the Iranian oil and gas sectors (Dorraj, 2013; Garver, 2011). Therefore, China's image has improved significantly in Iran in recent years.

China has upgraded its relations with Saudi Arabia to a new level of "comprehensive strategic partnership" that magnified the relationship beyond energy security and economic development into new inviolable strategic and political realms and paved the way for China's positive image projection in Saudi Arabia (Al-Tamimi, 2022; M. Chen, 2016; Macgillivray, 2019; Salman, 2016). President Xi Jinping and Saudi Crown Prince Mohammed bin Salman Al Saud have principally agreed to jack up China-Saudi relations to a new level of "comprehensive strategic partnership" and to integrate the BRI with Saudi Arabia's Vision 2030 (Foley, 2017; Fulton, 2020; Shay, 2018). As a result, Beijing and Riyadh signed a bilateral agreement of US$65 billion under the BRI framework to step up mutual cooperation in trade, economic development, space technology, renewable energy, nuclear energy, and petroleum engineering (Fulton, 2020; Shay, 2018). Chinese state-owned Railway Construction Corporation has recently completed a mega project "Haramain high-speed rail" worth US$16 billion in Saudi Arabia—the largest railway project in the Middle East that linked the two holy cities of Islam: Makkah and Madinah. It reduces the long road journey by two hours and makes it more comfortable and pleasant for more than 60 million Muslim pilgrims who travel between Makkah and Madinah for Hajj and Umrah (Islamic pilgrimage) every year. The project contributed economically and religiously to the well-being of the Muslim Ummah and added positive synergy to the Sino-Islamic relationship (Khan & Pratt, 2019). China has also become the largest importer of Saudi crude oil and conversely, the Kingdom has emerged as the single largest importer of Chinese goods in the Middle East and North Africa region. Saudi Arabia is also the fifth-largest importer of Chinese products at the global level (Elmagherbi, 2010; Elmagherbi & Wang, 2011; Foley, 2017; Hussain, 2016). The trade volume (both import and export) between the two countries has significantly increased in the last ten years from US$26.7 billion in 2007 to US$44.9 billion in 2016 (UN Comtrade, 2018). The bilateral trade between the two nations has now reached US$ 65.2 billion in 2022 (Al-Tamimi, 2022). The heightening economic, political, and strategic relationship between China and Saudi Arabia along with the geostrategic and geopolitical shift in the Middle East and tension in Saudi-U.S. relations pave the way for China's positive image projection in the Kingdom and also pacify Saudi's stance on Uyghur Muslim issues in Xinjiang, as it strongly criticized China's policies toward Uyghurs Muslims in Xinjiang in the past (Al-Sudairi, 2013; Al-Tamimi, 2022; Hussain, 2016). In addition, *Arab News* is published by the Saudi Research and Marketing

Group—a close ally of the Saudi regime and organ of softer power projection. Therefore, strong bilateral relations between China and Saudi Arabia may lead to a positive image construction of China in *Arab News* (Al-Sudairi, 2013).

China's image perception in Turkey and Egypt was reported negatively in the past (Al-Sudairi, 2013; Pew Research Center, 2017; Xie & Page, 2013). According to the Pew Research Center survey on China's global image, public perception of China in Turkey predominately remained negative from 2005 through 2019 (Table 5.1; Ergenc, 2015; Pew Research Center, 2017; Xie & Page, 2013). Historically, both countries have engaged in hostile relations due to Uyghur Muslim issues in China's Xinjiang. Uyghur has Turkish origin and therefore, Turkish President Tayyab Erdogan openly criticized China's alleged squelching of Uyghur Muslims during the ethnic violence in 2009, describing it as "a kind of genocide" (BBC News, 2009). Erdogan publicly commented to open doors for the Uyghur Muslims from Xinjiang, making the relations between the two countries even more fragile. In June 2015, the Turkish Ministry of Foreign Affairs alleged China of imposing a so-called "Ramadan ban" and not allowing the Uyghur Muslims in Xinjiang to fast during Ramadan resulting in an anti-China media campaign and an outbreak of large-scale anti-China public demonstrations in Turkey on July 5, 2015 (Chen, 2020). Turkey is also among the four Muslim countries (Egypt, Turkey, Jordan, and Palestine) where people showed distrust in Chinese leadership for making the right decision regarding world affairs (Figure 5.2). However, the relations between the two countries started to heal, particularly in the aftermath of a failed coup attempt in Turkey in 2016—Turkish President Erdogan openly praised China's friendly support and standing with the people of Turkey in their time of need. He stated, "We, the Turkish people, will never forget about it" (Chen, 2020, p. 784). Thereafter, President Erdogan visited China to participate in the First Belt and Road Forum for International Cooperation in Beijing in May 2017—repairing the stranded relations and recalibrating the new strategic relationship under the auspices of the BRI. The positive development in the relations between the two nations improved China's image projection in Turkish news media and the public negative sentiment toward China in Turkey declined from 54% to 44%. The favorability of China in Turkey increased from 33% to 37% between 2017 and 2019 (Table 5.1; Pew Research Center, 2019).

China's image perception in Egypt also encounters arduous challenges as the public perception of China's favorable image has declined from 65% to 46% and negative public opinion of China has increased from 29% to 53% in Egypt between 2007 through 2014 (Table 5.1). A majority of the Egyptian public did not agree with Chinese leadership's policies to "do the right thing regarding world affairs" (Figure 5.2). There are palpable public concerns about China's strategic and financial involvement in Egypt. Although a majority of the public (57%) perceived China-Egypt relations as "important" for the economic and infrastructural development of Egypt (Pollock, 2021), the favorability toward China's hefty infrastructural investments under the auspices of the BRI declined to 38% in Egypt (Lekorwe et al., 2016). There are concerns that China's massive infrastructural investments under the BRI will increase the burden of foreign debt as Egyptian foreign debt soars to US$137.85 billion in June 2020 (e.g., Elleithy, 2021; Hurley et al., 2019). Resultantly, the country will fall prey to a debt trap that may lead to conceding to Beijing's political and strategic influence as many of the Chinese infrastructural investments link to the Government's assets (Khan et al., 2023; Selim & Moaaz, 2021; Sun & Xu, 2022). The local industry is also voicing against the abundance of Chinese cheap products in the markets and demanding the government to protect the local industries that are unable to compete with big Chinese enterprises. The upsurge in imports from China also widens the trade deficit between the two countries. Egypt's imports from China rose to US$13.64 billion while exports stalled at US$0.92 billion in 2020, marking China as the largest contributor to the trade deficit in the Egyptian economy (Mena, 2021; Sun & Xu, 2022). Some of the strategic analysts in Egypt see Chinese massive investments in the Suez Canal region through the prism of seeking naval support bases to facilitate Chinese naval deployment in the Black Sea to manage their scattered naval deployment in the African countries (e.g., Somalia) (Al-Khair, 2021; Sun & Xu, 2022). There is also a collision of strategic interests between the two countries on some regional issues, for example, the Turkey-Egypt conflict over Libya and the Eastern Mediterranean gas fields and China's construction of the "Ethiopian Renaissance Dam" project that is perceived as a threat to Egyptian national interests and of its water security (Selim & Moaaz, 2021). Heeding those negative developments, the Egyptian mainstream newspaper—*Daily Egypt News* criticizes the Egyptian government's engagement with China during the study period (Khan et al., 2023).

China and Qatar have enjoyed positive and friendly relations since the founding of diplomatic relations in 1988. Both nations established a strategic relationship in November 2014 when the Emir of Qatar, Tamim bin Hamad Al Thani visited China and signed a strategic partnership agreement with China—paving the way to align Qatar National Vision 2030 with China's BRI to enhance bilateral cooperation in the field of energy, infrastructure, finance, economy, culture, and regional security. During the visit, President Xi appreciated Qatar's unique status and role in the Middle East and Gulf region and called it China's major economic and security partner in the region (Chaziza, 2020). However, the positive vibe in relations did not materialize into positive news coverage of China on *Al-Jazeera English*. The reason behind China's negative image projection in *Al-Jazeera English* may be the result of its independent editorial policy that is free from the Qatari government's control (Worth & Kirkpatrick, 2011). It follows the Western style of interpretative journalism and focuses more on political issues, providing a voice to the ignored, isolated, and unnoticed audiences in the Islamic world (El-Nawawy & Powers, 2010; Miles, 2006). The study noticed that *Al-Jazeera English* attributed 60% of its coverage of China to political issues (Table 7.15) which is the most susceptible and weak aspect of China's overall image (Ding, 2011; Xie & Page, 2013). *Al-Jazeera* repeatedly highlighted the Uyghur Muslim issues in Xinjiang and critically analyzed China's BRI projects in the Islamic world.

China's economic and technological development has significantly contributed to China's positive image construction in the Islamic world. The study found a positive correlation between China's positive image construction and economy, and China's technological coverage in Islamic English news media. In recent years, China's economic development and technological advancement have attracted global media attention and contributed positively to China's global stature and its positive image construction (Eichenauer et al., 2018; Kornphanat, 2016; Shambaugh, 2015). Xiang (2013) noted that China's economic and technological rise has contributed to its positive image construction such as a "fascinating China" and "innovative China" around the world.

China has earned a global reputation for its robust economic growth and poverty elevation efforts for uplifting the socio-economic standards of more than 800 million people in a short time (The World Bank, 2022) and it started to contribute to China's positive image promotion in the global news media (Aukia et al., 2017; Wu, 2008). China's pledges of hefty economic and infrastructural investments in the Islamic world under the BRI and its economic model of development have inspired many Islamic countries to follow the Chinese path of economic development, paving the way for China's positive image promotion in the Islamic world. Though China's growing economic engagements in the Islamic countries generated a positive vibe across the Islamic world, it also sprawled with sensitive issues related to trade deficits, debt distress, and an abundance of Chinese products in the local market that might challenge China's future image promotion in the Islamic world.

China's technological advancements and scientific innovations have improved its geopolitical standing and its role as a leading global competitor to the U.S. and Western technologies in the Islamic world. China's enormous investments in new and emerging technologies have not only improved its economic growth, social stability, military capabilities, infrastructural development, and scientific advancement in space and nuclear technologies but also boosted its global image, political outreach, and geostrategic influence in the developing world (Chhabra et al., 2021). China aims to dominate the world's advanced technology manufacturing industries by 2025, and therefore, President Xi launched a new Digital Silk Road (DSR) in 2015 as part of the BRI to accelerate Chinese investment in advanced and emerging technologies to "catch up with and surpass" the U.S and the West. The DSR kickstarted a new era of China's digital transformation in telecommunications, fifth-generation (5G) wireless technology, satellite navigation system (Beidou navigation system), artificial intelligence (AI), biotechnology, financial technology (e.g., Ant group digital payment systems), power grid cybersecurity, sea cables, and surveillance systems, semiconductors, weapons automation, nuclear and space technology, etc. and also strengthen China's digital footprint in the Islamic world, particularly in the Middle East and North Africa (MENA) region (Chhabra et al., 2021; Ridwan, 2022).

Since the launch of the DSR, China's digital giants Baidu and Alibaba have invested billions of dollars in digital infrastructure, telecommunication sectors, and e-commerce in the Islamic world. China's Huawei has emerged as the world's largest distributor of telecommunication equipment, the second-largest manufacturer of smartphones, and the global leader in 5G telecommunication networks. The Islamic world is a major beneficiary of Chinese digital investment and technologies. For example, China's investment through the DSR initiative is expected to contribute US$255 billion to the Gulf economy and will create more than 600,000 jobs in technology-related sectors in the Gulf region by 2030. China's technological giant, Huawei is also playing a major role in the digital transformation of the Arab Islamic world. Huawei installed a 5G network in Qatar in 2018 and signed a partnership agreement with Saudi's telecom giant Zain to launch a 5G network in the Middle East and North Africa in 2019. It also signed deals with Emirati telecom companies Etisalat and Du to provide 5G network services in the United Arab Emirates (UAE). Huawei also established the Cairo OpenLab to partner with regional universities to strengthen research and development in the MENA region. Whereas, China's BeiDou Navigation Satellite System provides useful information to the Islamic world in the fields of telecommunication, agriculture, maritime monitoring, climate change, disaster management, and regional security, etc. (Chaziza, 2022; Ridwan, 2022). In addition, Chinese projects, like "Haramain high-speed rail" between the two holy cities of Islam: Makkah and Madinah in Saudi Arabia and the Huawei digital infrastructure project in Saudi Arabia to promote religious pilgrimages have attracted great attention in the Islamic world and generated positive image of China in the Islamic world (Chaziza, 2022; Khan & Pratt, 2019). Among the others, the affordability and accessibility of Chinese digital technologies, particularly the popularity of affordable Chinese smartphones, Huawei, Vivo, OPPO, and Xiaomi have contributed significantly to China's image promotion in the Islamic world.

China's political image in the Islamic English news media was reported negatively. This may be the result of negative coverage of the global values frame (58.3%) in Islamic English news media that involved, human rights, civil rights, democratic rights, freedom of expression, religious freedom, environment protection, and copyrights issues in mainland China. A majority of these global values are shaped and developed on liberal principles propelled by Western liberalism and modernization since the start of the 20th Century. These values spread worldwide through Western democracies due to their dominance and victories in World Wars I and II. Particularly after the US' decisive win in World War II, it became the de facto champion and exponent of liberalism and its core values of freedom, equality, and democracy (Yan, 2020). Additionally, Westerners advocate for individualism, which prioritizes individuals' rights of freedom, self-expression, and autonomy in society. These Western values are further exemplified by the United Nations (UN) Charter, specifically Chapter 1, Article 1, Clause 2, which protects, encourages, and promotes an individual's fundamental human rights and freedoms without discrimination based on race, sex, religion, or language (UN Charter, 2023).

On the other hand, China is a prominent critic of Western liberal values and instead advocates for its version common values such as peace and development, equity and justice, democracy and freedom, pillars of Xi Jinping's vision of the global community of a shared future at the international level that are deeply rooted in the Chinese philosophy of Confucianism and nurtured through its long history and traditions. It focuses more on social harmony, group cohesion, maintenance of social order, respect for authority, filial piety, hierarchy, and collectivism to promote societal harmony (Yan, 2020). China's proposed alternative "common values" are based on the principles of equality, mutual respect, peaceful coexistence, social harmony, shared development for mutual benefits, and the principle of non-interference in sovereign states' internal affairs (Dunford, 2021;

Khan & Pratt, 2019; Liu & Dunford, 2016). The aim is to create an alternative normative structure (values, norms, and role expectations) that fortifies China's normative power and deters Western containment and criticism. This is in contrast to Western liberal values of freedom, democracy, and human rights (Zhou & Esteban, 2020). Therefore, China is trying to introduce these common values to the Islamic world through its grand foreign policy endeavor—the BRI.

Islamic countries have been resisting Western liberal values, particularly in response to recent incidents such as the Charlie Hebdo Cartoon Controversy (provocative cartoons of Prophet Muhammad) and the burning of the Holy Quran—a sacred Muslim religious book in Sweden and Denmark (Dogan, 2018; Khan et al., 2021). These actions are seen as provocative and discourteous towards the Islamic faith and the Muslim world. Additionally, the perception that Western countries have invaded sovereign Muslim countries on the pretext of human rights and democracy has further fueled this criticism. As a result, Islamic countries have become fierce critics of Western liberal values. However, China's "problematic political credibility, reviving popular nationalism, and some missteps in its foreign policies" are still negatively contributing to its political image in the Islamic world (Ding, 2011, pp. 302–304). For example, China's handling of Uyghur Muslims in Xinjiang, its support for Syrian President Bashar al-Asad, and its approach toward the Iran nuclear issue have been negatively perceived and reported in Ankara, Riyad, and Cairo (Colakoglu, 2015; Macgillivray, 2019; Mackerras, 2015). Researchers have noted that global media has remained critical of the Chinese government's alleged human rights violations and abridgment of the freedom of expression and democratic values in mainland China (Armony, 2012; Hayden, 2012; Kurlantzick, 2007). The study found that Islamic English news media has paid significant attention to global media's reporting of China's domestic political affairs and often reported China's alleged human rights violations, environmental pollution, climate change, freedom of expression, social justice, trade, and urban development negatively in the Islamic world (Armony, 2012; Ding, 2011; Shambaugh, 2013, 2015; Xu, 2014). China's image projection in the Islamic media is also influenced by the news media sources: If the media outlets use foreign news sources (e.g., Western journalists or news agencies—*Reuters* and *Deutsche Welle*) to report about China, the articulations of the news is more critical and negative as compared to the local journalists who use more positive or neutral tone to cover China-related news in the Islamic English news media (Khan et al., 2023).

Western news media and news agencies have a strong monopoly over the interpretation of news sources and information for global audiences. They control about 80–90% of the global news flow. China contributes only 5% to the global news flow, while the Afro-Islamic world controls the remaining 5%. Furthermore, Western media mainly presents China-related news to 78% of the global audience. Only 22% of the global audience receives China-related news from Chinese news media sources, while the remaining 10% of the global audience relies on Afro-Islamic news media. Even China's own mainstream news media often adopt international news from Western news sources (e.g., CNN, BBC, Reuters, AP, etc.) (Boyd-Barrett, 2000; Meng, 2020). Therefore, Western countries hold global discourse power to intentionally transmit their discourse system (social, political, and cultural values) to third-world countries to influence the country's public's perception, social psychology, and social, political, and cultural values there (Meng, 2020). Resultantly, Islamic news media often fall prey to Western logic and "discourse trap" about China's political image due to the lack of China's international discourse power in Islamic countries.

The study found a positive association between the country's political system and China's image construction in that country. The federal parliamentary system (Pakistan) and theocracy in Iran have shown a positive association with China's positive image construction in Pakistan and Iran respectively. Whereas absolute authoritarian monarchy in Saudi Arabia has shown a positive association with both positive and negative image construction of China. The presidential and semi-presidential systems in Egypt and Turkey have shown a positive association with China's negative image construction in Egypt and Turkey (Colakoglu, 2015; Macgillivray, 2019; Mackerras, 2015).

China's economic relationship also affected its image construction in Islamic English news media. This study found a positive association between China's export to the Islamic world and its negative image construction in Islamic English news media. However, China's imports from the Islamic world did not show any relationship with China's image construction in the Islamic world. The Islamic world faces a serious problem of trade imbalance with China. Resultantly, the trade deficit between Islamic countries and China is rising day by day. For example, Egypt's imports from China rose to US$13.64 billion while exports stalled at US$0.92 billion in 2020, marking China as the largest contributor to the trade deficit in the Egyptian economy (Mena, 2021; Sun & Xu, 2022). This largest trade deficit between China and Egypt provides an impetus for journalists to report negatively about the Egyptian government's economic engagement with China in the Egyptian mainstream media.

China's BRI has contributed positively to China's image construction in Islamic English news media. Particularly, BRI has been positively associated with China's positive economic and technological image construction in Islamic English news media. BRI offers considerable economic and political opportunities to the Islamic world. This multibillion-dollar initiative can boost the prospects of sustainable development goals in the Islamic world—that is, jobs creation, poverty alleviation, infrastructure development, and economic growth through regional and global connectivity that makes it more universally beneficial and inclusive (Bei, 2017; Khan & Pratt, 2019; Khan et al., 2018). Therefore, the Islamic world has openly embraced China's BRI and exhibited determination and enthusiasm to take maximum benefits from this mega project (Al-Ghwell, 2018).

Research implications

This research study analyzes China's image in the most influential and powerful Islamic countries that enjoy unique political, religious, and economic influence over the Islamic world and more specifically in the Islamic countries and Muslim Ummah as a whole. The findings provided evidence of China's growing political and economic stature and its image projection in the Islamic English news media. It provides a set of recommendations for China in its formulation of a set of useful policy guidelines for China's engagement in—and with the Islamic world. Theoretically, the study contributes to the literature on national image construction, interpretation, and dissemination and to the understanding of how the economic relationship, political system, and the implantation of the BRI projects in the different countries have influenced China's image construction, interpretation, and dissemination in the Islamic world.

Theoretical implications

This study offers valuable insights into the theoretical implications of China's image construction, interpretation, and dissemination processes in the Islamic English news media, particularly in the context of the Belt and Road Initiative (BRI) program in the Islamic world. Drawing on the framing theory, it sheds light on the role of Islamic English news media in shaping China's image-building processes in the Islamic world, which are deeply rooted in the historical relations between China and the Islamic world. The study also takes into account contemporary social and political realities, friendly diplomatic relations, geopolitics,

China's growing economic stature, as well as the positive coverage of China's related news in the Islamic news media.

China's image construction in the Islamic world seems to contradict many Western theories of national/global image construction, which heavily rely on neoliberal theories/thoughts such as advocating for human rights, freedom, and democracy. These theories emphasize the power of media discourse and communication for positive image building. However, China's favorable image construction, interpretation, and dissemination in the Islamic world seem to be less dependent on its communicative and discourse power. Instead, it is more related to China's constructive bilateral relations with Islamic countries, its approach to global diplomacy (based on non-interference in internal affairs, non-aggression, equality, and mutual respect for sovereignty and territorial integrity), and specifically its state economic statecraft, such as the Belt and Road Initiative (BRI).

US hegemonic foreign policies, invasions, and interference in sovereign Islamic countries in the name of freedom, democracy, and human rights have fueled growing anti-West, particularly anti-US sentiment and media framing in the Islamic world. This has resulted in a shift of positive public and media attention towards China as a reliable alternative political and economic ally in the Islamic world to address their political and economic issues. It is important to note that a nation's image construction is significantly influenced by geoeconomic and geopolitical realities that it faces while dealing with other nations (Coe & Neumann, 2011, p. 139). In the contemporary world, building constructive relationships and trust among nations has become the core strategy for managing a country's image. The relational paradigm, which emphasizes a foreign country's engagement in various fields such as politics, diplomacy, economy, culture, and host country-related affairs, largely influences how the media portrays the foreign country's image in the host country (Szondi, 2010). Therefore, the relational paradigm has become an overarching concept of public diplomacy, as it offers a more practical dimension for engaging in public diplomacy through relationship building, message exchange, and network creation between countries, rather than solely relying on the media to produce and disseminate information (Fitzpatrick, 2007; Zaharna, 2007).

China's constructive relationship with the Islamic countries, particularly, under the auspices of the Belt and Road Initiative (BRI), has provided positive input to China's coverage in the Islamic world. China's billions of dollars investment in energy, infrastructure, communication, and economic development in Islamic countries also boost public positive sentiments and media attention toward China's futuristic role in the Islamic world. More importantly, Islamic leaderships and political elites, who feel oppressed by the United States hegemonic foreign policies such as economic sanctions, political interference, threats, physical invasion, and war, have begun to view China as an alternative global power for political stability and economic development in the Islamic world. Therefore, they have adopted friendly foreign policies towards China.

A country's image construction is significantly related to the bilateral relations between countries. The way a country's image is portrayed in the media is often related to the host country's foreign policy towards other nations. For example, Mann (1999) observed that the framing of friend and foe in U.S. media significantly aligns with U.S. foreign policy towards China. Similarly, Chinese scholars like Cao (2014) and Zhang & Wu (2017) argue that China's image framing in Western media is predominantly influenced by the political relations between China and the West during different periods. Consequently, Islamic media outlets have started to align their editorial policies with their respective countries' foreign policy towards China. This has contributed to the construction, interpretation, and dissemination of a positive image of China throughout the Islamic world.

The cascading model also suggests that government administration and political elites are the most powerful suppliers of media news frames. Entman (2003, p. 420) argues that "The president [Head of the State] and top advisors [top government officials] enjoy the most independent ability to decide which mental associations to activate and the highest probability of moving their own thoughts into general circulation." These political elites often use media frames as a strategic tool to exercise power and convince target audiences to accept their interpretation that suits their aims or goals. Since people often have no personal experience in dealing with an issue, they seek information from the media portrayal. Therefore, political elites use framing as a strategy to shape public understanding and discourses to attain their interests and gain advantages, mainly to advance their future course of action (Benford & Snow, 2000; Entman et al., 2009).

The Islamic leadership and political elites have welcomed China's political and economic engagements in the Islamic world under the BRI framework. They have started to view China as a reliable political and economic ally, and a viable substitute for the U.S. in the Middle East. The Islamic leadership is also recalibrating its economic and political calculus, moving away from the U.S. periphery of influence to realign with China for economic and political advantages (Al-Ghwell, 2018; Cheng, 2016; Khan & Pratt, 2019; Lehr, 2018; Zambelis & Gentry, 2008). Consequently, Islamic news media, which is largely controlled by the state/government, follows a non-Western narrative of China and praises its unprecedented economic development and political rise in a short time. As a result, it often uses a positive and neutral tone to report China-related news. For example, a study on China's BRI and soft power framing in Pakistani news media shows that the local English news media endorses China's goodwill through positive framing of its culture, diplomatic relations, and economic investment of US$62 billion through CPEC—a flagship project of the BRI in Pakistan (Ittefaq et al., 2021).

Practical implications

The Islamic world is embroiled in geopolitical conflicts and geo-economic crises that offer abundant opportunities for China to raise its geopolitical, geoeconomic, and geostrategic capital through cementing strong political, socioeconomic, and strategic cooperation with the Islamic world. Beijing needs a well-thought-out strategy to serve its strategic goals, implement its ambitious BRI-related projects, and improve its global image throughout the Islamic world. Reciprocally, the Islamic world can effectively use China's economic and political capital to strengthen its strained economies and solve lingering political disputes. A few important practical implications for China and the Islamic world are as under:

1. The Islamic world is not a monolithic and homogeneous geographical identity but a collection of Islamic countries with diverse cultures, geographies, histories, and traditions. It's divided into ethnic, cultural, geographical, and sectarian lines. There are two major cultural blocs in the Islamic world: the Sunni and the Shia, controlled by two rival Islamic countries, Iran and Saudi Arabia, respectively. The conflicting national interests of both nations in the Middle East and North Africa (MENA) often accelerate the historical enmity between the two rival countries, particularly the strategic and political tension over the issues related to the Middle East and North Africa region, broadly, that is, to the armed conflicts in Yemen, Iraq, Libya, and Syria. Although China tries to maintain a diligent balance and adheres to the principle of non-interference in the armed conflicts in the MENA regions, anything less has potential consequences for China's fervent political and economic interests in the region and its favorable image promotion in the Islamic world. For example, China's support for Syrian President Bashar al-Asad in the Syria civil war

and its lenient stance on the Iranian nuclear program has been perceived negatively in Turkey and Saudi Arabia (Sunni Islamic states) (Colakoglu, 2015; Macgillivray, 2019; Mackerras, 2015).

2. The historical rivalry between Saudi Arabia and Iran offers an opportunity for China to enhance its global leadership role by mitigating the tension between Riyadh and Tehran. In the past, the U.S. and Russia failed to strike a balance between Riyadh and Tehran due to their conflicting interests in the region. However, China can take advantage of its perceived unbiased global power status that enjoys solid political and economic relations with both Saudi Arabia and Iran and can use its leverage to foster symmetrical communication between the two rival capitals. Such amity will enhance China's stature and leadership role in the Islamic world.

   The new developments in the Middle East, particularly China's successful mediation for a peace deal between Iran and Saudi Arabia, have significantly increased China's political leverage, stature, and leadership role in the Islamic world. This has sparked a global debate about China's emerging role as a global leader in conflict management, especially in the volatile Middle East region. While this peace deal signifies China's growing influence in Middle Eastern politics, it also presents new challenges for Chinese diplomacy. The Islamic world now looks to China to play a role in resolving the long-standing political dispute for an independent Palestine state between Israel and the Arab world. This task is far more complex and demanding than the bilateral dispute between Iran and Saudi Arabia, as it involves multiple actors such as Israel, the United States, Palestine, Saudi Arabia, Turkey, Jordan, and others. There is a significant risk of conflicting interests between China and other countries, particularly the U.S. and Israel, if China aligns itself with the Muslim world. However, if China manages to broker a peace deal between Israel and the Arab world, it will emerge as a "hero" in the eyes of the Islamic world.

3. China's understanding of Islamic socio-political culture is limited. There is mistrust and misunderstanding between China and the Islamic world on the issues related to the handling of Uyghur Muslims in Xinjiang. The perception of mistreatment of Uyghur Muslims in China's Xinjiang is still a major issue between China and the Islamic world (Kelemen & Turcsányi, 2020) and it can trickle the negative spillover on Sino-Islamic relations that might hurt the BRI projects in the Islamic world. Particularly, Turkey has shown great concern and displeasure over China's

alleged clampdown on Uyghur Muslims in Xinjiang due to their Turkic origins. Turkish President Tayyab Erdogan strongly condemned China's crackdown on Uyghur Muslims during ethnic violence in 2009, describing it as "a kind of genocide" (*BBC News*, 2009). Protest in support of Uyghur Muslim rights in Xinjiang has also been witnessed in a few other Islamic countries (e.g., Turkey, Malaysia, Kazakhstan, and Indonesia) in recent years (*Al-Jazeera*, 2022; Ezell, 2021). Iranian religious clerics, the public, and the media also disparage the role of the Chinese government in handling the Xinjiang Muslim issues (Singh, 2021b) and China's vote in support of a U.N. Security Council Resolution that levied economic sanctions on Iran in 2010 (Chen, 2011). China has also been criticized by the Islamic and Western media for its alleged confinement of Uyghur Muslims in "reëducation" camps (Clarke, 2015; Ezell, 2021). Though China defends its action as deradicalization efforts to curtail the growing extremism and radicalism in Xinjiang (Benabdallah, 2018; Dabashi, 2018; Page et al., 2018), the anger in a few Islamic countries is on the rise where more than 50% of the population hold an unfavorable opinion about China, mainly in four key Islamic countries (Egypt, Turkey, Jordan, and Lebanon) (Pew Research Center, 2017; Xie & Page, 2013). The negative public perception of China and criticisms of Chinese policies toward the Uyghur Muslims in Xinjiang in the Islamic world carry significant reputational, political, and economic costs for China in the Islamic world. Therefore, China can use the BRI projects as public diplomacy initiatives to dispel this negative public perception and present itself as a trustworthy and close comrade of the major Islamic countries such as Saudi Arabia, Pakistan, Turkey, Egypt, and Indonesia (Benabdallah, 2018). China can take several steps to enhance its engagement with the Islamic world. These include launching a strategic media campaign, promoting people-to-people contacts, and adopting effective public diplomacy mechanisms to engage politicians, scholars, journalists, students, and business enterprises from the Islamic world. By doing so, China can broaden its understanding of specific Islamic countries and strengthen its economic, political, and socio-cultural ties with the Islamic world as a whole.

4. China's economic relationship with the Islamic world also needs a reality check, as, the trade balance between China and certain Islamic countries (e.g., Turkey, Egypt, Pakistan) has largely inclined in favor of China in the past decade. The mounting trade deficit between China and Islamic

countries could potentially hurt China's image and its future relations with the Islamic world (Ergenc, 2015; Temiz, 2018; Zhu, 2010).

5. China's understanding of Islamic Banking and Finance (IBF) is limited and hurts its efforts to explore new opportunities and venues to use Islamic finance and banking channels in generating economic resources for BRI projects in the Islamic world. IBF holds huge potential for China's financial institutions to facilitate BRI-related projects both financially and economically in the Islamic world. Therefore, China's need to hire Islamic IBF experts and the appointment of a former governor of the Malaysian Central Bank such as Dr. Tan Sri Zeti, to AIIB's International Advisory Panel on Islamic Financing is a right step toward the integration of Islamic finance into the BRI projects that would significantly reduce the financial risk to the Chinese investments in the Islamic world.
6. Under the auspice of the BRI, China has signed a "comprehensive strategic partnership" agreement with different Islamic countries and enhanced its political, economic, and security engagements with the Middle Eastern countries in recent years. China's prominence has increased manifold and its fast-growing regional influence, and political, diplomatic, economic, and security-related activities are seriously posing challenges to the U.S. national interests and political hegemony in the Middle East and North Africa (MENA) region (Singh, 2021a). China's growing influence under the BRI framework in the MENA region can engender a clash of economic, political, and strategic interests between China and the U.S. in the region. For example, a former Chinese diplomat, Sun Bigan notes that the scrimmage between China and the U.S. will escalate over the political and economic influence and oil trade in the Middle East, and "Bilateral quarrels and clashes are unavoidable" in the future (Khan & Pratt, 2019, p.131; *The Daily Star*, 2009). For decades, Washington enjoyed the sole hegemonic power in the MENA region. It cannot overlook the Arabs' rising interest in viewing China as a possible substitute for the U.S. in the MENA region. Both China and the U.S. have divergent strategic interests, economic, and political priorities in the region, however, there are some common interests (e.g., counterterrorism) that can bind the two nations to work together. China should stick to a more balanced, and fair approach in regional political disputes and explore shared areas of mutual interests (e.g., counterterrorism, economic development) for healthy and productive engagement with the U.S. in the MENA region.

Beijing should evade conflict with the U.S. political, economic, and strategic interests in the MENA region while maintaining closed and cordial relations with Arab states. It will help significant reduction in tense competition between China and the U.S. in the MENA region.

7. The weak brand image of Chinese companies and the growing perception of Chinese products as "cheap and low quality" also pose a serious challenge to China's global image and reputation in the Islamic world. For example, public perception in all nine surveyed countries in the MENA region (i.e., Jordan, Palestine, Sudan, Morocco, Libya, Lebanon, Iraq, Tunisia, and Mauritania) indicates that the majority of the public preferred German or U.S. companies over Chinese companies for the construction of infrastructure projects in their respective country (Robbins, 2022). Chinese companies' poor performance and public perception of Chinese products and services as "Cheap and of low quality" can affect Chinese economic activities and damage China's national reputation in the MENA region. Global companies, their brands, and their products have a crucial place in people's daily lives and can potentially affect the national reputation and overall image of the country of origin (White, 2012). Therefore, Chinese companies need to strengthen their brand image and their product qualities to improve China's competitive reputation on a global scale.
8. Lastly, China needs to build strong Chinese media and communication infrastructure in the Islamic world to amplify its message and to counter the prevailing Western narrative about China in the Islamic English news media. Currently, the Islamic English news media mainly relies on Western news sources, namely, *Reuters* (UK), *Deutsche Welle* (Germany), *Associated Press* [*AP*] (USA), and *Agence France-Presse* [*AFP*] (France) to report on China and about the world affairs. China's global media presence in the Islamic world is negligible, and therefore, it should marshal its global media resources like *Xinhua* news agency, *China Daily*, *People's Daily*, *China Radio International*, *Global Television Network* (CGTN) to build strong global media and communication infrastructure in the Islamic world. It should also invest in local news media outlets or purchase airtime on local TV or Radio to promote its soft image and counter the Western narrative about China in the Islamic world. It is pertinent to mention that *Voice of America* [*VOA*] often purchases airtime in Islamic countries to present its perspective to the audience in the Islamic world.

Limitations of the study

This study has investigated China's image construction, interpretation, and dissemination in Islamic English news media. The researcher selected six newspapers from the six most prominent and powerful Islamic countries (Saudi Arabia, Pakistan, Turkey, Egypt, Iran, and Qatar). However, the Islamic world is comprised of 50 Islamic countries and their economic and political relationship with China are significantly different from one another. Therefore, China's image construction, interpretation, and dissemination in six prominent Islamic countries cannot be generalized to the whole Islamic world because the importance of a country and its relationship to other countries is significantly associated with the positive or negative media projection of that particular country (Brewer et al., 2003; Nisbet et al., 2004; Nisbet & Myers, 2011; Wanta et al., 2004).

The researcher selected English-language newspapers only from Saudi Arabia, Pakistan, Turkey, Egypt, Iran, and Qatar. However, a majority of local media in the Islamic world uses local or national languages to broadcast their content e.g., the national languages of Saudi, Egypt, and Qatar are Arabic, Urdu in Pakistan, Turkish in Turkey, and Farsi in Iran. Therefore, China's image construction, interpretation, and dissemination in English-language news media may be different from the mainstream media presentation of China in their local language for local audiences. Lastly, the researcher used a stratified random sampling technique and conducted manual content analysis to analyze a sample of 4,870 articles from the complete dataset of 43,286 articles related to China in the six prominent Islamic English news media that further restricted the researcher from generalizing its research findings.

Research directions and a way forward

Based on the limitations of this study, the researcher proposed the following recommendations for future studies related to China's image construction, interpretation, and dissemination in the Islamic world.

1. This study was conducted in six prominent and most powerful Islamic countries. The future researcher should include less prominent but emerging Islamic countries (e.g., Indonesia, United Arab Emirates, Malaysia) to broaden the understanding of China's image construction, interpretation, and dissemination in Islamic English news media.

2. This study examined China's image construction, interpretation, and dissemination in English-language Islamic English news media. Researchers (Willnat & Wilkins, 1998) argue that local and transnational news media have different impacts on the cultural and political attitudes of local audiences. More importantly, English language media is considered an elite medium in the Islamic world which only fulfills and caters to the needs of elites. Contrary to local media, which truly presents a public voice and demystifies international content for local audience consumption (Clausen, 2004; McLeod et al., 1996; Scheufele, 1999). Therefore, the future researcher should also consider the native language news media of the respective country to examine China's image construction in the Islamic world. The comparison of China's image construction, interpretation, and dissemination in native and English language news media will further increase the understanding of China's image in the Islamic world.
3. The emergence of social media has transformed the landscape of international communication and public diplomacy (Bjola & Holmes, 2015; Zhong & Lu, 2013). Xiang (2013) argues that social media has the potential to generate a far-reaching impact on audience perception of a country's economic, political, cultural, and social image. Therefore, future research should focus on comparative studies of China's image construction, interpretation, and dissemination through traditional news media and social media in the Islamic world.
4. This study provided a preliminary understanding of China's image construction, interpretation, and dissemination in Islamic English news media. However, Islamic English news media's effects on China's image construction on public perception in the Islamic world were not measured. Therefore, the future researcher should also consider the agenda-setting function and cultivation analysis of Islamic English news media by comparing China's image construction, interpretation, and dissemination in Islamic English news media and public perception of China in the Islamic world.

Conclusion

This study examines China's image construction, interpretation, and dissemination in the six most prominent and powerful Islamic countries i.e., Saudi Arabia, Pakistan, Turkey, Egypt, Iran, and Qatar. It uses the longitudinal content analysis as a research method to measure and assess the contents related to China's image in Islamic English news media in the six most influential and powerful Islamic countries, namely, Saudi Arabia (*Arab News*), Pakistan (*The Nation*), Turkey (*Daily Sabah*), Iran (*Tehran Times*), Egypt (*Daily News Egypt*) and Qatar for its vibrant global media outlet "*Al-Jazeera English*" for the period from January 1, 2009, through December 31, 2018. Twofold sampling techniques were used. *First*, the researcher used keywords to search ("China" or "Chinese") in the LexisNexis database and retrieved a total of 43,286 articles related to China published in Islamic English news media to measure the attention intensity paid to China's coverage in Islamic English news media. *Secondly*, the researcher used a stratified random sampling technique (that is, one hundred articles for each year) and collected 4,870 articles related to China to measure China's overall image and its precise dimensions e.g., political image, cultural image, economic image, technological image, and social image in the Islamic world.

Results indicate that China's significance and importance have increased in the Islamic world during the last decade. Islamic English news media has constructed, interpreted, and disseminated China's positive image in the Islamic world. However, China's image was not the same across all the Islamic countries. China's image in Saudi Arabia, Pakistan, and Iran was reported as positive. Whereas, China's image in Turkey, Egypt, and Qatar was reported as negative. This study found five prominent dimensions of China's image in Islamic English news media: political, economic, cultural, technological, and social image. China's economic and technological image was reported more positively. However, China's political image remained negative in Islamic English news media. China's Belt and Road Initiative positively contributed to China's positive image construction in the Islamic world. Particularly, BRI has improved China's positive economic and technological image in the Islamic world. BRI also contributed to China's positive image projection in Saudi Arabia, Pakistan, and Egypt.

The findings provided evidence of China's stature and image in the Islamic English news media and helped guide its policy in—and its engagement with—the Islamic world. Theoretically, the study contributed to the literature on national image construction, interpretation, and dissemination. It also provided an understanding of how the economic relationship, BRI and political system of the different countries have influenced China's image construction, interpretation, and dissemination in the Islamic world.

References

Afzaal, M., Hu, K., Ilyas Chishti, M., & Khan, Z. (2019). Examining Pakistani news media discourses about China–Pakistan Economic Corridor: A corpus-based critical discourse analysis. *Cogent Social Sciences*, *5*(1), 1683940. <https://doi.org/10.1080/23311886.2019.1683940>

Al-Ghwell, H. (2018, June 30). Why the Arab world should build bridges with China. *Arab News*. <http://www.arabnews.com/node/1330736>

Al-Jazeera. (2022, January 23). Uighurs in Turkey call for boycott of Beijing Winter Olympics. *Al-Jazeera English*. <https://www.aljazeera.com/news/2022/1/23/uighurs-in-turkey-call-for-boycott-of-beijing-winter-olympics>

Al-Khair, W. A. (2021, December 10). Chinese investment in Egypt comes at high price, analysts warn. *Al-Mashareq*. <https://almashareq.com/en_GB/articles/cnmi_am/features/2021/12/10/feature-01>

Al-Sudairi, M. T. (2013). China in the eyes of the Saudi Media. *Gulf Research Center*, *February*(February), 1–38. <https://www.ictsd.org/sites/default/files/downloads/2013/04/china-in-the-eyes-of-the-saudi-media.pdf>

Al-Tamimi, N. (2022). Saudi Arabia's once marginal relationship with China has grown into a comprehensive strategic partnership. In J. Gunter & H. Legarda (Eds.), *Beyond blocs: Global views on China and US-China relations* (pp. 73–79). Mercator Institute for China Studies. <https://merics.org/sites/default/files/2022-08/MERICS-Papers-On-China-Beyond-blocs-Global-views-on-China-and-US-China-relations-3.pdf>

Albæk, E. (2011). The interaction between experts and journalists in news journalism. *Journalism*, *12*(3), 335–348. <https://doi.org/10.1177/1464884910392851>

Almedia, M. (2018, July 14). China's "Marshall Plan" for the Arab world. *Arab News*. <http://www.arabnews.com/node/1338856>

Armony, A. C. (2012). A view from Afar: How Colombia sees China. *The China Quarterly*, *209*, 178–197. <https://doi.org/10.1017/S0305741011001536>

Aukia, J., Heimonen, J., Pahikkala, T., & Salakoski, T. (2017). Automated quantification of Reuters news using a receiver operating characteristic curve analysis: The Western media image of China. *Global Media and China*, *2*(3–4), 251–268. <https://doi.org/10.1177/2059436418754890>

BBC News. (2009, July 10). Turkey attacks China "genocide." *BBC News*. <http://news.bbc.co.uk/2/hi/8145451.stm>

Bei, J. (2017). Economic globalization 3.0 and the concept of interconnection under the Belt and Road Initiative. *China Economist*, *12*(2), 2–21. <https://www.proquest.com/openview/30d494a8ce126f40dab6b23cab730e39/1?pq-origsite=gscholar&cbl=1806366>

Benabdallah, L. (2018). China's relations with Africa and the Arab World: Shared trends, different priorities. *South African Institute of International Affairs*, *67*(November), 1–14. <https://www.jstor.org/stable/resrep25989>

Benford, R. D., & Snow, D. A. (2000). Framing processes and social movements : An overview and assessment. *Annual Review Sociologic, 26*, 611–639. <https://doi.org/10.1146/annurev.soc.26.1.611>

Bjola, C., & Holmes, M. (2015). *Digital diplomacy: Theory and practice*. Routledge.

Brewer, P. R., Graf, J., & Willnat, L. (2003). Priming or framing: Media influence on attitudes toward foreign countries. *Gazette (Leiden, Netherlands), 65*(6), 493–508. <https://doi.org/10.1177/0016549203065006005>

Boyd-Barrett, O. (2000). National and international news agencies: Issues of crisis and realignment. *Gazette (Leiden, Netherlands), 62*(1), 5–18.

Cao, Q. (2014). *China under Western Gaze: Representing China in the British Television Documentaries 1980–2000*. World Scientific.

Chang, T.-K. (1998). All countries not created equal to be news: World system and international communication. *Communication Research, 25*(5), 528–563. <https://doi.org/10.1177/009365098025005004>

Chaziza, M. (2020). China–Qatar strategic partnership and the realization of One Belt, One Road Initiative. *China Report, 56*(1), 78–102. <https://doi.org/10.1177/0009445519895612>

Chaziza, M. (2022, October 7). Gulf states go digital with China. *East Asia*. <https://www.eastasiaforum.org/2022/10/07/gulf-states-go-digital-with-china/>

Chen, J. (2011). *The emergence of China in Middle East* (Issue 271, pp. 1–8). National Defense University, Washington, DC. <https://doi.org/10.1111/j.1539-6975.2009.01318.x>

Chen, M. (2016). The economic adjustment of Saudi Arabia and the Docking of bilateral economy and trade between China and Saudi Arabia under the "One Belt and One Road" Initiative. *Journal of Middle Eastern and Islamic Studies (in Asia), 10*(2), 46–70. <https://doi.org/10.1080/19370679.2016.12023282>

Chen, Y. (2020). Developments in China–Turkey relations: A view From China. *Critical Sociology, 46*(4–5), 777–787. https://doi.org/10.1177/0896920519885001

Cheng, J. Y. S. (2016). China's relations with the Gulf Cooperation Council States: Multilevel diplomacy in a divided Arab World. *The China Review, 16*(1), 35–64. <https://www.jstor.org/stable/43709960>

Chhabra, T., Doshi, R., Hass, R., & Kimball, E. (2021). *Global China: Assessing China's growing role in the world*. Brookings Institution Press.

Clarke, M. (2015). China and The Uyghurs: The "Palestinization" of Xinjiang? *Middle East Policy, 22*(3), 127–146. <https://doi.org/10.1111/mepo.12148>

Clausen, L. (2004). Localizing the global: "Domestication" processes in international news production. *Media, Culture & Society, 26*(1), 25–44. https://doi.org/10.1177/0163443704038203

Coe, K., & Neumann, R. (2011). International identity in theory and practice: The case of the modern American presidency. *Communication Monographs, 78*(2), 139–161. <https://doi.org/10.1080/03637751.2011.564641>

Colakoglu, S. (2015). Dynamics of Sino–Turkish relations: A Turkish perspective. *East Asia, 32*(1), 7–23. <https://doi.org/10.1007/s12140-015-9225-7>

Dabashi, H. (2018, December 22). Muslim cleansing: A global pandemic? *Al-Arabiya English*. <https://www.aljazeera.com/opinions/2018/12/22/muslim-cleansing-a-global-pandemic>

Ding, S. (2011). Branding a rising China: An analysis of Beijing's National Image Management in the age of China's rise. *Journal of Asian and African Studies, 46*(3), 293–306. <https://doi.org/10.1177/0021909611405830>

Dogan, R. (2018). Respect for the sacred versus freedom of expression: Analysis from an Islamic perspective in the context of de-radicalization. *International Journal of Social Science Studies, 6*, 1.

Dorraj, M. (2013). *Iran's expanding relations with China and their strategic dimensions* (12th ed.). Emirates Center for Strategic Studies and Research.

Dunford, M. (2021). China's Belt and Road Initiative and its Implications for Global Development. *Acta Via Serica, 6*(1), 91–118. <https://doi.org/10.22679/avs.2021.6.1.004>

Ehteshami, A., Horesh, N., & Xu, R. (2018). Chinese-Iranian mutual strategic perceptions. *The China Journal, 79*(79), 1–20. <https://doi.org/10.1086/693315>

Eichenauer, V. Z., Fuchs, A., & Brückner, L. (2018). The effects of trade, aid, and investment on China's image in developing countries. *University of Heidelberg Department of Economics, 646*. <https://doi.org/10.2139/ssrn.3147206>

El-Nawawy, M., & Powers, S. (2010). Al-Jazeera English: A conciliatory medium in a conflict-driven environment? *Global Media and Communication, 6*(1), 61–84. <https://doi.org/10.1177/1742766510362019>

Elleithy, A. (2021, October 23). Despite reaching all-time high, Egypt's external debt is within safe levels. *Al-Monitor*. <https://www.al-monitor.com/originals/2021/10/despite-reaching-all-time-high-egypts-external-debt-within-safe-levels>

Elmagherbi, F. I. (2010). A case study of China's relations with the Arab World. *2010 2nd IEEE International Conference on Information and Financial Engineering*, 646–650. <https://doi.org/10.1109/ICIFE.2010.5609442>

Elmagherbi, F. I., & Wang, R. (2011). Optimum plan to improve the economic relation between China and Arab World. *Modern Applied Science, 5*(6), 181–187. <https://doi.org/10.5539/mas.v5n6p181>

Entman, R. M. (2003). Cascading activation: Contesting the White House's frame after 9/11. *Political Communication, 20*(4), 415–342. <https://doi.org/10.1080/10584600390244176>

Entman, R. M., Matthes, J., & Pellicano, L. (2009). Nature, sources, and effects of news framing. In K. Wahl-Jorgensen & T. Hanitzsch (Eds.), *The handbook of journalism studies* (pp. 175–190). Routledge.

Ergenc, C. (2015). Can two ends of Asia Meet? An overview of contemporary Turkey-China relations. *East Asia, 32*(3), 289–308. <https://doi.org/10.1007/s12140-015-9242-6>

Ezell, C. (2021). Human rights abuses in Xinjiang: Perspectives and responses from the Islamic World and the Middle East. In *Center for Open Science*. SocArXiv. <https://doi.org/10.31219/osf.io/mk7q6>

Fels, E. (2017). Pakistan: "Iron Brother" to Beijing, reluctant partner for Washington. In *Shifting Power in Asia-Pacific?* (pp. 437–505). Springer.

Fitzpatrick, K. (2007) "Advancing the new public diplomacy: A public relations perspective". *The Hague Journal of Diplomacy, 2*(3), 187–211.

Foley, S. (2017). When oil is not enough: Sino-Saudi relations and vision 2030. *Asian Journal of Middle Eastern and Islamic Studies, 11*(1), 107–120. <https://doi.org/10.1080/25765949.2017.12023296>

Fulton, J. (2020). China-Saudi Arabia relations through the "1+ 2+ 3" cooperation pattern. *Asian Journal of Middle Eastern and Islamic Studies, 14*(4), 516–527. <https://doi.org/10.1080/25765949.2020.1841991>

Galal, M. N. (2014). The China-Arab States Cooperation Forum: Achievements, challenges and prospects. *Journal of Middle Eastern and Islamic Studies (in Asia), 8*(2), 1–21. <https://doi.org/10.1080/19370679.2014.12023244>

Garver, J. W. (2011). *China and Iran: Ancient partners in a post-imperial world.* University of Washington Press.

Grey, F. (2017). How oil twists the Hegemon's Arm: The case of the United States and Saudi Arabia and their Ambivalent partnership. *Digest of Middle East Studies, 26*(2), 320–339. <https://doi.org/10.1111/dome.12108>

Guzansky, Y., & Orion, A. (2017). Slowly but surely : Growing relations between Saudi Arabia and China. In *Institute for National Security Studies* (Issue 891, pp. 1–5). <http://www.jstor.com/stable/resrep08664>

Hayden, C. (2012). *The rhetoric of soft power: Public diplomacy in global contexts.* Lexington Books.

Hurley, J., Morris, S., & Portelance, G. (2019). Examining the debt implications of the Belt and Road Initiative from a policy perspective. *Journal of Infrastructure, Policy and Development, 3*(1), 139–175. <https://doi.org/10.24294/jipd.v3i1.1123>

Hussain, Z. (2016). *Saudi Arabia in a multipolar world.* Routledge.

Ittefaq, M., Ahmed, Z. S., & Martínez Pantoja, Y. I. (2021). China's Belt and Road Initiative and soft power in Pakistan: An examination of the local English-language Press. *Place Branding and Public Diplomacy*, 1–14. <https://doi.org/10.1057/s41254-021-00212-8>

Jones, T. M., Van Aelst, P., & Vliegenthart, R. (2013). Foreign nation visibility in US news coverage: A longitudinal analysis (1950–2006). *Communication Research, 40*(3), 417–436. <https://doi.org/10.1177/0093650211415845>

Kamel, M. S. (2018). China's Belt and Road Initiative: Implications for the Middle East. *Cambridge Review of International Affairs, 31*(1), 76–95. <https://doi.org/10.1080/09557571.2018.1480592>

Kelemen, B., & Turcsányi, R. Q. (2020). It's the politics, stupid: China's relations with Muslim countries on the background of Xinjiang crackdown. *Asian Ethnicity, 21*(2), 223–243. <https://doi.org/10.1080/14631369.2019.1677145>

Khan, M. K., & Pratt, C. B. (2019). China's Belt and Road Initiative: Its landscape (and trajectory) in the Islamic World. In A. Visvizi, M. Lytras, X. Zhang, & J. Zhao (Eds.), *Foreign business in China and opportunities for technological innovation and sustainable economics* (pp. 117–142). IGI Global. <https://doi.org/10.4018/978-1-5225-8980-8.ch006>

Khan, M. K., Pratt, C. B., & Akhtar, N. (2023). China's public diplomacy for image making in Islamic North Africa: Frames of the Belt and Road Initiative in Daily News Egypt. In: A. A. Anani-Bossman, T. E. Mudzanani, C. B. Pratt, & I. A. Blankson (Eds.), *Public relations management in Africa Volume 1.* Cham: Palgrave Macmillan. <https://doi.org/10.1007/978-3-031-26704-8_5>

Khan, M. K., Sandano, I. A., Pratt, C. B., & Farid, T. (2018). China's Belt and Road Initiative: A global model for an evolving approach to Sustainable Regional Development. *Sustainability, 10*(11), 4234. <https://doi.org/10.3390/su10114234>

Khan, M. K., Wu, F., Pratt, C. B., & Akhtar, N. (2021). Satires, narratives and journalistic divides: Discourses on free speech in Western and Islamic news media. *The Social Science Journal*, *58*(4), 458–476.

Khan, Z., Changgang, G., & Afzaal, M. (2020). China-Pakistan economic corridor at the cross intersection of China, Central Asia and South Asia: Opportunities for regional economic growth. *The Chinese Economy*, *53*(2), 200–215. <https://doi.org/10.1080/10971475.2019.1688005>

Kornphanat, T. (2016). Culture and commerce: China's soft power in Thailand. *International Journal of China Studies*, *7*(2), 151–173. <https://icsum.org.my/wp-content/uploads/2020/02/kornphanat.pdf>

Kurlantzick, J. (2007). *Charm offensive: How China's soft power is transforming the world*. Yale University Press.

Lams, L. (2016). China: Economic magnet or rival? Framing of China in the Dutch- and French-language elite press in Belgium and the Netherlands. *International Communication Gazette*, *78*(1–2), 137–156. https://doi.org/10.1177/1748048515618117

Lehr, D. (2018, July 21). How China is winning over the Middle East. *The Diplomat*. <https://thediplomat.com/2018/07/how-china-is-winning-over-the-middle-east/>

Lekorwe, M., Chingwete, A., Okuru, M., & Samson, R. (2016). *China's growing presence in Africa wins largely positive popular reviews*. Afrobarometer. <https://afrobarometer.org/sites/default/files/publications/Dispatches/ab_r6_dispatchno122_perceptions_of_china_in_africa1.pdf>

Lim, A. C.-H. (2015). Iron Brothers': Sino-Pakistani relations and the China-Pakistan Economic Corridor. *Eurasia Review*. <https://www.academia.edu/12286990/_Iron_Brothers_Sino_Pakistani_Relations_and_the_China_Pakistan_Economic_Corridor>

Liu, W., & Dunford, M. (2016). Inclusive globalization: unpacking China's Belt and Road Initiative. *Area Development and Policy*, *1*(3), 323–340. <https://doi.org/10.1080/23792949.2016.1232598>

Liu, X., & Yang, Y. E. (2015). Examining China's official media perception of the United States: A content analysis of people's daily coverage. *Journal of Chinese Political Science*, *20*(4), 385–408. <https://doi.org/10.1007/s11366-015-9340-8>

Macgillivray, I. (2019). Maturing Sino-Saudi strategic relations and changing dynamics in the Gulf. *Global Change, Peace and Security*, *31*(1), 61–80. <https://doi.org/10.1080/14781158.2018.1475350>

Mackerras, C. (2015). Xinjiang in China's foreign relations: Part of a new Silk Road or Central Asian zone of conflict? *East Asia*, *32*(1), 25–42. <https://doi.org/10.1007/s12140-015-9224-8>

Mann, J. (1999). Framing China. In R. Giles (Ed.), *Media Studies Journal Covering China* (pp. 102–107.). The Freedom Forum.

McLeod, J. M., Daily, K., Guo, Z., Eveland Jr, W. P., Bayer, J., Yang, S., & Wang, H. (1996). Community integration, local media use, and democratic processes. *Communication Research*, *23*(2), 179–209. <https://doi.org/10.1177/009365096023002002>

Mena. (2021, March 29). Trade exchange between Egypt, China reaches $14.56B in 2020. *Egypt Today*. <https://www.egypttoday.com/Article/3/100267/Trade-exchange-between-Egypt-China-reaches-14-56B-in-2020>

Meng, X. (2020). *National image: China's communication of cultural symbols.* Springer. <https://doi.org/10.1007/978-981-15-3147-7>

Miles, H. (2006). *Al-Jazeera: The inside story of the Arab news channel that is challenging the West.* Grove Press.

Nisbet, E. C., & Myers, T. A. (2011). Anti-American sentiment as a media effect? Arab media, political identity, and public opinion in the Middle East. *Communication Research, 38*(5), 684–709. <https://doi.org/10.1177/0093650211405648>

Nisbet, E. C., Nisbet, M. C., Scheufele, D. A., & Shanahan, J. E. (2004). Public diplomacy, television news, and Muslim opinion. *Harvard International Journal of Press/Politics, 9*(2), 11–37. <https://doi.org/10.1177/1081180X04263459>

Page, J., Dou, E., & Shah, S. (2018, September 27). China's Muslim detention camps spark protests in Islamic World. *The Wall Street Journal.* <https://www.wsj.com/articles/chinas-detentions-of-muslims-trigger-protests-in-islamic-world-1538040605>

Pew Research Center. (2017). *China image: Do you have a favorable or unfavorable view of China?* <http://www.pewglobal.org/database/indicator/24/survey/17/response/Unfavorable/>

Pollock, D. (2021, December 15). Egyptians value United States and China equally, but dislike both Iran and Israel. *Washington Institute.* <https://www.washingtoninstitute.org/policy-analysis/egyptians-value-united-states-and-china-equally-dislike-both-iran-and-israel>

Richter, C., & Gebauer, S. (2011). The portrayal of China in German Media. *Berlin: Heinrich-Böll-Stiftung,* 1–10. <http://www.boell.de>

Ridwan, P. M. (2022, September 20). China's technology is a mixed blessing for MENA states. *East Asia Forum.* <https://www.eastasiaforum.org/2022/09/20/chinas-technology-is-a-mixed-blessing-for-mena-states/>

Rizvi, H.-A. (2016). The military and politics in Pakistan. *South Asia Journal of South Asian Studies, 31*(2), 65–76. <https://www.jstor.org/stable/41394233>

Robbins, M. (2022). Public views of the U.S.-China Competition in MENA. *Arab Barometer, VII,* 1–17. <https://www.arabbarometer.org/wp-content/uploads/ABVII_US-China_Report-EN-1.pdf?ct=t(EMAIL_CAMPAIGN_8_11_2022_14_10_COPY_03)>

Salgado, S., & Strömbäck, J. (2012). Interpretive journalism: A review of concepts, operationalizations and key findings. *Journalism, 13*(2), 144–161. <https://doi.org/10.1177/1464884911427797>

Salman, M. bin. (2016, September 3). Fusing Vision 2030 with Belt Road Initiative. *Arab News.* <http://www.arabnews.com/node/979346/saudi-arabia>

Scheufele, D. A. (1999). Framing as a theory of media effects. *Journal of Communication, 49*(August 1996), 103–122. <https://doi.org/10.1111/j.1460-2466.1999.tb02784.x>

Selim, G. M., & Moaaz, R. S. (2021). Sino-Egyptian relations post-2013: The dynamics and challenges of an emerging strategic partnership. *Arab Studies Quarterly, 43*(4), 349–370. <https://doi.org/10.13169/arabstudquar.43.4.0349>

Shah, A. R. (2018). How does China–Pakistan economic corridor show the limitations of China's "One Belt One Road" Model? *Asia & The Pacific Policy Studies, December 2017.* <https://doi.org/10.1002/app5.224>

Shambaugh, D. (2013). *China goes global: The partial power.* Oxford University Press.

Shambaugh, D. (2015). China's soft-power push: The search for respect. *Foreign Affairs, 94*(4), 99–107. <https://www.jstor.org/stable/24483821>

Shay, S. (2018). Saudi Arabia and the "nuclearization of the Middle East". *Institute for Policy and Strategy, March.* <https://www.runi.ac.il/media/bnbddxrh/shaul_shay18_03_18.pdf>

Singh, M. K. (2021a). China and the United States in the Middle East: Between dependency and rivalry. In A. Farhadi & A. J. Masys (Eds.), *The great power competition Volume 1* (pp. 369–395). Springer.

Singh, R. (2021b). Critical discourse analysis of Iran-China relations through Football Headlines. *English Linguistics Research, 10*(2), 1. <https://doi.org/10.5430/elr.v10n2p1>

Small, A. (2015). *The China-Pakistan axis: Asia's new geopolitics*. Oxford University Press.

Szondi, G. (2010). From image management to relationship building: A public relations approach to nation branding. *Place Branding and Public Diplomacy, 6*(4), 333–343. <https://doi.org/10.1057/pb.2010.32>

Sun, D., & Xu, R. (2022). China and Egypt's comprehensive strategic partnership in the Xi-sisi era: A "role theory" prism. *Mediterranean Politics, 00*(00), 1–21. <https://doi.org/10.1080/13629395.2022.2035139>

Temiz, K. (2018). An illustration of Sino-Turkish relations: The Cyprus question. *Insight Turkey, 20*(1). <https://www.insightturkey.com/articles/an-illustration-of-sino-turkish-relations-the-cyprus-question>

The Daily Star. (2009, October 1). What will China's rising influence mean for the Middle East region? *The Daily Star.* <http://www1.dailystar.com.lb/Opinion/Editorial/2009/Oct-01/119578-what-will-chinas-rising-influence-mean-for-the-middle-east-region.ashx>

UN Charter. (2023). Chapter I: Purposes and principles (Articles 1–2). <https://www.un.org/en/about-us/un-charter/chapter-1>

UN Comtrade. (2018, January 19). Trade statistics. *United Nations Statistics Division.* <https://comtrade.un.org/data/>

Vandewalle, L. (2015, June 18). Pakistan and China: "Iron brothers" forever. *Think Tank European Parliament.* <https://www.europarl.europa.eu/thinktank/en/document/EXPO_IDA(2015)549052>

Wanta, W., Golan, G., & Lee, C. (2004). Agenda setting and international news: Media influence on public perceptions of foreign nations. *Journalism & Mass Communication Quarterly, 81*(2), 364–377. <https://doi.org/10.1177/107769900408100209>

White, C. L. (2012). Brands and national image: An exploration of inverse country-of-origin effect. *Place Branding and Public Diplomacy, 8*(2), 110–118. <https://doi.org/10.1057/pb.2012.6>

Willnat, L., & Luo, Y. (2011). Watching the Dragon: Global television news about China. *Chinese Journal of Communication, 4*(3), 255–273. <https://doi.org/10.1080/17544750.2011.594552>

Willnat, L., & Wilkins, K. (1998). International and local media impact on cultural values and political attitudes: The case of Hong Kong. In B. T. McIntyre (Ed.), *Mass media in the Asian Pacific* (pp. 29–43). Multilingual Matters Ltd.

Worth, R. F., & Kirkpatrick, D. D. (2011). Seizing a moment, Al Jazeera galvanizes Arab frustration. *New York Times, 27.* <https://www.nytimes.com/2011/01/28/world/middleeast/28jazeera.html>

Wu, D. (2008). Glocalization and the discourses of cultural China: An introduction. In D. D. Wu (Ed.), *Discourses of cultural China in the globalizing age* (pp. 1–10). Hong Kong University Press. <https://doi.org/10.5790/hongkong/9789622099128.003.0001>

Xiang, D. (2013). China's image on international English language social media. *Journal of International Communication, 19*(2), 252–271. <https://doi.org/10.1080/13216597.2013.833535>

Xie, T., & Page, B. I. (2013). What affects China's national image? A cross-national study of public opinion. *Journal of Contemporary China, 22*(83), 850–867. <https://doi.org/10.1080/10670564.2013.782130>

Xu, S. (2014). *Chinese discourse studies.* Palgrave Macmillan.

Yan, X. (2020). Chinese values vs. liberalism: What ideology will shape the international normative order? In *Globalizing IR theory* (pp. 102–123). Routledge.

Zaharna, R. (2007). "The soft power differential: Network communication and mass communication in public diplomacy". *The Hague Journal of Diplomacy, 2*(3), 213–228.

Zambelis, C., & Gentry, B. (2008). China through Arab eyes: American influence in the Middle East. *Parameters, 38*(1), 60–73. <https://doi.org/10.55540/0031-1723.2412>

Zhang, C., & Meadows III, C. W. (2012). International coverage, foreign policy, and national image: Exploring the complexities of media coverage, public opinion, and presidential agenda. *International Journal of Communication, 6*, 20. <https://ijoc.org/index.php/ijoc/article/view/1424>

Zhang, L., & Wu, D. (2017). Media representations of China: A comparison of China Daily and Financial Times in reporting on the Belt and Road Initiative. *Critical Arts, 31*(6), 29–43. <https://doi.org/10.1080/02560046.2017.1408132>

Zhong, X., & Lu, J. (2013). Public diplomacy meets social media: A study of the US Embassy's blogs and micro-blogs. *Public Relations Review, 39*(5), 542–548. <https://doi.org/10.1016/j.pubrev.2013.07.002>

Zhou, W., & Esteban, M. (2020). Beyond balancing: China's approach towards the Belt and Road Initiative. In *China's new global strategy* (pp. 36–50). Routledge.

Zhu, W. (2010). On the strategic relationship between China and Islamic countries in the Middle East. *Journal of Middle Eastern and Islamic Studies (in Asia), 4*(3), 1–27. <https://doi.org/10.1080/19370679.2010.12023159>

Appendix A. Coding Sheet

1.	**Date of publication**	_____Day _____Month _______Year
2.	**Length of the Article**	Length: _______words
3.	**Type of the article**	a). News b). Column/Opinion c). Editorial d). Features e). Interview f). Letter to the editor g). Other
4.	**Name of the Country/ publication:**	a). Saudi Arabia (*Arab News*) b). Pakistan (*The Nation)* c). Turkey (*Daily Sabah*), d). Iran (*Tehran Times)* e). Egypt (*Daily News Egypt*) f). Qatar (*Al-Jazeera English)*

5.	**The overall tone of the Article**	a). Positive (friendly) b). Negative (hostile) c). Neutral (moderate)
6.	**Journalistic Attitude**	a). Positive (Descriptive) b). Positive (Analytical) c). Negative (Descriptive) d). Negative (Analytical) e). Neutral
7.	**Themes/Issues**	a) Politics b) Economy c) Culture d) Social Issues e) Science and Technology f) Misc.
8.	**Sub Themes/Issues**	
	1) **Politics**	a). Diplomatic relations b). Defence and Security c). Global values d). Other (Specify)______________
	2) **Economy**	a). Trade and investment b). Business c). Infrastructural development d). Natural Resources e). Economic Policies and Reforms f). Economic aid and loans g). Other (Specify)_____________
	3) **Culture**	a). Sport b). Tourism c). History and Artefacts d). Media and Entertainment e). Fine-Art f). Ethnicity g). Education h). Chinese Language i). Cuisines j). Other (Specify)_____________

4) **Social Issues**	a). Health b). Education c). Welfare d). Corruption e). Poverty f). Natural Disasters g). Crime h). Gender Gap i). Others (Specify)_____________
5) **Science and Technology**	a). Technology b). Science c). innovation d). Other (Specify)__________
6) **Miscellaneous/Others**	a). Other (Specify)__________

Index

The Belt and Road Initiative

Interdisciplinary Perspectives

Series Editor: Wenshan Jia

The Belt and Road Initiative (BRI) unveiled in 2013 by China has been gaining global traction and exerting global impact. Owing to the significance and impact of the BRI, there is a growing need for an academic book series that covers various essential topics related to BRI, such as five kinds of connectivity, BRI health initiatives, BRI digitization, and more.

This book series provides a scholarly and systematic understanding of BRI from global, multicultural, and interdisciplinary standpoints. It serves as a valuable resource for academics, think-tanks, policy makers, business leaders, and the public with objective, original, and cutting-edge knowledge on BRI above and beyond the existing fragmented information available through media coverages and think-tank reports.

For additional information about this series or for the submission of manuscripts, please contact:

editorial@peterlang.com

www.ingramcontent.com/pod-product-compliance
Ingram Content Group UK Ltd.
Pitfield, Milton Keynes, MK11 3LW, UK
UKHW020840290926
15470UKWH00004B/1454

9 781433 195570